MILLIONS

OF

JEWS TO RESCUE

A Bergson Group Leader's Account
of the Campaign to Save Jews from the Holocaust

BY SAMUEL MERLIN

EDITED AND ANNOTATED BY RAFAEL MEDOFF

Foreword by Seymour D. Reich • Afterword by Jeremy Ben-Ami

ISBN: 0615439101

ISBN-13: 9780615439105

LCCN: 2011920693

TABLE OF CONTENTS

ACKNOWLEDGMENTS

For the better part of three decades, Samuel Merlin labored on this manuscript, pouring his heart and soul into what was clearly a labor of love as much as it was a painful revisiting of the most difficult episodes in his life. The process of shepherding his work to publication has been made possible with the help of a number of individuals and institutions, to whom I am deeply grateful. Jack Yampolsky, Phyllis Yampolsky, Dr. Becky Kook, Nili Kook, and the Institute for Mediterranean Affairs provided the assistance that made it possible to undertake this project.

Simone Schliachter and her colleagues at the Central Zionist Archives, in Jerusalem, and Amira Stern and her colleagues at Metzudat Ze'ev (the Jabotinsky Archives), in Tel Aviv, were extremely helpful in facilitating my access to relevant documents. Additional documents were made available by the families of Hillel Kook, Baruch Rabinowitz, and Harry Selden.

Professors David S. Wyman, Monty N. Penkower, and Bat-Ami Zucker offered valuable suggestions about various aspects of the manuscript. Elisha Yalin-Mor, Miriam Chaikin, Nisan Teeman, Uri Avnery, Yisrael Medad, Ruth Tamir, and Ehud and Noga Duchovni kindly shared their memories of Merlin. Photographs were generously provided by Ruth Tamir, Ehud and Noga Duchovni, Nili Kook, Jack and Judith Yampolsky, and Miriam Chaikin.

Rafael Medoff
Washington, D.C.
June 15, 2011

FOREWORD

by Seymour D. Reich

In the pages to follow, Samuel Merlin presents his remarkable history of the Bergson Group's struggle to save European Jewry from the Holocaust. He also describes some of the attempts by mainstream Jewish leaders to interfere with the Bergson campaign. As a former chairman of the Conference of Presidents of Major American Jewish Organizations and former president of B'nai B'rith International and the American Zionist Movement, three of the leading Jewish establishment organizations, I have always found this aspect of the story particularly unsettling.

The central figure in the Jewish establishment's fight against Bergson and Merlin was Rabbi Stephen S. Wise, leader of a long list of organizations, including the American Jewish Conference and the American Zionist Emergency Council, forerunners of two of the organizations that I later chaired. Considering the enormous range of responsibilities that Wise shouldered in the Jewish community, it is astonishing how much time and energy he diverted to trying to thwart the Bergson Group.

Wise was deeply bothered by Bergson's success in attracting the support of prominent non-Jews. "They are a disaster to the Zionist cause and the Jewish people," he wrote to one colleague in 1944. "Yet see how many names they capture who are well-meaning and are friendly to the Jews! It is too sad for words." There are letters from Wise to such notables as Interior Secretary Harold Ickes and Bishop Henry St. George Tucker, pressing them to cut their ties to Bergson. To their credit, both men refused to heed Wise's plea. But others did succumb to the pressure.

It is sad to note that fighting Bergson was seemingly elevated to one of the top items on the Jewish leadership's agenda. In May 1944, Wise's American Zionist Emergency Council sent an urgent message to its chapters around the country, telling them it was "mobilizing all responsible groups in American Jewry to combat [Bergson's] activities." At one point, the Council managed to persuade 46 rabbis to withdraw their support from the Bergson Group. That was no mean feat in an era without email or fax machines.

Jewish leaders also tried to incite the U.S. government against Bergson. On May 19, 1944, Nahum Goldmann, who with Wise was co-chair of the World Jewish Congress, met with State Department officials and urged them to draft or deport Bergson. Goldmann told them that Wise "regarded Bergson as equally as great an enemy of the Jews as Hitler, for the reason that his activities could only lead to increased anti-Semitism."

The timing of Goldmann's action is astounding. On Monday, May 15, 1944, the mass deportation of Hungarian Jews to Auschwitz began. Three days later, the *New York Times* reported that the first transports of Jews had left the Carpathian provinces, and were being taken to "murder camps in Poland." It boggles the mind to think that on Thursday, Goldmann read in his morning newspaper that Hitler was shipping Hungarian Jews to death camps, and on Friday, he went to the State Department to declare that Bergson was as dangerous as Hitler!

There were a number of reasons for Wise's opposition to Bergson. None of those reasons was irrational, but it seems to me they were exaggerated beyond the point of common sense.

For example, Goldmann mentioned the fear of "increased anti-Semitism." There certainly was a great deal of anti-Semitism in those days. But that does not mean Bergson's newspaper ads or rallies would lead to a wave of attacks on Jews.

Rabbi Wise was a strong supporter of President Franklin Roosevelt. So were most American Jews. But Wise should not have let his feelings about FDR cloud his judgment as a Jewish leader. It was not his job to shield the president from criticism over America's refugee policies.

Some Jewish leaders resented Bergson and Merlin because of their connection to Ze'ev Jabotinsky, leader of the Revisionist Zionists. Those Zionist rivalries certainly could provoke passionate feelings. It was tragic that Zionist political differences were allowed to get in the way of the issue that should have been uppermost in everyone's mind, the mass killing of Jews in Europe.

Another important reason, perhaps the most important reason, for the Jewish leaders' campaign against Bergson, was the fear that the Bergson Group was usurping their positions of leadership in the community. I winced when I first saw the press release from a Jewish organization in 1944 accusing Bergson of "usurpatory aspirations," and the memo in which a top official of the World Jewish Congress, in 1943, warned that the Bergson Group was "stealing the thunder" of the established Jewish groups.

The time has come to acknowledge, unequivocally, that Rabbi Wise and his colleagues were wrong. They should not have devoted their resources to attacking Bergson. They should have focused on persuading the Roosevelt administration to bring about the rescue of Jews from Hitler's Europe. That was their obligation, and they failed.

We cannot change the past. But we can learn from the past, first and foremost by acknowledging the mistakes that were made. By setting the historical record straight and shining a powerful spotlight on events that must never be forgotten, Samuel Merlin's history of the Bergson Group is a vitally important step in that direction.

Seymour D. Reich is a veteran Jewish communal leader. He has served as chairman of the Conference of Presidents of Major American Jewish Organizations, president of B'nai B'rith International, president of the American Zionist Movement, and president of the Israel Policy Forum. He is an attorney with Gallet Dreyer & Berkey LLP, in New York City.

EDITOR'S PREFACE

Rafael Medoff

Samuel Merlin played an important role in events leading to the rescue of 200,000 Jews from the Holocaust. He served in Israel's First Knesset. He helped ignite a series of major controversies in the American Jewish community both in the 1940s and four decades later. Yet outside the small circle of his collaborators and adversaries, Merlin's name was barely known either in his heyday or in subsequent years.

Smil (in Hebrew, Shmuel) Merlean was born in the Russian city of Kishinev on January 10, 1910, and raised in a traditional Orthodox Jewish home.[1] He described his childhood as "the dull existence of a Jewish boy in a small town in Russia, a boy forced by circumstances to earn his livelihood at a very early age."[2] As a teenager, he attended the Magen David school and at some point during his adolescence worked as a reporter for a local newspaper. In 1930 and 1931, Merlin studied at the University of Paris (the Sorbonne), focusing on modern history. It was during this period that Merlin became attracted to Zionism, in particular the militant wing of the movement, Revisionist Zionism, headed by the fiery Vladimir Ze'ev Jabotinsky. The Revisionists advocated energetic political efforts to advance Jewish statehood, military training for Jewish youth, and mass Jewish emigration from Europe to Palestine. They regarded the mainstream Zionist leadership's more accommodating approach to the British authorities in Mandatory Palestine as excessively cautious. Merlin joined the Revisionist youth movement, Betar, and undertook a number of visits to the Kishinev region and elsewhere to develop local Betar chapters.[3]

By 1932, Merlin decided to leave the Sorbonne without completing his degree, in order to accept a full time position as secretary-general of the Revisionist Zionist movement in France. The following year, Merlin was promoted to secretary-general of the World Zionist-Revisionist Executive and appointed secretary (senior aide) to Jabotinsky. He shuttled between Warsaw, Paris, and London. It was on one of his visits to Warsaw in 1935 that Merlin made the acquaintance of a local Betar leader named Natan Friedman-Yalin, whose fine penmanship, Merlin decided, made him eminently suitable to create membership cards for the movement. They would soon leave the movement together.[4]

In the early 1930s, in response to Palestinian Arab violence and a steady British retreat from earlier promises to facilitate creation of a Jewish national home, a number of Jabotinsky followers established an underground militia in Palestine called the Irgun Zvai Leumi (National Military Organization). Its members undertook counter-terrorism actions against Arab targets while simultaneously organizing the smuggling of European Jews to Palestine in defiance of British immigration restrictions. By 1938, Merlin had become disillusioned with Jabotinsky's exclusive reliance on politics and diplomacy. Convinced "that political activity had run its course," Merlin decided the time had come to prepare for an armed revolt against the British. He resigned from the Revisionist movement and shortly afterwards joined the Irgun, where he was named coeditor, along with Friedman-Yalin, of *Die Tat*, the Irgun's Warsaw-based Yiddish-language newspaper.[5]

Merlin soon became closely acquainted with a group of emissaries who had been sent from Palestine to Europe by the Irgun to organize immigration transports, known as *aliyah bet,* or alternative—that is, unauthorized by the British—immigration.[6] This group included Hillel Kook (who later adopted the pseudonym Peter Bergson), Yitshaq Ben-Ami, Eri Jabotinsky (son of the Revisionist leader), and Alex Rafaeli. During 1939-1940, the Irgun sent these young men to the United States to undertake political activity and fundraising to support the *aliyah bet* campaign. As for Merlin, by chance he left Warsaw for Paris on the morning of September 1, 1939, just hours before the German invasion of Poland. According to his account, he subsequently persuaded French government officials to send him to the United States to carry out anti-Nazi propaganda there. He arrived at the New York harbor on February 26, 1940, just ten weeks before the German invasion of France. The German occupation put a swift end to his mission in the United States.[7]

Jabotinsky himself traveled to the U.S. in March 1940, to organize a campaign for the creation of a Jewish army to fight alongside the Allies against the Nazis. Merlin soon became active in this effort. He later recalled with pride that Jabotinsky introduced him to a number of people as "one of my most intimate collaborators."[8] After Jabotinsky's sudden passing in August of that year, Merlin, together with Bergson, Eri Jabotinsky, Ben-Ami, and Rafaeli, decided they could be more effective politically if they operated independently of the U.S. wing of the Revisionist Party. Initially they worked within the framework of the American Friends of a Jewish Palestine, a small political action committee that Ben-Ami had set up in New York City the previous year.

In mid-1941, the American Friends group transformed itself into the Committee for a Jewish Army of Stateless and Palestinian Jews. It focused exclusively on promoting the Jewish army idea, until late 1942, when news of the Nazi genocide was verified by the Allies. At that point, the activists set aside the Jewish army campaign and, operating as the Emergency Committee to Save the Jewish People of Europe, focused their attention on pressuring the U.S. and Great Britain to rescue Europe's Jews. Later, they established two more organizations, the American League for a Free Palestine (est. December 1943), to mobilize American support for Jewish statehood, and the Hebrew Committee of National Liberation (est. May 1944), to serve as a government-in-exile for the Jewish rebels fighting the British in Palestine and those European Jews trying to reach the Holy Land. Because the leadership of the groups overlapped, they were often referred to collectively as the Bergson Group.

These action committees utilized political protest tactics that were uncommon at the time, especially among Jewish organizations. They sponsored several hundred full-page newspaper advertisements, organized rallies and marches, lobbied in Washington, and used theatrical productions to promote their message. They were particularly successful at winning the endorsement of non-Jewish political and cultural figures, including prominent actors, writers, artists, musicians, and other celebrities.

Bergson was the group's leader and chief public spokesman. Merlin was his close collaborator in formulating and implementing political strategy. Merlin was also the group's chief propagandist; he "wrote or edited most of the ads, memoranda, and pamphlets" for the group, as he once put it.[9] He also served as editor of its magazine, *The Answer*. Merlin generally operated behind the scenes and was almost completely unknown to the public, yet played a central role in all that the Bergson committees achieved. Every bit the stereotypical starving Jewish activists, Merlin and Bergson shared a small apartment, lived extremely frugal lives, and took just $25 each as their weekly salaries.[10]

In the spring of 1948, the Bergson Group purchased and outfitted a ship, which it named the *Altalena* (one of Jabotinsky's literary pen names). It reached the coast of Palestine in June, loaded with weapons for the Irgun to use against the Arab armies invading the newborn State of Israel. Merlin, who intended to settle permanently in the new state, was one of the passengers. Prime Minister David Ben-Gurion, claiming the weapons were intended for an Irgun coup against his government, ordered his troops to fire upon the ship. Fifteen of the passengers were killed and a number were wounded. Merlin was shot in the left heel, an injury which would bother him for the rest of his life.

Samuel Merlin's identification card as a Member of Knesset, 1949.

Merlin collaborated closely with Irgun commander Menachem Begin to create Herut, the main nationalist political party, which was based on the principles of the Revisionist movement. Merlin became the party's first secretary-general and served as editor of its newspaper, also called *Herut*. In 1949, he, Eri Jabotinsky, and Bergson—now reassuming his real name, Hillel Kook—were elected to the First Knesset as Herut representatives.

It was not long, however, before the three former 'Bergson Boys' were at odds with Begin. Part of the problem was a clash of personalities. Begin was strong willed and insisted on strict party discipline, while Kook, Merlin, and Jabotinsky prided themselves on being independent thinkers. There were also differences with regard to the nature of the new state. Kook, Merlin, and Jabotinsky were staunchly secular and envisioned the rise of a new "Hebrew" culture and nation that would be largely separate from world Jewry. Begin, by contrast, felt close to the world of traditional East European Jewish culture and favored strong ties between the Jewish State and the Diaspora. There were strategic differences as well. While Begin wanted Israel to remain neutral between the Soviet Union and the United States, Merlin and his friends—no doubt influenced by their years in America—argued that Israel should adopt a strongly pro-American orientation.

Tensions between the trio and Begin soon reached the boiling point. In the autumn of 1949, Begin brought about Merlin's ouster as party-secretary. The following year, Merlin and his close friend Shmuel Tamir, a Herut party activist, created a separatist faction within Herut called *LaMerhav* (To the Region). Their choice of that name emphasized their belief that Israel should separate itself from world Jewry and become more integrated in the Middle East. In early 1951, Kook and Jabotinsky broke away to serve as independent Knesset Members separate from Herut.[11] When Begin selected candidates to run on the Herut list in the next Knesset elections, in 1953, Kook, Merlin, and Jabotinsky were not included. Not that any of them would have wanted to stand for election again, even if Begin had offered; it seems they had their fill of Begin, Herut, and Israeli politics in general.[12]

Jabotinsky stayed in Israel. Kook went to the United States for a number of years to undertake various business ventures, but later returned to Israel permanently. Merlin, however, chose a different path. In 1956, Merlin and his wife, Winona Weber (whom he met when she worked for the Chicago chapter of the Bergson Group) moved back to the United States. His friends say that Merlin "never quite fit in as an Israeli" and "never seemed to really find his place in Israel." Others point to his disillusionment that the new state did not turn out as he had hoped. Interestingly, however, the Merlins kept an automobile and apartment in Israel; they spent two months there each summer and did not sublet it during the rest of the year. Friends speculate that the residence and car served as

a kind of cushion against the feelings of remorse that must have
accompanied Merlin's decision to
leave Israel.[13]

At various times over the
years, Merlin wrote a column for
the Israeli daily *Ha'aretz,* as well
as articles for other Israeli periodicals. He also taught political science part-time at Farleigh
Dickinson University. But his
main vocation was directing
the Institute for Mediterranean
Affairs, a small educational organization that he and Kook created,
and which Kook and other friends
financed. The Institute held occasional seminars concerning the

*Left to right: Merlin (with pipe), his wife Winona,
and their friends Shmuel Tamir and Mordechai
Ra'anan, at a party in the 1950s.*

future of the Middle East; Merlin turned the proceedings of one of them into a
book. He also authored a book about the 1965 Mideast peace plan proposed by
Tunisian President Habib Bourguiba.[14]

At some point in the 1960s, Merlin set to work on a book-length history
of the Bergson Group. Books about modern American Jewish history, American
Zionism, or America's response to the Holocaust that were published in the late
1960s and early 1970s included little or nothing about the Bergson activists.[15]
Merlin's account thus would have represented an important first step in bringing the Bergson story into the historiography of the period.

Advocates of the Jewish establishment's perspective on the 1940s held
a distinct advantage in the effort to shape the public's view of that period.
Mainstream Jewish and Zionist leaders (Stephen Wise, Nahum Goldmann,
and others) enjoyed sufficient stature to secure major publishers for their autobiographies,[16] and large Jewish organizations possessed sufficient resources to
commission scholars to write their histories.[17] The Bergson Group, having dissolved shortly after Israel's creation, was not in a position to do likewise. Merlin
was the obvious choice to redress this imbalance and write the Bergson committees back into history. He was an experienced writer; he had been active
continuously as a member of the Bergson Group's leadership through all of its
organizational reincarnations, from 1940 to 1948; and he was the keeper of the
group's voluminous files, situated in the office of the Institute for Mediterranean
Affairs, which would provide much of the material needed for such a
project.[18]

Bergson Group alumni eagerly awaited completion of the book. As the activists married and raised families, they remained in close contact and at periodic social gatherings of the old comrades, Merlin fielded inquiries about the book's progress with assurances that the project was well underway. As the years passed with no end in sight, however, they began to doubt Merlin would ever finish it. Yitshaq Ben-Ami's son Jeremy recalls that after a while, the idea that Merlin would never complete the book became so much a part of their circle's conventional wisdom that the phrase "Merlin's book" became virtually a synonym for something that would never happen.

From Merlin's correspondence with Kook in the 1970s and 1980s, one might come away with the impression, again and again, that the book was just inches from the finish line. As early as 1972, Merlin reported to his old friend that "I am so engulfed in the work about the Committee, I do nothing else and neglected the Institute completely and I am afraid that I may endanger its status..."[19] Two years later, Merlin wrote that he had "started, at long last, to write my history of the Committee in final draft—to be ready for the publisher."[20] But another two years passed before he informed Kook that he had "just finished" what he called "the second draft." He added: "I hope to live long enough at least to finish the history of the Committee."[21] Health problems undoubtedly made the task harder. He suffered his first heart attack in 1975, his second in 1977. Other medical problems developed in the years to follow.[22]

Despite the earlier letters about his "second draft" and his "final draft," in the spring of 1979 Merlin was telling Kook that "The 'History' though I work on it daily and almost exclusively—is a slow process, and it is difficult for me even to explain...I feel bad that it took and takes so long to wind up. I wish anybody would advise me how to do it faster."

In the meantime, the question of American Jewry's response to the Holocaust was arousing growing interest in the Jewish community. In September 1981, Arthur J. Goldberg, a former associate justice of the Supreme Court, announced he would chair a private commission of prominent American Jews that would examine the American Jewish community's response to the Nazi genocide. The commission, funded by Holocaust survivor Jack Eisner, would be assisted by a research team headed by Prof. Seymour Maxwell Finger of the City University of New York. The thirty-four members of the commission, including senior leaders of the World Jewish Congress, B'nai B'rith, Hadassah, and other major Jewish organizations, did not know that Finger hired Merlin to serve as one of the key members of the research team.

Merlin delivered the draft of the research team's final report to the commission in late 1982. Not surprisingly, it was strongly critical of the major Jewish organizations' response to the Holocaust. The commission members were furious both at the content of the draft and the realization that Merlin, an interested party, was its primary author. At a stormy meeting, commission members accused Merlin of allowing his partisan view of the 1940s conflicts to color the report. They rejected the draft, and Merlin resigned in protest. Fisner accused the commission members of being unwilling to face the harsh truth about Jewish leaders' response to the Holocaust, and withdrew his funding from the entire project. Shortly afterwards, however, Goldberg announced he would personally provide the funding to resume the commission's work. A year later, Finger's research team released a new report, still somewhat critical of the Jewish leadership's actions during the 1940s, but less so than the Merlin version. The rise, fall, and revival of the commission were chronicled in a series of front-page articles in the *New York Times* and provoked widespread discussion in the Jewish community and beyond. Two decades after he and his comrades labored to influence the American, and American Jewish, response to the Holocaust, Merlin had managed to take center stage in the public debate over that response.[23]

In early 1983, on the heels of the controversy over the Goldberg Commission, Kook inquired in a letter as to what Merlin was working on. With more than a trace of testiness, Merlin replied:

> You ask me what I am doing. Well, I am doing the history. It took many years to write mainly because we were such an extraordinary, in fact a unique phenomenon, which does not lend itself to simple narrative or explanation. Yet I am confident that something will come out of it, and I don't share the views of those who think, but who don't tell me, that I got stuck. Through the years I didn't get stuck for one day, and what I did and do is clear to me.[24]

For all his denials, however, it seemed Merlin was indeed stuck, and finally, in a May 1983 letter to Kook, Merlin addressed the matter with a little more than the usual bland reassurances. It was now eleven years since Merlin's 1972 letter about being so "engulfed" in working on the book that he was "neglecting the Institute completely." Kook had again inquired about the delays. Merlin conceded the matter had become "embarrassing." By way of explanation, Merlin wrote Kook about "three characters I encountered in literature which may be relevant to our, or rather my, condition."

The first was an elderly man who appeared in a short story by A. J. Liebling in *The New Yorker*:

> The old man [was] always carrying with him a briefcase stuffed with paper. He claimed that he is writing the history of the

twentieth century in the form of personal memoirs. He claimed
that when it will appear in print, it will revolutionize historiography, and it will be the greatest book ever written, or words
to that effect. But in the meantime he needs a dollar or two to
buy a drink. Somehow everybody believed him that he is writing a long manuscript (30 volumes?) but the nature of that Mss
nobody knew because he refused to tell. Not only because out
of fear that his deeds will be stolen, but also because the events
and his evaluation of them are so sensational that they cannot
be revealed except in the framework of their totality. When he
died it was discovered that he did not write a word...his brief
case was stuffed with old newspapers.

The second character Merlin found relevant to his own situation appeared
in *The Plague*, by Camus:

He has there a man who wrote a novel. And he composed
the opening paragraph. He read it to the people who worked
with the doctors and nurses and volunteers to overcome the
epidemic. But each time he read this first paragraph, it was
somewhat rephrased, only a nuance, sometimes only a word
placed in the same paragraph, changed its place in it. What is
remarkable is that the people listened to him and were interested in this single paragraph. There was no sarcasm about it—
it appeared to them aesthetically satisfactory; the main problem: what about the continuation—the novel itself was never
raised. He died in the epidemic and did not go further than a
revised version of this single paragraph.

The third character was "from Thomas Wolfe, the American Novelist I am
mad about." Wolfe once described a drama class that he taught in Boston. In one
class, among the aspiring young actors and actresses, sat an older man, with grey
hair, who "followed the course with the greatest attention, and never missed a
class."

The instructor...was curious why a man of such an age decided to
take this course. Once after class he called him aside and asked
him the question, and he said that since he was a youngster, he
wanted to be a playwright, but he had no chance, he always had
to earn a living, and life was not kind to him. He never made
enough money to take time off—a year or so—to write the play.

But recently he retired, has a pension and plenty of time (the children are married) and he is writing the play. But he thought he may learn something about the techniques, the rules, if there are any, of writing a play so that he could apply them to the work he is working on. Sure enough after a few months he finished the play and showed it to the instructor. The latter was very impressed—in many respects it was perfect—the plot, the dialogue, the unexpected revelations, the dramatic encounters, and the climax. However it had one fatal weakness; he wrote a play for an audience that is dead—for an audience of 40 years ago.

Perhaps Merlin cited these examples because it was finally beginning to dawn on him that he would never complete his book. It may be that he was too close to the subject matter to ever feel satisfied that he had told the story completely or as effectively as he felt necessary. Perhaps the experience of reliving those events in his mind was too stressful. Or it could be that his disillusionment over the Goldberg Commission experience left him too bitter to revisit the subject matter. Whatever the reasons, he passed away in 1996 without ever finishing his long-awaited book. He did, however, leave behind multiple versions of his manuscript, close enough to completion to make the reconciling of the texts feasible and to enable Merlin's story to be told at last.

Readers will notice that Merlin himself is almost completely absent from the narrative, even though he played a central role in the events which he describes. This is by Merlin's design. "This man, who speaks through memoranda to Governments, and through ads to millions of people—is the shyest man in the world!," a Bergson Group magazine asserted in 1944, in what was probably the only instance any of its publications ever offered any substantive information about Merlin. "This expert in political publicity hates publicity for himself. On all occasions, and there are many, at conferences, dinners, meetings, when the photographers appear—Merlin disappears."[25] In this manuscript, too, Merlin has managed to almost completely disappear. His own role is hardly mentioned as Merlin recounts the amazing story of a handful of young Jewish activists who forced the Allies to take steps, however belatedly, to rescue Jews from the Nazis. I am grateful to have been granted the opportunity to help make Merlin's voice heard at long last.

1 ON THE EVE OF CATASTROPHE

The Jews of Europe found themselves in a cul-de-sac even before the Nazi volcano erupted. All the political theories propounded by the Zionists and anti-Zionists alike proved bankrupt by events. All the panaceas were illusions. The anti-Zionists, although divided into two parties—the Bundists[26] and the Volkists[27] (the former hitched their wagon to the socialist star, and the latter had no star to hitch onto)—both represented fundamentally the same ideology: that the Jews are a national entity and as such they should live and develop in the countries of their habitation and as such they should fight for national minority rights along with other ethnic minorities in Eastern Europe. These rights were guaranteed by the Principal Allied Powers at the Paris Peace Conference.[28] But these recognized and "guaranteed" rights were of no avail, and were considered by the governments concerned, especially in Poland as a provocation, an insult to their dignity and sovereignty, and interference in the internal affairs of their state. Thus these rights more often than not were a source of friction rather than harmony and cooperation.

The incorrigible hope of Jews the world over that socialism, or liberalism, or enlightenment, will bring about the millennium was shattered by historical reality. This ideology and program did not meet with a sympathetic response either in the liberal circles of Poland, or among the working classes, even those that sympathized with socialism. The environment in those countries remained hostile regardless of party or class.

The controversy that raged among Jews in Eastern Europe concerning "giving up positions" was pathetic and confusing. The arguments for national autonomy were solid and plausible, but outside the context of realities. In the long run, it could not have worked even had Adolf Hitler not appeared on the scene. The Jews were not only faced with prejudice and hatred, but economic problems which had no solution in an unfriendly environment.[29]

The argument that one should fight for individual rights was of course incontrovertible, yet there was a speciousness about it because the case of East European Jewry was not like that of Western, emancipated Jews in France or England. The Jews in Poland or Rumania did not argue that they were Poles or Rumanians in every respect. They did not say, "We are born here; this is our country, our language, our culture, and we will fight for our right to stay here because this is our nation ('although our religion is Jewish and we are proud of our spiritual heritage')." The Polish or Rumanian Jews could not say all this. They could not and did not (with a small number of exceptions) because they considered themselves a national minority with their own language (or languages, in case they were Zionists and knew Hebrew), culture, and aspirations. The majority were more or less inclined to emigrate overseas, many of them to Palestine if it would be possible.

The Jews of interwar Europe were not comparable to the black minority in the United States, even long before the civil rights movement triumphed. Even rabid segregationists refrained from saying the blacks should be expelled from America. They did not want to treat blacks as equals. They wanted to relegate them to an inferior status.

With regard to the Jews in Poland and other East European countries, it was not only a matter of rights, but chiefly a mass refusal to accept them on any basis; not even on a basis of inferior rights, status, and opportunity.

As for Zionism, its political bankruptcy became no less evident. The programs of all the Zionist parties—from the leftwing Poale Zion [Labor Zionists][30] to the maximalist Revisionist Zionists[31]—were tried but with no visible success. Money was raised through the Keren Kayemet (Jewish National Fund)[32] to buy land, and the Keren Hayesod[33] to build on the land; youths were trained on a mass scale for pioneer life and work in Palestine; they learned to adapt to arduous physical labor as farmers; they learned Hebrew; they attended protest meetings and signed petitions; members of Betar,[34] the youth wing of the Revisionist Zionists, were instructed in military discipline: how to use weapons, and jiujitsu in self-defense. The socialist Zionists cultivated friendship and connections with their comrades, the socialists in England and France. Revisionist leader Ze'ev Jabotinsky[35] tried to stir up public opinion in practically all the countries of Europe and beyond, winning friends in Great Britain—in parliament and the press. But it was to no avail. The British White Paper of May 1939 choked off nearly all Jewish immigration to Palestine, thus for all intents and purposes, sealing the doom of any hopes for the Zionists to ever attain a Jewish National Home in Palestine, whatever the 1917 Balfour Declaration, which first used that term, meant by it.[36]

Vladimir Ze'ev Jabotinsky

The British Mandate over Palestine became a scrap of paper, while in London and Jerusalem, antisemitic British politicians and officials pursued a policy of conniving, consciously or unconsciously, with Hitler's war against the Jews. This was the time, 1939, when the Fuhrer had already ruled over

Germany for six years and had absorbed Austria.[37] This was the time of contagious madness on an international scale, barbarism was rampant, and humanity abdicated decency and common sense in the most elementary way. It was the time of a wholesale sellout by everybody. On September 29, 1938, the betrayal in Munich took place. On May 17, 1939, Chamberlain's White Paper was issued. On August 23, 1939, the Hitler-Stalin nonaggression pact was signed. In the beautiful spring of that same year, the ghost ship *St. Louis,* with nine hundred Jewish refugees from Germany, sought entry in Cuba—where the government canceled the Cuban entry visas that the passengers possessed—and the United States and, despite all the pleas and despair, was sent back to Hitler's Europe.

Three Fatal Weaknesses

On the very threshold of total crisis in Jewish history, it was proven once more that the Jews, talented in so many ways and having made tremendous contributions to human civilization throughout the ages, suffered from three disastrous weaknesses.

First, they lacked to an astounding degree a sense and an understanding of political and social realities around them. Their genius stopped short of that. They had no built-in alarm mechanism or, if they had, something went wrong with it and it ceased functioning.

The second weakness was their mystique of timelessness; the Zionists and the Orthodox preferred to call it "a sense of eternity." It was a tendency to expect good things to happen; an assumption that the inevitable will be avoided, that one should have patience to weather the storm, if a storm is expected, and that the proper opportunity will offer itself at some indeterminate point in the future. This counsel of patience and waiting was at the root of the history of all Jewish trends and movements for the past hundred years or so. The advocates of emancipation counseled their fellow-Jews in Eastern Europe to wait for the rise of liberalism and enlightenment. Socialists (the Bund and others) waited for the revolution. The Orthodox waited for the messiah. The mainstream Zionists always recommended waiting for the outcome of some diplomatic scheme or overture, or until the world war (First and Second) is over. This author heard with his own ears Dr. Chaim Weizmann,[38] president of the World Zionist Organization, tell an audience of American Zionist leaders in 1943 that British Prime Minister Winston Churchill asked him to personally convey the message to American Jews not to embarrass the British (and the Allies) with their political agitation during the war. After the war, Churchill promised, he would see to it that the aspirations of the Jewish people would be satisfied.

Franklin D. Roosevelt spoke to American Zionists in the same vein. This was the slogan, the catchword, the promise: If you don't embarrass us now, then after the war, the problems will be solved satisfactorily. Most American Zionists, most American Jews in general, fell for this until it was too late. Then they woke up—and this, too, with great difficulty. The sequence was disastrous: even when absentmindedly becoming aware of the dangers ahead, they nonetheless were patiently and fatalistically waiting for things to take a turn for the better. This left the Jewish people unprotected and unprepared when the volcano erupted.

President Franklin D. Roosevelt with Ibn Saud, king of Saudi Arabia, in 1945.

Bontzie Schweig[39]

The third weakness was their uncritical trust in the established leadership. This is puzzling. In antiquity, the Jews were considered, and with a great deal of justification, as a spiritually and intellectually independent, if not rebellious, people. Most called them both rebellious and stiff-necked. Yet throughout their long dispersion and persecution, they seem to have undergone a radical change of character as far as attitude to their leadership is concerned. Whoever appeared as their representative and *shtadlan* [the Jews' liaison to the Gentile authorities], usually self-styled, was accepted gratefully and with a feeling that the leader or *shtadlan* knew best what was good for them. Throughout the centuries, they became conditioned to the almost absolute prohibition of questioning not only the motives but even the wisdom of their leaders.

This unqualified acceptance of leadership throughout the ages, but especially in the twentieth century, plagued not only the Jews but much of mankind. This attitude inevitably leads to trouble, upheaval, and often to revolution and war. When a man as an individual, or men as a group, a party, or a nation, begins unquestionably and unconditionally to say "Aye, aye!" to their leaders, it is almost like issuing a death sentence upon themselves. Freedom and survival are conditioned upon refusing to take things for granted. Policy and leadership must be scrutinized. When one risks one's life in the process of examining the important issues of existence, as Socrates did, his death becomes immortal.

Between the Devil and the Deep Blue Sea

The Jewish people of Europe found themselves caught between British denial that Palestine was ever intended as a solution to the Jewish problem, and Hitler's determination to get rid of the Jews by any means. For lack of an alternative in Hitler's fiendish mind, the solution was the gas ovens.

Only one man of stature, Jabotinsky, saw the situation realistically, and warned the Jews of Eastern Europe that they were living on the edge of a live volcano. He called for mass evacuation of the Jews from Europe, and offered a political plan to achieve it. This vision by necessity and logic implied a readiness to win the cooperation of the East European governments, first and above all the Polish government. The organized spokesmen of the full gamut of the Jewish organizations, from the Communists to the Zionists,[40] raised such a hue and cry with accusations of betrayal, that Jabotinsky once more became an outcast from the Jewish consensus. The Zionists as well as the anti-Zionists were against any hint of the necessity of Jewish mass emigration because, according to their views, this meant giving up the struggle and renouncing the "national" rights of the Jews in the countries of their dispersal. If this animosity towards Jabotinsky by the anti-Zionists was at least consistent with their ideology, then that of the Zionists must remain puzzling unless one attributes it to their perennial inclination to have their cake and eat it too.

Jabotinsky's most important innovation was the sense of urgency he tried to impart to the Jews in Europe. Most of them were confident that eternity was on their side. He felt that time was running out on them. His insistence that it was imperative for the Zionists to at least define their "final aim" did not make him *meshuga l'oto davar*, a man with an *idée fixe*, as his opponents claimed. He thought that defining the final aim in unambiguous terms was the only way of forcing the Zionists to apply means which would influence the course of immediate historic events. The Zionists thought they had at their disposal all the time they needed. Therefore they advocated the approach of "another dunam, another cow." By the same token and in the same spirit, they preached *geulat haprat*, the redemption of one person, and then another person, or small groups, to reside, if possible, in kibbutzim. Simultaneously, the Socialist Zionists preached world revolution. They didn't know that as far as the Jews were concerned, there just was no time for all that. Jabotinsky tried to convince them that the hour was late, to make them snap out of their stupor. He believed that if only he could persuade them of the "final aim" imperative, they would, in the nature of things, begin to concentrate their energies on practical ways and means to obtain that goal. He tried to impress them as to the imminence of the disaster, and appealed to them to prepare quickly for a mass evacuation. It was to no avail.

Setting the Stage for Hitler

A crucial decision in the months preceding the outbreak of the war was taken not by the Nazis but by Great Britain, by issuing the White Paper[11] on May 17, 1939, precisely when the survival of the Jews under Nazism hung in the balance. In a sense it was the British who showed the world—and Hitler took notice of it—that as far as the Jews were concerned, one could with complete impunity violate solemn international commitments, defy world public opinion (and, to a great extent, opinion in one's own country), act in defiance of explicit decisions of the international community, and ultimately get away with murder. The Jewish people and world public opinion understood Britain's 1917 Balfour Declaration, pledging to facilitate the establishment of the Jewish national home in Palestine, as an internationally sanctioned commitment. The League of Nations in 1922 conferred the Palestine Mandate on Great Britain as a trustee on the basis of the Balfour Declaration. This was widely understood to mean the eventual implementation of Jewish national sovereignty and independence. The British, however, built into the Balfour Declaration and other relevant policy documents a series of loopholes and deceptive ambiguities.

The White Paper of 1939 was a reversal of Britain's original pledges regarding Palestine. Now the British government, second only to Hitler, demonstrated that in the wider scheme of British imperial interests, Jewish survival was of little or no consequence. More than that, to sacrifice Jewish survival on the altar of the unappeasable gods of Empire was seen as serving the best interests of their colonial hold over vast territories.

Thus the January 1942 Wannsee Conference, at which the Nazis organized the administrative machinery to carry out the mass murder of Europe's Jews, should be viewed against the background of Great Britain's policy towards the Jewish people. The Nazi policy of total extermination would probably have been inconceivable without the British having set the stage for it both in the sacrifice of Czechoslovakia in the September 1938 Munich agreement and then in the Chamberlain government's May 1939 White Paper.

The British pronouncement that Jews are undesirable in Palestine (of all countries!) may have sparked Hitler's fiendish imagination: if they are not wanted in Palestine, the Promised Land of their National Home, then *a fortiori* he could argue with greater vigor that they are not wanted in the countries where they may be considered, and many did perceive themselves, to be foreigners.

In the years of Munich, the White Paper, and the Holocaust, there was a frightening similarity between the British and German peoples; in each case, the vast majority supported their respective governments. Of course in Germany the support was frenzied, hysterical, and nearly total, and those who did not share the enthusiasm cowered in silence, while in Great Britain there were many loud and eloquent voices of dissent. But they were in the minority and ineffective; they did not cause any changes in government policy. Even worse, as was later discovered, much of the opposition was opportunistic and partisan: the same Labour Party leadership that denounced the White Paper in 1939, continued implementing the White Paper, with staggering brutality, when it came to power in July 1945. Ernest Bevin, the foreign secretary and dominant figure of that government, revealed himself to be a notorious antisemite, crudely admonishing the pitiful remnant who survived the crematoria and wished to go to Palestine to live out the remainder of their traumatized lives, not to push to the "head of the queue." (What queue?)

Winston Churchill, who considered himself a stalwart Zionist, criticized the White Paper when it came up for debate in the House of Commons (on May 22, 1939) with his usual rhetorical power:

> The pledge of a home of refugees, of an asylum, was not made
> to the Jews of Palestine, but the Jews outside Palestine, to that
> vast, unhappy mass of scattered, persecuted, wandering Jews
> whose intense, unchanging, unconquerable desire has been for a
> National Home...That is the pledge which was given, and that
> is the pledge we are now asked to break...I feel bound to vote

against...As one intimately and responsibly concerned in the earlier stages of our Palestine policy, I could not stand by and see solemn engagements into which Britain has entered...set aside for reasons of administrative convenience or—and it will be a vain hope—for the sake of a quiet life. I should feel personally embarrassed in the most acute manner if I lent myself by silence or inaction, to what I must regard as an act of repudiation...a plain breach of a solemn obligation...a breach of faith...

What will the world think about it?...What will our potential enemies think?...Will they not be encouraged by our confession of recoil? Will they not be tempted to say, "They're on the run again. This is another Munich," and be more stimulated in their aggression by these very unpleasant reflections which they make?...May not this be a contributory factor...by which our potential enemies may be emboldened to take some irrevocable action and then find out, only after it is too late, that it is not this government, with their tired Ministers and flagging purpose, they have to face, but the might of Britain and all that Britain means?

By the end of May, the House of Commons approved the White Paper by a slim majority: out of a total strength of 413 members, 268 voted in favor, 179 against, and 110 abstained (such a large number of abstentions was unprecedented).

Chamberlain's government also needed the approval of the Mandates Commission of the League of Nations. It convened in June 1939 and devoted three sessions to the subject. Though the Colonial Secretary, Malcolm MacDonald, appeared in person to plead the case, the commission did not accept his arguments. In their report to the League Council, they declared that "the policy set out in the White Paper was not in accordance with the interpretation which, in agreement with the Mandatory Power and the Council, the Commission had placed upon the Palestine Mandate." But the British government paid no attention. With the outbreak of World War II, the League was dead.

On September 1, 1939, the Germans invaded Poland. Two days later, Great Britain and France declared war on Germany. The same day, September 3, Churchill joined Chamberlain's administration as First Lord of the Admiralty, that is, head of the navy. On May 7, 1940, less than a year after his aforementioned speech against the White Paper, Churchill became prime minister and formed a new government, most of whose members were on record as having voiced bitter, often devastating denunciations of the White Paper. Churchill remained in power until the end of July 1945, when the war was over and Hitler committed suicide. Throughout all the years of the Holocaust, under Churchill, the White Paper was rigorously and mercilessly enforced. In the meantime, Jews perished by the millions.

Martin Gilbert, the definitive biographer of Churchill, views him not only as a great leader on a global scale and intrepid commander in chief, but also as a moral figure of rare ethical and spiritual qualities. He seems to regard it as one of his tasks to rehabilitate Churchill's behavior and policies concerning the Jews during the Holocaust.[42] In March 1978, Gilbert appeared before an audience of survivors of Hitler's death camps and told them that according to documents newly made available to researchers by the British government, Churchill's cabinet colleagues and subordinate officials kept from him vital information concerning the mass destruction of the Jews. As a result, according to Gilbert, he really did not know the true story and the nature of the Holocaust. As Gilbert tells it, the policy of these officials generally was to keep secret the events of the Holocaust. The pertinent documents requiring Churchill's opinion were not shown to him. And if a question of possible rescue policy came up, knowing their boss's sense of compassion for the Jews and his hatred of Hitler, they found a way to deal with it on an administrative rather than political level.

Whenever by chance Churchill heard or read something about the unspeakable atrocities and brought the information to the attention of cabinet members or other senior officials of the government, they invariably tried to explain it away as propaganda, or as exaggerations, and otherwise minimized the significance of the news story—and besides, they argued, even if it were true, what could be done? Nothing, except to fight until Hitler, the scourge of the human race, was removed.

They never failed to point out that any concern with alleviating the plight of the Jews would inevitably lead to the question of admitting numbers of them to Palestine. Were the British to launch upon such a policy it would lead to disaster. The Arabs, to a man, would rise up in arms and join the enemy. This certainly is not what the prime minister wished. As a result, according to Gilbert, while Churchill tried hard, he never succeeded in convincing his colleagues of the necessity to do something to stop the slaughter.

Although the outrageous behavior of the British cabinet ministers and high officials is certainly true—and this we have from a plethora of public and primary documentary sources—it does not stand to reason that this was enough to keep Churchill ignorant of what ordinary citizens knew well to be the reality. A similar school of historiography tried to prove that Hitler did not know what his subordinates were doing to the Jews, and that he learned about the horrors of the Holocaust only in October 1943. When David Irving's controversial book[43] came out in 1977 containing the assertion that Hitler was ignorant of the

Holocaust, historian A.J.P. Taylor, reviewing the book, sarcastically asked: "Is it really conceivable that Hitler was the only man in Europe who did not know what was happening to the Jews or that the gas chambers existed?" Without trying to make invidious comparisons, and being fully aware of the main differences between the British leader and Hitler, who were separated by an unbridgeable abyss, it is difficult to resist the temptation to paraphrase Taylor's question and ask whether it was possible that only two people were not aware of the nature and dimensions of the Holocaust: Hitler and Churchill.

Yet it would be incorrect to look at it as an exclusive British-German duet. Not only Palestine was shut off: all the gates of escape and rescue were closed. The hearts of those in power, almost everywhere, who could help, were like stone; their consciences dead. It was one of the bleakest eras in the annals of man.

2 THE JEWISH RETURN TO POLITICAL ACTIVISM

The slow emergence of the Hebrew liberation movement was a reaction, indeed a rebellion, against the illusions and false hopes of all the Jewish political factions, including the Revisionists. The young pre-World War II generation which Jabotinsky inspired knew that the Jewish people were faced with a total crisis, and the only thing left to do was to take fate into their own hands. Theoretically, this was not an entirely new perception. No doubt the seminal Zionist thinkers Leon Pinsker,[44] in his pamphlet *AutoEmancipation*, and Theodor Herzl,[45] in his *Der Judenstaat (The Jews' State),* and some of the Hebrew poets, novelists, and publicists from the last quarter of the 19th century onward, were all prompted by the same psychological impulse and gave expression to the same awareness. What was new and revolutionary in the 1930s and 1940s was the means to be employed: active resistance which included violence. Ultimately, the Jews would have to rely upon their own determination to fight with weapons in their hands and be willing to risk their lives in the struggle for liberation.

Such an idea could hardly have occurred in Pinsker's time or Herzl's, when the mere concept of a political campaign on behalf of the Jews as a national entity was new and untried. The founders and shapers of Zionism were revolutionary in two respects. First, conceptually: auto-emancipation—not to wait for outside help to bring salvation, but achieve it by the efforts and will of the Jews themselves. Second, the means—by international diplomatic, political, and propaganda efforts. Half a century passed and there was little to show for the effort. Not that the results were not of great value; they were, but not in proportion to the need. They did not advance the cause of the Hebrew nation towards national independence.

The young generation of the 1930s threw themselves body and soul into the battle for a new type of political activism initiated by Jabotinsky. These young men and women who flocked with enthusiasm to Jabotinsky's banner were a new breed of Jews never known in the history of the Diaspora. Disciplined, wearing uniforms, undergoing paramilitary training for the defense of the nation (in Palestine), they were incorporated in units of a military pattern. They marched in parades. They transformed their manner and body posture. They learned to take orders from superiors. They prepared for *aliyah*. Politically, they were the backbone of Jabotinsky's movement, the Revisionist Zionists. They organized mass meetings, engaging in a recruiting campaign on an unprecedented scale. More than one million Jews in Eastern Europe became supporters of Jabotinsky, listened to his oratory, sang his songs, were enthralled by his personality. It lasted for more than a decade, but slowly it became clear to some of his most ardent and loyal followers that even his activist Zionism did not achieve a break-through. This, despite the fact that it captured the imagination and enthusiasm of a great many of the masses, with its bold proclamation of statehood as the aim of Zionism (something which other branches of the Zionist movement refrained from saying), its creation of a mass movement of Jews to identify themselves with this aim, its mass propaganda campaign to make the world understand it, and its independent diplomatic activities based on the goal of statehood. Despite all this, the Revisionist leader saw no way to transform the World Zionist Organization from within, and consequently seceded from it. In 1935, he created the New Zionist Organization. Some 713,000 people voted in the election to the NZO's Constituent Congress, which convened in Vienna in September of that year. (By comparison, the 19th World Zionist Congress, held at about the same time in Lucerne, was elected by 635,000 voters.) Yet this extraordinary demonstration of mass support and organizational strength did not bring the hoped-for results. On the contrary, the new movement began somehow to share the fate of the old organization led by Chaim Weizmann and the Socialist Zionists, and to end up in the same blind alley into which the Zionism of the official, traditional school had maneuvered itself.

From the Jewish Legion to the Revolt

What was the magic which drew so many of the young to Jabotinsky, and what was it that later caused their disenchantment, which gradually turned into a discreet and muffled rebellion?

The idea of Jewish armed resistance and violence was the brainchild of Jabotinsky. He fired the imagination of the young Jews in Eastern Europe with the idea that in their struggle for liberation, they must not only include the military factor, but make it their cornerstone. He preached this idea with the full force of his personality. Probably 95 percent of the young who joined one of his organizations, but especially Betar, did so because of this vision of Jews wielding military force. This was the great emotional impulse that impelled them to gather around his banner. For Jabotinsky, Jewish militarism was an expression of two related concepts. One was that a military force, an army, both symbolizes and concretizes the notion of nationhood. Even in the process of achieving legal international status, a nation can best be characterized by its ability to take care of its own military security.

The second concept was self-defense: to defend Jewish life whenever and wherever attacked by enemies. This was purely a humanist attitude: Jewish life is of the greatest importance and must be defended under all circumstances, even if it involves making a deal with the devil. This was the case in December 1921, when Jabotinsky attempted to come to an agreement with Simon Petlura, the White Russian general whose armies engaged in systematic pogroms while fighting the Bolsheviks. He did not care who Petlura was, what his feelings were, or his political ambitions. He wanted to make a deal with him that Jewish gendarmerie should defend the Jews against his own soldiers. Nothing came of it. But late in his life, he said that if asked what epitaph he wished on his tomb, he would suggest "This was the man who made the pact with Petlura."

In the spring of 1903, at the age of 23 and not yet a Zionist, Jabotinsky organized the first Jewish defense group in his native Odessa, in anticipation of a pogrom. Since that date, he remained dedicated to Jewish military defense. Years later, again anticipating anti-Jewish outbreaks by Arab mobs in Palestine, he organized the first Haganah units which he led during the bloody Jerusalem riots in April 1920. A military court sentenced Jabotinsky to fifteen years at hard labor. He became the first *Asir Tzion*, Prisoner in Zion.[46]

These were all bold, innovative, heroic moves—but defensive in nature. Their aim was the protection of Jews. At the same time, he considered his initiatives not only a practical means to defend Jewish lives, but also a matter of pride and morale. He hated to see Jews attacked, humiliated, cringing, waiting for the Russian policeman or soldier to save him. Or, in Jerusalem and Jaffa, Jewish pedestrians consciously walking close to the front doors of buildings to make it easier to escape Arab pogromists.

During World War I, Jabotinsky fought almost single-handedly to bring about the creation of Jewish units within the British army, known as the Jewish Legion. His personal campaign exemplified heroism and vision, a determination to crusade for an issue against all odds, against emancipated Jews and fellow Zionists, against the reluctance of the British government—and even against the stateless Jews from Eastern Europe who immigrated to England before and during the war, and who simply did not want to be inducted into the British army because, like most Jews everywhere, they did not consider the Entente with the hated Czarist Russia as an ally on their side. Their enemy then was not Germany, but Russia—the Russia of the pogroms, of the Pale of Settlement, of the persecutions, of official antisemitism. Jabotinsky, with his vision, saw the Entente victorious and the partition of the Ottoman Empire as a foregone conclusion, and was sure that if the Jews participated in the war, especially in the conquest of Palestine, it would be counted in their favor during postwar deliberations about the future status of Palestine. The Jewish units did play a major part in shaping the political and psychological climate in which Zionism was viewed in England, and had an impact upon some of the British statesmen who were responsible for the Balfour Declaration.

But Jabotinsky's hope and dream that the Jewish Legion would remain a permanent institution after the war, with a role in the occupation and then defense of the country, did not materialize. The British disbanded the Legion. Why did Jabotinsky's plan for the Legion fail? For the same reason that so little in many Zionist enterprises succeeded as hoped: because everything was contingent upon the good will, honor, and friendship of the British. Britain displayed neither good will, honor, nor friendship. It was, in fact, with some notable exceptions, anti-Zionist and at some junctures even antisemitic.

Jabotinsky continued during all his life to fight for the Jewish Legion, and made it the central plank in his political platform. But it was an object to be achieved by British consent. He wanted a Charter for the Legion, as Herzl wanted a Charter from the Turkish Sultan for a Jewish state, in whatever guise it was deemed possible. It did not work.

The idea of conquering Palestine by military force was not foreign to Jabotinsky. More than once it crossed his mind, but somehow he could not reconcile the violence it involved with the legality of his approach—his conviction that the aim of national independence in the last account could be achieved politically. He thought perhaps a symbolic act should be undertaken—for instance, a military attempt to occupy Jerusalem, or part of it, to raise the Hebrew flag and hold it for a short time, if only for a few hours, and he himself would be in command of the operation. This would symbolically set the precedent for Hebrew sovereignty in Palestine. It never came to fruition. He always reverted to his credo that the main thrust of the movement must be political. It could to some extent be supported by controlled acts of violence. But when he listened to the arguments of his young disciples, they angered him and almost drove him to despair. At times he thought they were absurd.

This does not diminish Jabotinsky's greatness as the father of the Hebrew liberation movement and its spiritual commander in chief. He was a hero. In Jabotinsky one could find the virtues and talents of all the other Zionist leaders combined and multiplied many times over. He remains a giant, standing head and shoulders above the rest. But he did not come to the last logical, if desperate, conclusion: that the liberation of the Jews was contingent upon an independent military force, organized not by permission or "charter" from the British, but forged independently. His disciples and followers of the young generation of the emerging Hebrew nation, both in Palestine and in Eastern Europe, whose imagination was fired by the idea of a Jewish Legion, came to a completely unexpected revolutionary conclusion: this military force has to be organized independently, with or without British consent. It must not be only defensive. It has to be the instrument and means to liberate Palestine from British rule altogether. This was the aim and therein was the solution.

Simultaneously they came to the conclusion—also inspired by Jabotinsky—that a military force fighting to liberate the country from colonial rule could succeed only if accompanied by a vigorous propaganda and diplomatic campaign to explain and back up the military activities. The imperative was to put the British on the defensive diplomatically, disarm them politically, and pillory them morally. All this was achieved in a comparatively short time by the combined efforts of a military struggle by the Hebrew underground in Palestine, and the political, diplomatic, and propaganda campaigns undertaken by the Bergson Group in the United States and later in France.

The Formative Years of the Jewish Resistance

When did the Jewish resistance movement in Palestine begin? Chronologically, the answer is clear: when Abba Achimeir[47] organized the first anti-British demonstration in 1930, on the occasion of the visit to Palestine of the Undersecretary of State for the Colonies, Drummond Shiels. But ideologically and politically, the answer is less clear. The genealogy and evolution of ideas and concepts is always more difficult to establish than that of events. It is difficult to state which came first, the deed or the idea.

Jabotinsky liked to quote from Goethe the lines about Faust's uncertainty as to how to translate the opening verse of St. John:

It says: "In the beginning was the word."
Already I am stopped. It seems absurd.
The Word does not deserve the highest prize.
I must translate it otherwise.
If I am well inspired and not blind.
It says: in the beginning was the Mind.
Ponder that first line, wait and see.
Lest you should write too hastily.
Is mind the all-creating source?
It ought to say: In the beginning there was Force.
Yet something warns me as I grasp the pen,
That my translation must be changed again.
The spirit helps me. Now it is exact.
I write: In the beginning was the Act.

If Jabotinsky was enchanted with this passage it is because it reflected his own doubts, though more often than not he was inclined to accept that at the beginning was the word, the concept, which is the father of the deed. This is a moot theory, unless it means that in order to be of significance, every deed must stem from a concept. But it definitely does not mean that every concept leads to action.

Hegel claimed, and rightly so, that in a man's mind all kinds of ideas cross and crisscross, but so long as they are not related to a concrete deed to follow, the ideas mean nothing. Actually, man often acts out of intuition rather than rational thought, out of obscure, inexplicable promptings. Perhaps it would not be a wild statement to say that all knowledge, or most scientific achievement, is a result of experimenting on hunches rather than *a priori* conceptions. Life and history probably result from that composite dynamism that makes up man's essence, which is both thought and intuition, which are inseparable and unreal in isolation.

In the formative years of the Hebrew movement of national liberation, the ideas and concepts were vague, inarticulate, somewhat self-contradictory, still overlaid with traditional Zionist preconceptions, terminology, and inherited clichés. In some instances, it was influenced, to a degree, by the then-current slogans of various European nationalist movements. But its inspirations, though varied, sprang from original Hebrew sources and personalities. Apart from Jabotinsky—the spiritual father and idol of the national liberation movement— there were the Hebrew poets, such as Chaim Bialik, who castigated the Jews of the Diaspora for passively accepting their oppression. In the style of the ancient Hebrew prophets, he fulminated against Jewish cowardice and lack of dignity, extolling the heroism and daring of the mythological giants who rebelled against Moses and attempted to take Palestine by storm, before the time was ripe. There was Tschernichowsky, perhaps the greatest poet of the early decades of the 20th century, who extolled the virtues of the ancient Greeks, along with the heroic deeds of the ancient Hebrew heroes. Dr. Joseph Klausner wrote a multi volume history of the commonwealth during the Second Temple, from the beginning until the country was conquered by the Romans. In his books, he vividly described the zealots' fight for freedom. A poet of lesser stature, Ya'akov Cahan, coined the phrase "In blood and fire, Judea fell, in blood and fire it will rise again."[48] It became one of the unofficial anthems of the liberation movement.

Drawing its inspiration from poetry and history, rebellious youth, who for the most part belonged to the movement created by Jabotinsky, engaged in a campaign of resistance and then of violence against the British. Its purpose was to let the authorities know how the Jews felt about their policy. It had no clearly defined philosophy or aim. The ideological and conceptual crystallization was a slow process.

The various and consecutive avatars of the Hebrew national resistance movement may be divided roughly into three phases. First came *The Romantic*, from 1930 to 1937, initiated by Abba Achimeir. The second was *The Break* with the past, and the decision to become organizationally, militarily, and ideologically self-reliant. This period began in 1937 with the establishment of the independent military organization, the Irgun Zvai Leumi. This period lasted until the outbreak of World War II. The third phase was that of *Crystallization*. This was during the years 1939-1944, when a coherent and integrated philosophy of national liberation was formulated.

Achimeir, a militant anti-Socialist, spearheaded the first revolt against conventional Zionist methods. He organized the first anti-British demonstration in Jerusalem and became the first political prisoner in British Mandatory Palestine. He formed an illegal group called *Brit ha-Biryonim* (the name of the extreme zealots who fought the Romans in the First Century CE). His organization was small but undertook several spectacular demonstrations against the British. (They also later tore down the swastika flags flying above the German Consulate in Jerusalem.) These activities, although limited in scope and nonviolent, gained renown throughout Palestine and the Diaspora as expressions of a new spirit and a fresh form of struggle. The British harassed and repeatedly arrested Achimeir and his comrades. When Dr. Chaim Arlosoroff, prominent Labor Zionist and chief of the Jewish Agency's Political Department, was murdered in June 1933, the British authorities arrested Achimeir, accusing him of being the "spiritual instigator" of the killings because of his militant writings. Although acquitted of the charge, he was re-arrested for belonging to an "illegal terrorist organization."[49]

Jabotinsky's attitude towards Achimeir was somewhat ambiguous, as was his later attitude towards the underground resistance movement. He enthusiastically approved of what Achimeir did—and even referred to him as *morenu v'rabenu* (our teacher and mentor)—but not of what he wrote. Achimeir's journalistic diaries indulged in extremism and occasionally conveyed some sympathy for Fascist Italy under Mussolini. Of course, at that time such sentiment was not an unheard-of phenomenon in the Western world, and more than a few well-meaning democrats expressed admiration for aspects of the Italian dictator's rule. But that was not Jabotinsky's taste or philosophy; he was an inveterate liberal of the 19th century school of Mazzini,[50] and an uncompromising libertarian. In any event, the arrests and trials took their toll and Achimeir's group faded from the scene after a few years, giving way to groups of a blatantly military character.

In 1931-1932, a split ruptured the Haganah, the Labor Zionist-controlled underground defense militia. A group of Haganah members who belonged to non-Socialist parties seceded, and under the leadership of Avraham Tehomi created a second clandestine group, which they initially called Haganah Bet. Although the vast majority of the rank and file of the new group were followers of Jabotinsky, it was an independent, nonparty entity in every respect. It was not controlled, officially or unofficially, by the Revisionist Party or by Jabotinsky

personally. Soon, however, Haganah Bet shifted from being nonpartisan to acting in accordance with Jabotinsky's views. In December 1936, Jabotinsky officially appointed Tehomi commander in chief of the Irgun, as it was now known.
Within months, though, Tehomi had reached agreement with the leadership
of the Haganah to merge the two militias. Most of the Irgun's approximately
three thousand members refused to follow their commander. In April 1937, they
expelled Tehomi, officially launched the Irgun, and asked Jabotinsky to serve as
their commander in chief.[51] After some hesitation, he agreed to an arrangement
according to which his orders on major policy would be obeyed and he would
appoint a commander in Palestine to lead day to day operations.

This arrangement did not go smoothly. Tensions between the Palestine
Command and the commander in chief were exacerbated by the fact that
Jabotinsky was banned by the British from entering Palestine. Communications
between the local commander and Jabotinsky were poor, not merely because of
technical problems but because the Command in Palestine sometimes tried to
circumvent the need for Jabotinsky's approval in instances where they suspected
(for good reason) that he might disapprove. Some of the operations they undertook went against his grain and his inner convictions on ethical and not only
political grounds. Rivalries developed between the Palestine Command of the
Irgun and the executive committee of the Revisionist Party, on the one hand,
and with the leadership of the Revisionist youth movement, Betar, on the other.
Since all three organizations were interested in taking an active part in 'illegal
immigration,' there was a need for active coordination but it did not always
proceed harmoniously.

Jabotinsky never tried to return clandestinely to Palestine, because he
regarded himself primarily as a political leader rather than the head of an
underground military organization. He never wavered from the Zionist saying,
Bereshit bara elokim et ha-politika, i.e. "In the beginning, God created politics." It
became increasingly difficult for him to reconcile the two positions he held. In
the end, the Irgun's relationship with him was not only strained but artificial,
and his authority was nominal. When Jabotinsky passed away in August 1940,
the Hebrew underground which he inspired and helped bring into being was
fragmented and demoralized at the very nadir of its history.

The Irgun's Young Leadership

Among the young militants who created the Irgun were a number who later
became historic figures, among them David Raziel, Avraham Stern, and Hillel
Kook. They did not begin at the top of the hierarchy. The first commander of
the Irgun was Robert Bitker, who was soon replaced by Moshe Rosenberg. In

late 1937, Raziel, who had been commander of the IZL's Jerusalem district and a member of the High Command, became commander. In addition to his military qualifications, Raziel was a natural leader of men, an intellectual, a Hebrew scholar, a stylist of exceptional eloquence, and a powerful personality of character and inspiration. It has been reported that Jabotinsky, after meeting Raziel and hearing of his exploits, remarked: "This is the man for whom I was waiting these last fifteen years."

Stern, also known as Yair, was a poet, a linguist, a theoretician and a man of great personal charm. One of his songs, *"Chayalim Almonim"* (Unknown Soldiers), a composition of exceptional beauty and power, became the hymn of the fighting underground. On occasion the song was erroneously attributed to Jabotinsky, prompting him to publicly assert that he wished he could write such an excellent poem. As for Hillel Kook, more about him below.

Raziel and Stern, who together with other members formed the High Command, succeeded in instilling in the rank and file a new spirit of dedication and morale as well as an increased intellectual and ideological level. They increased membership, intensified the activities of the underground in Palestine, and successfully expanded their work into the Diaspora.

At that point, during the last two and a half years before the outbreak of World War II, the Irgun leadership did not fall into a mood of despair, despite the fast-deteriorating situation for Jews in Palestine and the Diaspora, and despite their frustration at the lack of tangible achievements from Jabotinsky's political offensive. On the contrary, because they were educated and inspired by Jabotinsky, they refused to share the fatalism of the Zionists and the Jews in general, and to feel defeated before the battle was really underway. They did not reconcile themselves to the idea that nothing could be done. They grew ever more conscious of the underground's potential military strength and its growing popularity in the *yishuv*, which increased in numbers (by the late 1930s it numbered about 600,000 strong). The bleaker the conditions of the Jews in Europe became, the greater was the appeal of the Irgun to the younger generation both in Palestine and the Diaspora.

Yet the break with the mainstream Zionist movement and the increased alienation from Jabotinsky and the Revisionist Party made the Irgun's task seem almost impossible. Its commanders had placed the movement outside the perimeters of most of Jewish and Zionist life and thought. The decision to make that break, to take that leap in the dark, refusing to recognize any authority except their own consciences, raised the danger that the Irgunists would behave irresponsibly—that they might become anarchists or lawless desperadoes, as the British and the Zionist leadership were wont to characterize them. In that formative phase, none of these fears materialized. The young Irgun commanders realized from the beginning that whatever they intended to undertake could not be achieved in an atmosphere of moral and political chaos. They knew that they would have to act as fighters for the survival and freedom of an ancient people.

It was at this second phase that the Irgun was already engaged in a struggle in three different but related fields: acts of violence in Palestine; defying and breaking the British blockade against Jewish immigration by bringing in Jews "illegally," despite the White Paper regulation (which is why it was known as *Af Ai Pi*, i.e. "despite all obstacles"); and organizational, military, and propaganda training in Poland, as well as diplomatic contacts with East European governments, especially with the regime in Warsaw. Out of this range of activities, undertaken out of necessity and under the pressure of external events, there emerged a pattern of thought and a conceptualized approach to the crisis in which the Jewish nation found itself, both in Palestine and in East Europe.

Reevaluating Zionism's Major Premises

The Hebrew liberation movement rejected nearly all the major premises of the Zionist movement. It saw the root of Zionism's failure in its unconditional focus upon one power: Great Britain. Even the Revisionists, let alone the mainstream Zionists, never questioned the justification of British rule in Palestine. They claimed only that Britain abused this right, and that with the White Paper of 1939 it flagrantly betrayed its trust. But it was always their idea that whatever the policy of this or that British government may be in Palestine, the basis of Jewish claims was still embodied in the Balfour Declaration and the Mandate. Hence the political aim of all the Zionists, and foremost of the Revisionists, was to bring about a revision of British policy in favor of Zionism. But in essence, the aim still was to perpetuate British tutelage over Palestine, at least until such time as the Jews will be strong enough—that is, enjoy a majority—to rule Palestine as a Jewish state.

Jabotinsky did believe the Jews should not consider themselves irrevocably bound to the fact of a British presence in Palestine. He did argue, although somewhat forlornly, that it was unwise for the Jews to lock themselves into the idea of the British Mandate. He suggested instead that the Jews look to another power that might be available to take over the Mandate, perhaps Poland or a group of nations. In his view, the Jews should behave like a young woman being courted by a suitor, who had not yet made up her mind and let it be known that she was still open to the wooing of other suitors. In his testimony on February 11, 1937, before Britain's Peel Commission—which had been sent to investigate the Palestine problem following Arab riots that erupted in 1936—Jabotinsky made it clear that the bond between the British and the Jews in Palestine was not some kind of unbreakable Catholic marriage:

> What will happen if what the Jews desire cannot be conceded
> by Great Britain?...[T]hen we shall expect Great Britain to act
> as any Mandatory who feels he cannot carry out the Mandate:
> give back the Mandate. [T]he Mandatory together with the
> Jews will look for the alternative; we will sit down together
> and think what can be done; but not that Great Britain should
> go on holding the Mandate and pretend it is 'fulfilled' while
> my people are still suffering in the Diaspora and still only a
> minority in Palestine.

What he hoped was that under such circumstances the British would become worried, have a change of mind if not of heart, and hence become more willing to live up to their original pledges under the Mandate to help create a Jewish national home. If worse came to worst, Palestine should perhaps be entrusted to another, more suitable, friendly, interested Mandatory. From a practical point of view, there was little chance in the middle and late 1930s that anybody would agree to take over the Mandate. But the point here is that Jabotinsky took it for granted that although it might become necessary to replace the British with another ruler, Palestine would still remain under foreign tutelage. In the minds of the commanders of the Hebrew underground and their emissaries and supporters abroad, however, a new attitude gradually developed: Why should Palestine be ruled by a foreign power and not by the Hebrew nation itself?

The rebellious generation which brought into existence the Hebrew liberation movement was not inhibited by political sophistry and legalistic double talk about British rights and prerogatives in Eretz Yisrael, except those conferred upon her by the League of Nations to sponsor and facilitate the building of the Jewish National Home. Regardless of what the term "national home" implied, one thing it certainly could not mean: exclusion. Nor could it mean that the Jews already living in Palestine should be left to the outrages of Arab terror and not be protected. Jabotinsky pleaded with the British to permit the Jews to defend themselves legally. In his testimony before the Peel Commission, he said:

> As to keeping the country quiet and avoiding disturbances:
> [T]ry reestablishing the Jewish Regiment [Legion] as part and
> parcel of the permanent garrison. Try legalizing Jewish self-
> defense...Why should the impression be created in this country
> that we want Johnny, Tommy, and Bobby to defend us? We
> do not. If, in the building of Palestine, sweat and gold have to
> be employed, let us give the sweat and let us give the gold; if
> blood has to be shed by the defenders of Palestine, let it be our
> blood and not English blood.

The Haganah, the self-defense organization controlled by the Labor Zionists, practiced *havlagah*, a term meaning to restrain oneself from reacting, in this case from reacting to the Arab terrorists who made the highways and marketplaces in Palestine extremely dangerous for the Jews in the mid and late 1930s. The Irgun rejected *havlagah* and answered terror with terror: as long as the highways and marketplaces remained unsafe for Jews, they would also be unsafe for the Arabs.

This was not the only objective of the Hebrew resistance movement. A second goal was to remove from the hands of the British the jurisdiction over Jewish immigration. Arab terror was aimed chiefly at forcing the British to close the gates of Palestine to any Jewish immigration, which they finally succeeded in doing. The Irgun decided to take the matter of immigration into its own hands by bringing in Jews "illegally" on chartered ships. The Hebrew resistance forces could not accept the British argument nor those of the Arabs that this would unfairly change the demographic balance between Jews and Arabs and eventually affect the political status of Palestine. All legal and international considerations apart, regardless of whether or not the apprehensions of the Arabs were justified (and they certainly were), the Jews had no choice; the alternative was death. They literally ran for their lives. The right to live transcends every other consideration. For the Jews who tried to flee, it was a matter of life and death, as subsequent events proved beyond a shadow of a doubt. From this sense of desperate urgency was born *aliyah bet*, the "other" *aliyah*, unauthorized by the British but endowed with the moral authority of the right to life.

3   RESCUE ON THE EVE OF THE HOLOCAUST

As the *aliyah bet* campaign intensified, the Irgun found itself in desperate need of funds to support these efforts. Funding this rescue activity became the burning task, transcending everything else. With the Jewish communities of Europe under siege, the United States was the obvious place for such work. Between the spring of 1939 and the summer of 1940, the Irgun sent a handful of its most talented and promising activists from Europe and Palestine to America. Ultimately these young men would succeed in altering the course of American foreign policy and influencing the fate of Jewish Palestine, despite the fact the governments of mighty nations, as well as the Zionist leadership, devoted an inordinate amount of time and energy to trying to liquidate the activists.

Peter Bergson (Hillel Kook)

In the Yiddish and Anglo-Jewish press, they were often referred to as "the boys," because they were so young to become major players in the world of American and Jewish politics: they were all in their twenties or, at most, early thirties. They displayed the toughness and recklessness of underground fighters, combined with the polish, wit, and graceful manners of intellectual men of the world, a rare combination. All were educated; most were former university students. They spoke multiple languages. Most were good speakers and writers. Their reasoning and dialectics were most persuasive. They had a flair for public relations, a knack for propaganda. Some were natural born diplomats; their commander, Hillel Kook—who used the name Peter H. Bergson while in the United States[52]—excelled at this art. All were indomitable; even when faced with tremendous odds, they were fearless. They never took no for an answer. They refused to accept defeat, yet none ever panicked. They were also individualists. After the establishment of Israel, they remained creative in their various fields, whether academia, finance, industry, or international commerce. Three of them—including this author—served in Israel's first Knesset, but then decided against careers in politics.

Samuel Merlin in 1943.

This nucleus was joined, in the group's inner leadership circle, by a small number of Americans who were not famous but dedicated themselves to the cause of rescue and liberation. Editor and author Harry L. Selden;[53] Philadelphia businessman Alex Wilf;[54] Rabbi Baruch Rabinowitz;[55] Canadian businessman Sam Dubiner and his wife Betty;[56] dentist Irving Shendell, inventor Nathan Horwitt;[57] Judge Esther Untermeyer;[58] Louis Yampolsky, who was the group's accountant as well as a leader of the Philadephia branch together with his wife, Betty;[59] and many others, who literally gave up their businesses and became full time champions of the Jewish struggle. They did so at great personal sacrifice, not only because they did not attend to their businesses but because they were also among the largest financial contributors to the movement. Each of these men and women had his or her own spark of genius. In all probability, the successes of the Bergson Group would never have been achieved without their involvement.

Harry Selden

Baruch Rabinowitz

Louis and Betty Yampolsky, who were among the leaders of the Bergson Group's Philadelphia chapter. (Louis was also the national group's pro bono accountant.)

Bergson, who was the chief officer of the Irgun in the Diaspora, arrived in New York from London in July 1940. Also arriving that spring or summer were Arieh Ben Eliezer,[60] Alex Rafaeli (who sometimes went by the name Hadani),[61] Eri Jabotinsky (son of Vladimir Ze'ev Jabotinsky),[62] and this author. The group functioned as a military unit, although of course they never indulged in any military or illegal activities in the United States. One of their guiding principles was that there was a commander who had the last word, and the last word was the equivalent of a military order. This does not mean that there were no lively discussions which lasted for days, even weeks. Bergson, although of a stubborn character and a man of deep, almost unshakable convictions, was nonetheless open to the ideas of his colleagues and often accepted their views, retreating from his own position. If, however, he was convinced of something, it was his opinion which prevailed and his decision that was carried out. Whatever the flaws inherent in such a system when applied to political rather than military activities, it was justified by the results.

Following the German annexation of Austria, the *Anschluss*, in March 1938, the SS and the Gestapo actually cooperated with the Irgun's *aliyah bet* agents, since German policy at that point was to encourage Jewish emigration from Europe. The Nazis provided travel documents and permitted Jewish émigrés to take some money with them (although the sum they allowed quickly shrank and then ceased altogether). As a result of the Germans' eagerness to get rid of as many Jews as possible, tens of thousands reached Palestine in defiance of British restrictions. Hundreds of thousands more could have been saved if not for the obstructionist attitude of the Zionist establishment. At first the Zionist leaders opposed *aliyah bet* because they wanted to cooperate with the British, not clash with them. Later, when the leaders themselves undertook *aliyah bet* work, they acted without the necessary sense of urgency. Moreover, they foolishly insisted on trying to monopolize the field, as they did in all their endeavors. They controlled "legal" *aliyah*—by serving as the intermediary with the British in the allocation of immigration certificates—so naturally they wanted to control "illegal" *aliyah* as well. This would have been impractical and certainly unnecessary. But it was the product of a certain mindset that regarded anything they did not control as being wrong and harmful.

As of May 1939, England's White Paper policy limited Jewish immigration to just 15,000 per year. The new policy was implemented precisely at the time that escape from Europe was becoming a matter of life and death for the Jews. The few entry certificates allocated by the British were insufficient for even a tiny fraction of those in desperate need to flee. The British gave the certificates to the Jewish Agency and, by a viciously-devised system of partisan distribution, the precious lifesaving documents were given, first and foremost, to those affiliated with the Labor Zionist movement. The Jewish Agency thus became a political monopoly with the power to determine who would be saved and who would be left behind. Followers of Jabotinsky—an enormous number of European Jews—were almost totally excluded, because the Revisionists were regarded by the Zionist leadership as dissidents and troublemakers who were not part of the legitimate Zionist movement. Other groups were also excluded because they did not belong to the "approved" Zionist party or faction. In despair, the masses of European Jews rebelled against the British restrictions and against the Jewish Agency, and decided to go to Palestine without asking anyone's permission.

Eri Jabotinsky, who was a leading activist in organizing *aliyah bet*, later described the situation in these terms:

> The Jewish people awoke to the realization that they were no longer the subjects of any country; that no government was ready to protect them; that their fate lay in their own hands. Their decision to proceed to Palestine, by any means available, was not reached at any conference or Congress. It was the mute, almost instinctive resolution of a terror-stricken multitude. At the time I believed that we [Irgun emissaries in Europe] were instrumental in unleashing that flood. Since then, I have often

wondered. It seems to me now that we were the servants of this human stampede, rather than its leaders and captains.[63]

Yet the Zionist establishment did not regard *aliyah* as a way to rescue Europe's Jews from a raging inferno. They saw *aliyah* as a means to gradually build up their version of a Jewish state, through the "selective" admission of young pioneers trained for kibbutz life. They were ready to write off a substantial portion of the Jewish masses, as is clear from the remarks made by Dr. Chaim Weizmann, president of the Jewish Agency and World Zionist Organization, at the 1937 World Zionist Congress, in Zurich.

The date was August 4. The delegates were debating the report of Britain's Peel Commission, which had recently concluded its investigation of the causes of the Arab riots in Palestine. The report recommended the partition of western Palestine into a tiny Jewish state, a larger Arab state, and British zones of control.[64] Weizmann spoke in favor of the principle of partition, although he believed the Jews could negotiate for improved borders. He spoke emotionally about the grim conditions that Jews faced in Europe, and the enormous responsibility which the Zionist leadership had to assume for the fate of millions of Jews.

In his remarks, Weizmann divided European Jewry into two categories: those whom the Zionists should try to save by bringing them to Palestine; and those who would have to be abandoned and wait for the arrival of the Messiah. He recalled that when he testified before the Peel Commission, the commission members had asked him, "But can you bring six million to Palestine?" Weizmann's reply, which he recounted to the delegates assembled in Zurich and was recorded by the stenographer there:

> "No." He was acquainted with the laws of physics and chemistry and he knew the force of material factors; in the depth of the Jewish tragedy he wanted at least two million of youth, with their lives before them...to be saved. The old ones will pass; they will bear their fate, or they will not. They were dust, economic and moral dust, in a cruel world...*She'erith hapleytah*—only a remnant, a branch, shall survive: two million, perhaps less. They had to accept it. The rest they must leave to the future—to their youth... *Be'ackhrith Hayamim*—in the end of days, after suffering, they must find the way to redemption.[65]

How did the elected delegates to the World Zionist Congress respond? They rose to a man and sang *Hatikvah*, the Zionist national anthem. Weizmann's address and the subsequent ovation are frightening, almost incomprehensible.

Here a revered leader, celebrated for two decades throughout the world as the great champion of the Jews, revealed in a speech before the elected representatives of the Zionist movement that he was aware that millions of Jews in Europe, in fact the majority of Europe's Jews, were facing destruction. But instead of seeking a solution to save them, he offered a vision of doom, as if their demise was inevitable so there was no use fighting it. "Jewish history," he asserted at one point in his speech, "is not ours to mold." He surrendered in advance to the supposedly preordained catastrophe. He psychologically and morally prepared his followers for this outcome, in a sense almost justifying the cruel destiny that Jewry faced, by characterizing them as dust, moral and economic dust, and proclaiming that the aim is to save just a remnant. At the same time, he in effect demanded from the Jewish masses that they accept the fate he prophesied for them.

While the Zionist establishment leaders claimed their aim was to liberate the Jewish people from oppression and save them from cataclysm, their ideology was in a sense anti-humanist. They viewed the Jewish masses as unworthy, unproductive human beings whose ultimate fate was of limited interest to them. The ideologues of the mainstream Zionist leadership strove for the spiritual and economic transformation of the Jews into a productive, morally superior, nationally self-conscious and proud people who in Palestine would practice social justice, free from the vices prevalent in other societies. Since such a transformation would require generations to achieve, they were psychologically geared for a very gradual, drawn-out process. They were not ready to deal with an urgent situation involving imminent danger. They were preoccupied with their plan for educating a relatively small group of pioneers to become worthy of redemption, an elite who would set an example for others to imitate, or to be left to their own fate. It was a highly ideological approach, completely inappropriate for dealing with reality.

Obviously Weizmann was well intentioned. Of course he did not want to see millions of Jews annihilated. He believed he was focusing on the best prospects for saving at least two million. Certainly that was a substantial number and had that aim been achieved, the dimensions of the disaster would have been that much less. But the principle of selectivity, of choosing the "best" portion to be saved, was both heartless and self-defeating. "Two million, perhaps less," he said. The principle was what counted the most; the moment he accepted it, the numbers became a matter of secondary consideration. The estimates of how many could be saved would diminish continuously as the tragedy enveloped European Jewry. By 1944, a Hungarian Zionist establishment figure, Dr. Rudolf Kastner, was selecting 1,600 Jews, out of the 800,000 Jews of Hungary, to be put on a train to Switzerland and saved as part of a deal with the Nazis which, in effect, sealed the doom of the rest of Hungarian Jewry. Kastner justified his action on the grounds that 1,600 was the most that could be saved. One may draw a direct line from Weizmann's prophecy of saving two million to Kastner saving 1,600, a line representing the vicious ideology of "selectivity."

The Tragedy of the Sakarya

In early 1939, an unlikely trio of activists arrived in New York City to begin planting the seeds for a movement to support *aliyah bet*: Col. John Henry Patterson,[66] a Christian Zionist and famed British lion hunter who had commanded the Jewish Legion that Jabotinsky had convinced the British to create in World War One; Robert Briscoe,[67] the Jewish mayor of Dublin, Ireland; and Chaim Lubinsky, an officer of the Irgun. The young dynamo who followed the delegation to the United States one month later, and began creating the organizational apparatus for what was to become the Bergson Group, was Yitshaq Ben-Ami, known to his colleagues as Mike. He set up a small office for his American Friends of a Jewish Palestine at 285 Madison Avenue and set to work building contacts, educating the Jewish community about the need for *aliyah bet*, and raising the first small sums for rescue activity.

Ben-Ami's first major test came at the end of 1939, when 2,400 Jewish refugees became marooned in ice-trapped barges at the mouth of the Danube River. During the summer and autumn of that year, Jews had streamed to the area because they heard there would be ships to take them to Palestine. Some came by land. Some came on river boats that were not allowed to dock when they approached the gathering point. They came from Vienna and Bratislava, Budapest, Belgrade, and other Bulgarian and Rumanian ports, or from Nazi-overrun Poland. They camped throughout the little city of Salina, waiting for a ship.

Yitshaq Ben-Ami

Lying out in the Black Sea, just beyond the limit of Rumanian territorial waters, was the *S.S. Sakarya*, a forty year-old freighter, displacing 3,000 tons and flying the Turkish flag. The ship was ready to take on refugees and run the gauntlet of the British navy guarding the shores of Palestine—to land them on a dark night at some deserted Palestinian coastal location. The only problem was money. The owners of the vessel, aware of the danger that their boat could be seized by the British, insisted on an additional $10,000 to insure against that risk. Raising the funds was a matter of utmost urgency; every day counted in human suffering and tragedy. It was December, and the Danube near Guirigi had frozen. The refugees were stranded, and no nearby port would admit them, even temporarily. The refugees, one third of whom were women and children, had already suffered unimaginably just to reach this point. The stories of their experiences were hair-raising.

Ben-Ami and his colleagues, including Rabbi Baruch Rabinowitz, frantically sought to persuade major American Jewish organizations to supply the $10,000. Rabinowitz's appeal to Henry Montor, executive vice president of the United Palestine Appeal (later known as the United Jewish Appeal), elicited an extraordinary response which presented the ideology of selectivity at its most grotesque. Explaining why the UPA would not fund the "illegal" voyage of the *Sakarya*, Montor wrote to Rabinowitz:

> "[S]electivity" is an inescapable factor in dealing with the problem of immigration to Palestine. By "selectivity" is meant the choice of young men and women who are trained in Europe for productive purposes either in agriculture or industry and who are in other ways trained for life in Palestine, which involves difficulties and hardships for which they must be prepared physically and psychologically. Sentimental considerations are, of course, vital and everyone would wish to save every single Jew who could be rescued out of the cauldron of Europe.
>
> But when one is dealing with so delicate a program as unregistered immigration, it is obviously essential that those people sent to Palestine shall be able to endure harsh conditions under which they must live for weeks and months on the Mediterranean and the difficulties which shall await them when they land on the shores of Palestine...
>
> [E]ven among the 2,000 people who were assembled by the Revisionists on the Danube...a great many of the passengers were old men and women, whose fate must be the sincerest concern of every Jew, but who were, obviously, not fitted for the hazardous journey across the Mediterranean in boats whose captains consented to this traffic only because of the exorbitant amounts they could command...
>
> In public discussion, it is considered inadmissible for a Jew even to conceive of the possibility of criminals in Jewish ranks, but inasmuch as this is a confidential letter, I think it is

fair...to point out that many of those who have been brought into Palestine by the Revisionists have been prostitutes and criminals—certainly an element which cannot contribute to the upbuilding of a Jewish National Home in which Jews everywhere might take pride.

Note the date on the letter: February 1, 1940. Poland had been overrun by the Nazis. Millions of Jews, all the Jews, were caught in the same trap, whether they were world famous hasidic rebbes, professors, writers, poets, artists, community leaders, millionaires and paupers, industrialists and petty street vendors and, yes, thieves and prostitutes. Saints and sinners alike were eager to escape. There was no time to investigate the moral background of someone seeking passage on a ship bound for Palestine. Nor would it have been practical or justified to do such investigating even before the war.

With crucial help from Louis I. Newman,[68] a Reform rabbi who supported Jabotinsky and was a leading American advocate of *aliyah bet*, Ben-Ami succeeded in raising the sum, ironically enough, from two prominent non-Zionists, Lucius Littauer and David Donneger.

Within weeks the *Sakarya* reached Palestine. Four passengers died en route; four babies were born; thirty-seven couples were married by the Turkish ship captain. Upon arrival, the British allowed the women and children to disembark freely, but the men were held in the Atlit detention camp for six months before being released to start new lives. Eri Jabotinsky, for his part, was arrested and imprisoned for the crime of "illegally" bringing Jews to their homeland. He was set free on August 6, one week before his prison sentence was due to conclude, upon receiving the news that his father had passed away.

Aliyah bet ground to a halt following the entry of Italy into the war in June 1940 and the subsequent outbreak of hostilities in the Aegean. It simply became physically impossible to move large numbers of civilians through the area. The narrow window of opportunity had closed before the Zionist establishment, with its enormous resources and manpower, had taken on a serious role in the campaign. The thousands whom they brought to Palestine could have been tens of thousands, even hundreds of thousands, had they displayed a little vision, determination, and political and psychological courage.

4 THE CAMPAIGN FOR
   A JEWISH ARMY

Surveying the American Jewish scene upon their arrival in 1940, the Irgun emissaries found a number of troubling anomalies. One was the self-segregated nature of the community and its activities. The segregation was organizational, geographical, and ultimately psychological as well. Jews defined themselves according to the synagogue where they prayed, the *landsmanshaften* (organized groups of people who originated from the same town in Eastern Europe) to which they belonged, or the neighborhood, the Lower East Side, in which they resided and from which they did not often venture forth. The segregation was reflected in daily activities: Jews spoke to Jews, Jews quarreled with Jews, Jews pleaded with Jews, one Jew asked another for money for some purpose. The discussions, the disputes, the exchanges of information, were all served up in the Yiddish press, with its circulation of about 250,000 in the interwar years and a readership of at least one million. Unlike the Hebrew press in Palestine, which for a long time paid relatively little attention to the Jewish disaster in Europe, the Yiddish press in the United States was from the beginning of the war quite well informed about what was happening in Nazi-occupied Europe, especially Poland, and presented the information on their front pages and in great detail. But it consisted of Jewish reporters speaking to Jewish readers.

The established Zionist leaders prided themselves on their supposed success in becoming part of American society. They were confident that they had "risen above" the world of the ghetto. Yet to a significant degree, their approach and activities still represented the segregated ghetto mentality. They largely kept Jewish concerns within the fold, that is, within the Jewish community, instead of actively bringing Jewish problems to wider attention and trying to influence general public opinion. On occasion they made a brief stab in that direction, as for example when, in 1941, they created a Christian Council on Palestine.[69] But this, too, smacked of the mistaken principle of segregation, the core assumption that the plight of the Jews of Europe and Palestine was a problem of the Jews alone rather than of all of humanity, and that protests should be organized along separate Jewish and Christian tracks, instead of in a coalition of all decent people. Perhaps it was no surprise that the general press typically put Jewish news in the back pages, even on the obituary page, or at best among other "religious" news items. The Jewish leaders made no serious effort to show them why news about the mass killings deserved to be on the front pages where everyone would see it, not only on page forty-seven where only those with a special interest (Jewish readers) would go looking for it.

The Irgun emissaries who came to America in 1940, and would soon be known as the Bergson Group, faced the unenviable task of trying to bring about the psychological desegregation of the Jews from the confines of the ghetto, the Lower East Side, the Yiddish press, and the *landsmanshaften* and to integrate the Jewish agenda into the framework of world problems. It was no mean feat to sever a tradition of more than a hundred years. One could not merely explain to the Jewish leaders, rabbis, and institutional bureaucrats that their approach was wrong and ineffective. This would only enmesh the activists in endless arguments with the establishment at a time when the ground was burning under everyone's feet. They needed to find a system that would work fast, a key to open the gates of the voluntary ghetto, and another to open the minds and hearts of the American people at large, to break the conspiracy of silence, the indifference surrounding the disaster of the Jewish people in Europe, and somehow convey the cry of agony which rose from the valley of tears to an unperturbed humanity in the free and civilized world.

This struggle to arouse a world immersed in moral torpor was extremely complex, especially since the Jewish leadership itself was part of that moral atrophy. The Bergson activists used various means to form a number of organizational, propagandistic, and political-diplomatic instruments, but above all it was imperative to devise a fresh approach. The single most effective instrument by which to achieve it was the idea of nonsectarianism. Whatever the Bergson Group thought should be undertaken, must be the concern and duty not only of Jews but Americans of various denominations. They understood that one has to reach public opinion in general; one has to establish contact with leaders, statesmen, politician, shapers of opinion, and decision makers of the American people on the highest level of their cultural, social, professional, and political life. One must not only inform them and gain their sympathy, but get them personally involved in a practical way.

Before long, as we will see, their efforts were crowned with success and news of the Jews began to appear on the front pages of the most important newspapers. Some New York dailies of large circulation not only reported events connected with the Jewish cataclysm, but gave close and constant attention, treating it with all the seriousness it deserved. Newspapers of such opposing views and policy as William Randolph Hearst's *Journal American* and the *Daily Mirror*, at one end of the spectrum, and the liberal *PM* and *New York Post* at the other, emerged as loyal and constant supporters of the ideas, political approach, and various campaigns of the Bergson committees.[70]

Soon there were hardly any important personalities in any walk of life or in government who had not been approached by the Irgun emissaries. Many were influenced and expressed willingness to help. Many joined and became active, giving of their time and experience. Not only was the cause of rescuing the Jews and establishing a Jewish homeland transferred from the ghetto to the reality of America at large, but it was placed, with respect, in the center stage of public awareness and concern.

* * *

To a dangerous extent, the mainstream Zionists inherited from the previous ghetto generations the instinct that for Jews, the best thing is not to draw attention, not to be spoken of, not to be at the center of public interest. Despite all the boasting by Labor Zionists that they were forging, in Palestine, a "new Jew" who would be free of ghetto fears and complexes, they often displayed precisely these complexes when dealing with the world outside the Jewish community. One of the most characteristic and, frankly, embarrassing traits of some Jews, even in their private conversations when only two participate, is their pronunciation of the word "Jews" or "Jewish" in a hushed whisper which betrayed self consciousness. With the outbreak of World War II, the situation was quite complex and made worse by the Nazi propaganda claims that the democracies were fighting a "Jewish war," that is, fighting at the behest of world Jewry. Therefore many Jews in America felt it was important to do nothing that could conceivably lend credibility to such accusations. The governments of the Allied nations, who were forced to fight Hitler in self-defense, insisted on abstaining from any acts or even pronouncements that might give the public the impression that they were engaged in a war at the instigation of the Jews. Of course this fear betrayed not only moral stupor but, primarily, absurd thinking. Hitler's strategic aim was to conquer the world for the benefit of the Third Reich, regardless of what happened to the Jews. As it was, the Allies' official attitude of ignoring the Jewish catastrophe paradoxically enjoyed the simultaneous support of rabid antisemites and frightened Jewish leaders.

Reaching Public Opinion Through Advertising

One of the most important innovations of the Bergson Group in the areas of propaganda, mass education, and mobilization of public opinion, was the use of paid messages, usually in the form of full page advertisements in prominent daily newspapers and weekly magazines from coast to coast. Subsequently this tactic became commonplace—mainstream Zionist organizations took out large newspaper ads, as did other advocacy groups such as trade unions, political candidates, and the like. But at the time the Bergson Group did it, it was a sensation in two respects: first, because it was so rarely used before; second, the shock of bringing the Jewish problem into the open in such an uninhibited manner.

The Bergson Group's first full page ad appeared in the *New York Times* on January 5, 1942, headlined "Jews Fight for the Right to Fight," and published under the name Committee for a Jewish Army of Stateless and Palestinian Jews. The ad included a list of board members and supporters of the committee, among them many leading political figures, writers, and other figures of renown.[71] The Bergson Group's office was flooded with thousands of sympathetic letters, telegrams, and phone calls, as well as many financial contributions. The common sentiment of the messages was one of admiration for the group's courage in speaking out so explicitly without self-consciousness or embarrassment. To the Bergson activists, this was the most surprising aspect. Coming from the very different worlds of Europe and Palestine, the group's leaders could not understand why the placing of a newspaper ad should be regarded by anyone as an act of daring and courage, almost bordering on the heroic. The "Jews Fight" ad and the hundreds of ads which followed, achieved their purpose: they brought the news of European Jewry's plight, the campaign for rescue, and the struggle for Jewish independence in Palestine, to the breakfast tables of millions of Americans, reaching into their collective conscience and urging them to live up to their moral responsibilities as civilized men and women.

Some of the early advertisements were written by Pierre van Paassen, the noted author and Christian Zionist. Others were composed by this author, or by Victor Ratner, who at the time was the highest paid copywriter on Madison Avenue, who volunteered his talents. The best known of the ads were the work of the journalist, playwright, and screenwriter Ben Hecht, whose dramatic abilities helped make the Jewish issue compelling and moving to ordinary Americans. The famous artist Arthur Szyk[72] created original illustrations to enhance a number of the ads. During 1942, the ads concentrated on the demand for creation of a Jewish army to participate in the war against the Nazis. Beginning in early 1943, the focus of the ads shifted to breaking the conspiracy of silence around the Holocaust and pressing the Roosevelt administration to take concrete action to save the Jews of Europe. In later years, many of the ads concentrated on winning the sympathy of the American public and political leadership for the need for Jewish national independence.

As published in The New York Times, January 5, 1942.

JEWS FIGHT FOR THE RIGHT TO FIGHT

"The vast majority of the members of the human race are on our side. Many of them are fighting with us, all of them are praying for us." —Franklin Delano Roosevelt.

The Jews of Palestine and the stateless Jews of the world do not only want to pray—THEY WANT TO FIGHT!!!!

"ANY NATION, ANY MAN WHO FIGHTS AGAINST NAZIDOM WILL HAVE OUR AID." — *Winston Churchill.*

200,000 JEWS OFFER THEIR SERVICES.

What are the Jews doing in this war?

In England, the United States and in Russia this question has an easy answer:

They are fighting.

But there are thousands upon thousands of Jews who are not fighting.

135,000 Fearless Palestinian Jews registered as volunteers for war service as soon as the war broke out. They want to defend their homeland and their very lives from attack by aggressors.

They are still waiting to be called to the colors.

Then there are the stateless Jews, the disinherited Jews, the ones driven from their homes by the great and evil violence of the Axis Powers.

They are scattered in every part of the world, young and courageous, who have only one dream—to fight under a flag that will carry them against the armies of Hitler.

They were the first victims of Hitler's hatred and aggression. Their relatives, their people are the most persecuted, the most starved, the most tortured under Hitler's yoke; they paid and are paying in actual human suffering infinitely more than any other people on earth.

They are eager to fight back and to avenge.

There is still another category of Jews—from countries not yet involved in the war—from South America and the Middle East. They feel that they, too, should have a part in the world struggle to defeat the enemies of civilization.

All of them are convinced that the Jewish people's place is on all the fronts where the democracies are fighting for those very foundations of society whose Magna Charta is the Bible.

They all want to unite in their own Freedom Army and to fight under their own Liberty Flag, under the supreme Allied Command.

There is nothing unprecedented in this demand: Jewish Legions fought in the last World War and participated in conquering Palestine.

To urge the materialization of this demand a Committee For a Jewish Army was organized and inaugurated on December 4, 1941, in Washington, D. C., a committee composed of men from all walks of American life who passionately believe in the victory of democracy and through that victory, in a better world for all, regardless of race or creed.

This Committee believes that with America's entrance into the war against the Axis, the question of a Jewish Army, based on Palestine, has become a direct and vital concern to the United States, since this army, 200,000 strong,

Will consolidate the Allied positions around the Suez Canal;

Will release a considerable part of the Anzac forces from the Middle East for combat in the Pacific, and thus

Will strengthen the defenses of this hemisphere.

In these historic days when the greatest leaders and animators of world democracy, President Roosevelt and Prime Minister Churchill, are deliberating the vital problems of world strategy, this Committee wants to express its conviction that the organization of a Jewish Army will be of great strategic importance to the strength of the United Nations and an additional proof that this titanic struggle will be decided not solely by brute force, but by principles of justice and honor.

Churchill gave expression to this conviction in these immortal words:

"Without honor we could neither hope nor deserve to win this hard war."

Therefore, this committee feels that humanity, Christianity, the very ideals for which we are fighting this war, are embodied in the demand for a Jewish Army.

It is the conviction of this Committee that the Jewish flag must fly in this ultimate clash, that will probably be fought out in the Middle East, over the evangelic hills of Galilee.

This Committee demands the right for the Jews to go and fight for freedom under the walls of Jerusalem.

This Committee demands that the Jews be not slaughtered in Palestine as helpless children, but that they will be trained and will be given arms in their hands—arms, airplanes, tanks and guns.

This Committee demands that the Jewish People be heard, that the Jewish People takes its place in the ranks of free peoples of the earth.

This Committee demands that the Jews the world over should be given a chance to express and to demonstrate their solidarity with the great American nation which became the standard-bearer of the fight for freedom and justice everywhere and for everyone. This chance should be given to them by enabling them to form an army of Palestinian and stateless Jews, who will fight side by side with the American people and her allied nations.

Many American strategists and many of America's most far-seeing statesmen are already convinced of the righteous of this plan and have endorsed it. Secretary of War Stimson has wired to the inaugural session of this Committee the following encouraging and inspiring words:

"Free men everywhere are arming for the defense of democracy. I send my best wishes for the success of your movement."

A powerful and courageous army ready to give its life for the ideals that mark the Allied cause lies waiting to be born.

The Committee asks that men and women of all creeds come to its aid by a determined effort in the creation of this first great modern Jewish Army.

With your help and cooperation the cause of the Jewish Army will be victorious. It will be victorious not only in the interest of the Jewish people but also in the interests of world democracy. Because ours is a struggle for right and justice—and right and justice are indivisible—they should be for all and everywhere.

COMMITTEE FOR A JEWISH ARMY

NATIONAL HEADQUARTERS

285 Madison Avenue   New York, N. Y.

LEx. 2-7644

Washington Office: Willard Hotel

REGIONAL OFFICES:
Philadelphia, 716 Walnut St.
Chicago,   139 No. Clark St.

HELP MAKE THE JEWISH ARMY A REALITY NOW!

THE AIM:

To bring about, by legal means and in accordance with the laws and foreign policy of the United States, the formation of a Jewish Army, based on Palestine, to fight for the survival of the Jewish people and the preservation of democracy. This army, composed primarily of Palestinian Jews and refugees as well as of volunteers from other countries, will fight on all required battlefields side by side with the United States, Great Britain, and the other Allied nations.

I wish to help the Committee in its work for the formation of the Jewish Army. My contribution is enclosed.

Name

Address

City   State

Make Checks Payable To:
Committee for a Jewish Army

The key to breaking through the wall of indifference to the Jewish disaster was to move away from the old pattern of speaking to fellow-Jews and instead appeal to the general public, while at the same time creating the necessary instruments through which non-Jews could become active participants rather than just passive sympathizers.

Ben Hecht addressing a Bergson Group event. To his left are
Peter Bergson and Rose Keane. To his right is Billy Rose.

This does not mean the Bergson activists did not value the importance of Jewish opinion. On the contrary, they solicited the support of a broad range of Jewish figures, including hundreds of prominent rabbis, led by the renowned Rabbi Eliezer Silver; stars of stage and screen, such as Paul Muni, Edward G. Robinson, and three members of the famous "first family of the Yiddish theater," Stella Adler, Luther Adler, and Celia Adler—with Stella, in turn, playing a key role in recruiting many other figures from the entertainment world; political leaders such as Congressmen Emanuel Celler[73] and Samuel Dickstein;[74] and such diverse personalities as author and attorney Louis Nizer,[75] boxing champion Barney Ross,[76] and composer Kurt Weill.[77] Beyond these celebrities, a core of full-time American Jewish activists, among them Harry Selden, Alex Wilf, Baruch Rabinowitz, Maurice Rosenblatt,[78] Louis and Betty Yampolsky, Maurice Rifkin,[79] Michael Potter,[80] and Betty and Rose Keane,[81] together with hardworking staff members such as Miriam Chaikin, did the gritty everyday work that kept the movement surging forward.

Arthur Szyk

Maurice Rosenblatt

Miriam Chaikin

Yet with all the support the Bergson committees received from these and many other American Jews, the work would have been of little avail had the Bergson Group followed the model of the major Jewish groups and organized itself on a sectarian basis. It was precisely the Jewish activists' partnership with non-Jews in a common, nonsectarian framework that made such a powerful impression on both public opinion and the Roosevelt administration, as well as on the governments of Great Britain and the other Allied nations.

The non-Jews who supported the Bergson Group in one or another of its campaigns were remarkable for their prominence, influence, and numbers. There was First Lady Eleanor Roosevelt, who attended and publicly praised the Bergson Group's *We Will Never Die* pageant. There was a former president, Herbert Hoover, who served as honorary chairman of the group's Emergency Conference to Save the Jewish People of Europe, in July 1943. There were members of President Roosevelt's own cabinet, including Secretary of War Henry Stimson and Secretary of the Navy Frank Knox, both of whom endorsed the Jewish army proposal, and Secretary of the Interior Harold Ickes, who chaired the Washington, D.C. branch of the Emergency Committee to Save the Jewish People of Europe, and the Assistant Secretary of the Interior, Oscar Chapman. Other government officials were likewise supportive, such as the chairman of the War Production Board, Donald Nelson, who wrote that he was "100% in accord" with the Jewish army campaign, and Fowler Harper, a solicitor general in the Interior Department, who helped draft the Bergson Group's rescue resolution that was introduced in Congress 1943 (more on that below).

There were numerous Christian leaders, such as the Presiding Episcopal Bishop, Henry St. George Tucker, who addressed the 1943 rescue conference. There were labor leaders, such as AFL president William Green and CIO president Philip Murray, who lent their names to the Jewish army cause. There were prominent newspaper publishers, from conservative William Randolph Hearst (owner of dozens of newspapers) to the liberal Ted O. Thackery, publisher of the *New York Post*. There were prominent literary figures, including Nobel Prize winning novelist Sigrid Undset and John Gunther, who later wrote *Death Be Not Proud*. There were leading entertainers, among them Bob Hope, Jack Benny, Milton Berle, Paul Robeson, Dean Martin, and Jerry Lewis, who took part in benefit shows to raise money for the Bergson campaigns.

A fascinating array of foreign diplomats also made common cause with the Bergson Group. For example, the activists met frequently with André Philip,[82] head of the Free French Mission in Washington. At one point, when unfriendly Roosevelt administration officials quietly ordered the interception and inspection of the French delegation's mail, the Bergson committee leaders undertook to send and receive mail for the French in ways that could not be traced. Philip reciprocated during the period just before Israel's creation when, as a member of the French cabinet, he provided certain assistance to the Bergson Group in its efforts to support the Irgun's fight for independence. The Bergson activists also had close relationships with Swaran Singh,[83] a future cabinet minister in India; Syngman Rhee,[84] who later became president of South Korea; Count Carlo Sforza,[85] leader of the Italian antifascists; and Charles Davila,[86] former Rumanian ambassador to the United States.

The alliances that the Bergson Group developed, and the coalition of supporters that it built, would prove crucial in its series of political action campaigns, beginning with the campaign to establish an army of stateless and Palestinian Jews.

Fighting for the Right to Fight

What would have been more natural and just than to permit the Jews of Palestine, together with stateless European Jews who fled Hitler, together with volunteers from neutral countries, to form an army and fight under their own flag and insignia against their mortal enemy, Nazi Germany, and thereby contribute to Allied victory? Yet logic and justice did not always count for much, especially when American political interests and British imperial interests were involved. Millions of Jews fought in the various regular armies of the Allies; and thousands more fought with the underground resistance organizations in the occupied countries, or with the partisans in Eastern Europe. They fought anonymously, as individuals, as it should have been. But the Palestinian and stateless Jews were not allowed to fight in an organized manner in an army of their own, except for a fleeting moment near war's end, in a small brigade, as we will see. As soon as the war broke out in Europe, 136,000 Palestinian Jews, out of a population of about 550,000, registered for military service, eager to be trained and sent to the battlefield to fight the Axis. They were never called up. Their service was considered dispensable.

This, despite the fact that the Jews of Europe, almost ten million strong, were the greatest single victims of both world wars. The first resulted in the Bolshevik takeover in Russia, and thus an Iron Curtain was lowered over the millions of Jews living behind it, bringing to an end Jewish culture in all its manifestations in that part of the world. The second ended in the Holocaust.

In World War I, the Western democracies and the United States were allied with the greatest enemy of the Jews, Czarist Russia. In their hearts, it was very difficult for the Jews anywhere, principally in America, to identify with the cause of the Entente since that would mean identifying also with one of the main partners of that alliance, Russia. In World War II, their dilemma was even more terrible. In each of the opposing camps they were confronted by enemies. Among the Axis, the Germans vowed to destroy them; among the Allies, there was Great Britain, determined to put an end to Jewish national aspirations and barring their entry to Palestine. Yet the Jews did make a choice and take sides, because they thought, and rightly so, that there was no alternative. Between the Axis and the Allies, they threw in their lot with the latter, whose leading power in the first years of the war was Great Britain, under the leadership of Winston Churchill.

But neither Jabotinsky, in the last few months of his life, nor the Bergson Group considered this choice as an act of desperation only. In a sense, they also saw in it a great opportunity to utilize the storm and steer the ship of Jewish national freedom in the desired direction. They reasoned that in the war, with the Allies as unprepared as they were, manpower would count for a great deal. The Jews were in a position to offer that manpower. If utilized in a large Jewish army, perhaps a quarter of a million strong, to fight against the Nazis on whichever front—and especially to defend the Middle East with its Suez Canal, oil and strategic sites—it would contribute significantly to Allied victory. This fact would then have overwhelming repercussions; it would force Great Britain to change its policy in Palestine. But, as we will see, it was not meant to be. The Allies recoiled from the idea of a Jewish army, offering all kinds of excuses, each more disingenuous and foolish than the next.

The Jewish army campaign was initiated by Jabotinsky upon his arrival in the United States in March 1940. During those first months, it was organized under the aegis of the American Friends of a Jewish Palestine, then later as the Committee for a Jewish Army of Stateless and Palestinian Jews. The Jewish establishment soon attacked. On June 18, 1940, the Jewish Telegraphic Agency published a dispatch from Washington under the headline "Zionist Leaders Here

Stephen S. Wise

Frown on Jabotinsky's Army Plan." It reported that a delegation of American Zionist leaders, headed by Dr. Stephen Wise as president of the Emergency Council for Zionist Affairs, met with the British ambassador to the United States, Lord Lothian, and afterwards issued a statement "disassociat[ing] themselves from the plan of Vladimir Jabotinsky to create a Jewish Army as part of the Allied Forces."

The Zionist leadership appears to have been motivated by three factors. First, a determination to combat Jabotinsky, regardless of the merits of his project, because he was a rival who posed competition for the hearts and minds of Jewry. Second, a fear that since the United States was still neutral, a campaign for a Jewish army might cast a shadow over their patriotism as Americans. Third, some kind of breakdown in communication between the American Zionist establishment and the London and Jerusalem offices of the Zionist movement, since the latter favored the creation of a Jewish military force within the British army, an idea not so distant from Jabotinsky's.

As in World War I, so too in 1940 there were also radical Zionists who were opposed not only to creating a Jewish army but to the very idea of taking sides in the war. The collegiate division of the Zionist Organization of America, known as Avuka, denounced the Jewish army idea and issued a four-point plan urging "Strict American neutrality; No aid—no men, no money, no ammunition to belligerents; Guard against war propaganda and hysteria; Provide for a war referendum amendment." Even though the Nazis had conquered much of Europe and were laying waste to the Jewish communities there, these students wanted the United States to remain neutral rather than join England in fighting Hitler.[87]

As Nazi atrocities multiplied, as the Palestine Jewish leadership embraced the army idea, and as the indefatigable campaign of the Committee for a Jewish Army gained ground, the Zionist organizations gradually changed their position regarding the formation of a Jewish army. But they were not able to easily solve the prickly problem of how to respond to the activities of the Bergson Group. Even after officially adopting a resolution advocating creation of a Jewish division in Palestine, under British command, they still faced the dilemma of how to promote the idea while at the same time combating the Committee for a Jewish Army, which they saw as their rival and enemy.

The Bergson activists, for their part, proceeded with care and deliberation, contrary to the accusation later hurled at them by the Jewish establishment that they were "rash." If anything, one could say they were too slow to arrive at some of their decisions. The campaign in the United States for a Jewish army, which continued in earnest after Jabotinsky's sudden death in August 1940, began under the auspices of the American Friends of a Jewish Palestine. But as the campaign intensified throughout 1941, the Bergson Group leaders realized that the Jewish Army concept should not be tied up so specifically with the future of Palestine or with an organization whose very name proclaimed a clearly political intent. A Jewish army should transcend the politics of the Palestine controversy, and should be available to fight on any front to which it would be assigned by the Allied High Command. They therefore decided to establish an organization whose name expressed the goal of an army of stateless and Palestinian Jews, without identifying with any political group or party. It would be a framework in which people of various political opinions and aspirations, including even those who were not Zionists or even Palestine-oriented at all, could participate.

The campaign was formally launched in early December 1941, with a proclamation in the House of Representatives, the introduction of a congressional resolution, and a public conference in Washington, D.C. The proclamation was made on the floor of the House on December 2 by Rep. John Dingell of Michigan. "Recently," Dingell announced,

Mr. Churchill declared that by 1942 there will be a shortage of manpower [for the war effort]. We here must also be concerned with another factor. Tomorrow, the Committee for a Jewish Army will convene here in Washington, and I declare to bring before the House certain aspects to be considered. That Committee for a Jewish Army is a nonpartisan, nonsectarian group calling upon all humanity now engaged or supporting those engaged in a great struggle, to recognize that the pioneer Jews of Palestine and the stateless Jews of Europe constitute a nation and hence must be allowed to fight as a nation. My colleague [Rep. Andrew Somers, D-New York] has introduced a bill for the purpose of allowing lend-lease equipment to be utilized for the Jewish Army. I trust we shall pass that bill.

The Jewish Army committee held its first public event at the Willard Hotel in Washington, D.C. on December 3. Hundreds of delegates from coast to coast participated in the sessions, which were presided over by Samuel Harden Church, president of the Carnegie Institute. Numerous diplomats representing foreign countries or governments-in-exile attended as an expression of sympathy for the cause. Secretary of War Henry L. Stimson sent a message of encouragement. "Free men everywhere are arming for the defense of democracy," he wrote. "I send my best wishes for the success of your movement." Behind the scenes, unfortunately, Stimson was not a serious advocate of the army idea. When the issue came up in internal government discussions, he agreed with the various disingenuous excuses that the critics made about the supposed lack of equipment, lack of ships, bad timing, and so on. Still, his message of support to the December 1941 conference spoke for itself, and the Jewish army activists, both in the United States and in Great Britain, frequently cited that message, to great effect, in their lobbying efforts. Stimson never once asked the committee to refrain from quoting him.

Other public figures of significance likewise sent messages of support. The Secretary of the Navy, Frank Knox, wrote: "In Palestine, Hitler faces the wrath of the people he has starved and tortured and degraded. Jews over half a million strong, many of whom know the ache of a storm trooper's kick, the agonies of the Schutzstaffel's lash. The Jewish haven in peace time has become a bulwark for democracy in war time. Lend it your strength." The chief justice of the Supreme Court, Harlan Stone, wrote: "I am entirely in sympathy with the proposal to raise a Jewish Army to fight side by side with the English Army."

The sessions of the conference received national press coverage, and the impressive roster of the CJA's National Committee lent strength and prestige to the movement. The 186 members of the National Committee included six

United States Senators, twenty-seven Representatives, eighteen prominent clergymen, and dozens of military officials, diplomats, labor leaders, educators,
authors, journalists, artists, actors, and business executives. Pierre van Paassen
was named chairman of the CJA, industrialist Alfred Strelsin became chairman
of the executive board, and veteran Zionist leader Meir Grossman was chosen as
its vice-chairman. The CJA's declared aim was clear:

> To bring about by legal means and in accordance with the laws
> and foreign policy of the U.S. the formation of a Jewish Army,
> based on Palestine, to fight for the survival of the Jewish people
> and the preservation of democracy. The Army, composed pri-
> marily of Palestinian Jews and refugees as well as of volunteers
> from free countries, will fight on all required battlefields side by
> side with the U.S., Great Britain, and the other Allied nations.

In contradistinction to the Zionist establishment, the Committee emphasized, first and foremost, that the Jewish problem needed to be brought into
the open. Among the Allies, there had been an unspoken resolve to ignore the
Jewish problem. Arthur Szyk, the artist and CJA activist, once remarked that
the Allies treated the plight of the Jews like pornography—"one does not discuss it in polite society."[88] The CJA was determined to change all that.

Moreover, if the Jews were singled out by Hitler as a special target of his
global war against the Free World, the Jews must be accorded the elementary
right to fight back as Jews. With regard to Palestine, the Jews there should be
permitted to defend their country in case of Axis attack—something which, in
late 1941, seemed entirely possible, even probable. The CJA also argued that the
idea of a Jewish army was not just a matter of moral value, a symbol for justice,
but was of practical, strategic importance. An army of at least 200,000 strong
young men, powerfully motivated by self-preservation and hatred of the enemy,
would constitute a formidable force and could play a significant part in bringing
about Allied victory in multiple crucial arenas of battle.

The Jewish Army committee sponsored full-page advertisements in leading daily newspapers around the country, to explain its position. This was not
the sort of thing Jewish organizations did in those days. The opening paragraph
asked, "What are the Jews doing in this war? In England, the U.S., and in Russia
this question has an easy answer: they are fighting." The question, then, was not
about them, but about the tens, perhaps hundreds, of thousands of other Jews
who were not fighting—but wanted to. Who were they? The ad explained:

> 135,000 fearless Palestinian Jews registered as volunteers for
> war service as soon as the war broke out...Then there are the

stateless Jews...driven from their homes by the great and evil violence of the Axis Powers. They are scattered in every part of the world, young and courageous, who have only one dream—to fight under a flag that will carry them against the armies of Hitler...There are still another category of Jews—from countries not yet involved in the war—from South America and the Middle East. They feel that they, too, should have a part in the world struggle to defeat the enemies of civilization. All of them are convinced that the Jewish people's place is on all the fronts where the democracies are fighting for those very foundations of society whose Magna Carta is the Bible. They all want to unite in their own Freedom Army and to fight under their own Liberty Flag, under the Supreme Allied Command.

By the time this message was published, the United States was already at war with the Axis. The ad thus explained to public opinion how a Jewish army would be in the best military interests of the U.S.:

...[W]ith America's entry into the war against the Axis, the question of a Jewish Army based on Palestine has become a direct and vital concern to the U.S. since this Army, 200,000 strong,
     Will consolidate the Allied position around the Suez Canal;
     Will release a considerable part of the Anzac forces from the Middle East for combat in the Pacific, and thus
     Will strengthen the defenses of this hemisphere.

The Zionist Establishment's Position

The Zionist leaders were, as usual, of two minds. On the one hand, they supported the idea of creating Jewish military units. Yet their demand remained modest, almost inconspicuous. They believed it should not be too dramatic or arouse undue suspicion. They opposed the very term "Jewish army." Dr. Weizmann, president of the World Zionist Organization, in May 1942 referred to the idea as "somewhat pretentious and somewhat fantastic." The debate seemed to be a replay of the arguments in 1917 over the formula to be submitted to the British urging a declaration endorsing Zionist aspirations: should the Zionist leaders tell Britain that their aim was a Jewish state, or should they hide behind the nebulous and almost deceptive term "National Home"? Their thinking in the 1940s unfortunately mirrored that of 1917; they were afraid that asking for too much would result in getting nothing. They really believed that the more modest their demands concerning a Jewish military force, the greater the chance of receiving British approval.

The wording used to describe their aim was not the only issue. There were also differences between the Zionist establishment and the Bergson Group concerning the methods to be used to reach their goal. The Zionist leaders believed in secret diplomacy, in strictly private approaches to British officials, and pleading or reasoning with them. The Jewish Army activists did not believe Great Britain would agree to anything, unless it was subjected to constant public pressure. Zionist leaders, by contrast, thought such tactics would actually be harmful; they feared the British would take umbrage and react negatively.

The key substantive difference had to do with the size of the army. The Jewish leaders asked for nothing larger than a division. The Committee for a Jewish Army spoke of a military force of such a size that it would make its weight felt in the strategic planning of the Allies. The Committee called for creation of an army of ten to fifteen divisions, perhaps a quarter million strong. Zionist leaders called this unrealistic. In fact, it was unrealistic only so long as they accepted the nonsensical excuses put forward by the British (and later of the Roosevelt administration as well), who were against it not because it was impossible but because they saw it as dangerous, for reasons to be described below.

There were two additional differences between the establishment and the Bergson Group on the army question. One was the issue of command: the Zionist leaders spoke of a Jewish unit that would be under British command; the Jewish Army committee emphasized that it should be under Allied command. The other was the question of where the army would be deployed. The Zionist leaders were primarily interested—and not without justification—in obtaining British permission to organize military units, regardless of the exact size and numbers, to protect the Palestine Jewish community in case of attack. The Bergson activists believed that, under the prevailing circumstances, it would be easier to convince public opinion of the merit of the army idea if they downplayed the angle of defending Palestine and instead emphasized the concept of a large Jewish army to be deployed anywhere the Allied High Command chose.

The Debates in Congress and Parliament

On November 28, 1941, Rep. Andrew L. Somers (D-New York), one of the most stalwart friends of Jewish rescue and liberation, introduced a resolution asking President Roosevelt to intercede with the British government to permit the organization of all-Jewish military units in Palestine. This resolution, introduced just before the founding conference of the Committee for a Jewish Army, had two purposes: first, to begin to involve the U.S. government, and especially the president, in the Jewish army project; second, to promote the idea that military and strategic interests should have priority over the narrow political and imperialist interests of the British Empire. In his remarks on the floor of the House, Somers said:

> [T]he President of the United States [should] at the earliest pos-
> sible date negotiate with the British government in an effort to
> utilize [Jewish] manpower. And [he should] assign an American
> general to the task of effectively using this Army, in the hope
> that military considerations will prevail and that we may drive on
> to victory and realize in the shortest possible time the complete
> destruction of the despotic forces that we are called upon to fight.

To buttress his argument and make clear how foolish the British position was, Somers quoted from a speech made by Winston Churchill that same day, in which the British leader declared that "we are likely to lose the war unless we use our combined overwhelming strength and use the multiplying opportunities that will present themselves to us." Therefore, Somers asked his colleagues, why not utilize the opportunity of a Jewish army?

Congressional supporters of the Bergson Group. Right to left: Sen. Guy Gillette, Rep. Andrew Somers, Rep. William Bennett, Sen. Francis Myers, and Sen. Warren Magnuson

The immediate mobilization of these people must suggest itself as a wise course to all who want to see America win this war quickly. Many of our generals and admirals tell us that such an Army is essential to the protection of the Suez Canal. I don't know whether or not we are sending any men into that section of the globe now, but I venture to assert that it is only a question of a few weeks when American boys will be sent to Palestine to protect that region. Obviously there is an available army there now: a fierce Army of traditional soldiers, for Jewish people, throughout the history of their existence, have been a fighting people. Why not use it?

A similar debate was initiated across the Atlantic by the London branch of the Jewish Army committee. The British division had been founded by the colorful and heroic Irgun naval leader Captain Jeremiah Helpern, was chaired by Lord Strabolgi, and included among its supporters Aneurin Bevan, leader of the Labor opposition in the House of Commons; Lord Davis; Lord Josiah Wedgwood, Commander Locker-Lampson, Geoffrey Mander, and *Jewish Chronicle* editor Ivan Greenberg.

On June 9, 1942, Lord Wedgwood and Lord Strabolgi discussed it in the House of Lords, and on August 6, 1942, Conservative MP Ian Hannah made similar remarks in the House of Commons. Hannah declared:

There is a broad feeling in Britain and in the U.S. that we are not making the most of the reservoir of good will that exists among Jews in Palestine. The Committee for a Jewish Army has strong support in the U.S. and has received the blessing of members of the American Government and Mrs. Franklin D. Roosevelt.

Why, indeed, was Great Britain indifferent if not averse to the Jewish Army proposal? The most outspoken opponent was Lord Moyne. In the June 1942 debate in the House of Lords, responding to Lord Wedgwood's motion in support of a Jewish army recruited from European Jewish refugees and Palestine, Moyne launched into an anti-Zionist tirade:

The Zionist claim has raised two burning issues—first the demand for large-scale immigration into an already over-crowded country, and secondly, racial domination by the newcomers over the original inhabitants...If comparison with Nazis is to be made it is surely those who force an imported regime upon the Arab population who are guilty of the spirit of domination and aggression.

Churchill, for his part, on some occasions made remarks sympathetic to the Jewish army idea, but he evidently did not feel strongly enough to make a serious effort to prevail over the likes of Moyne and other opponents. Churchill's support for Zionism in general was inconsistent, and when it came to the crunch, on issues such as the White Paper, he permitted the anti-Zionists and anti-Semites in his government to have their way. For all of Churchill's pro-Zionist rhetoric, the White Paper remained in force throughout his years as prime minister.

The American and British wings of the Jewish Army campaign were in close contact and at one point in mid-1942, Bergson and three colleagues—*Protestant Digest* editor Kenneth Leslie, Congressman Andrew Somers, and industrialist Alfred Strelsin—requested the administration's permission to fly to London to discuss the army plan with British officials. Assistant Secretary of State Adolph Berle complained to his superiors that Jewish Army supporters were "besieging the White House" for approval of the London trip, but saw no reason to deny them their passports. Undersecretary of State Sumner Welles disagreed. In view of the fact that "the British Ambassador Viscount Halifax is very much exercised about the whole matter," Welles opposed allowing the Bergson activists to make the journey. In a meeting with Halifax in September, Berle said the State Department was "worried about the [Jewish Army committee's] agitation and that the best thing that could be said for allowing these men to go would be that it might conceivably quiet down the agitation here..."[89]

Halifax not only opposed letting the Bergson delegation go to London, he was anxious for the Roosevelt administration to invoke its wartime prerogatives in order to put an end to Jewish army activities in the United States. Halifax complained bitterly to Welles about "propaganda appearing in the American press recently, clamoring for the creation of a Jewish Army." Welles tried to console him by pointing out that "there were many Jews in this country who were opposed to the kind of propaganda that was going on..." At Welles's suggestion, Halifax sent his deputy Harold Butler to urge Elmer Davis, director of the Office of War Information, to help publicize the British perspective on the Jewish army controversy.[90]

By the summer of 1942, senior State Department officials, operating at Secretary of State Cordell Hull's instructions, drafted a proposed statement by FDR to suppress public promotion of Zionism in general and the Jewish army idea in particular. "The agitation for the formation of a Jewish Army in Palestine is having such alarming effects in the Near East and Middle East that I am impelled to draw your attention to the matter," Hull explained to President Roosevelt in his cover note. "This agitation which has recently taken the form of full-page advertisements in the metropolitan areas advocating the formation of a Jewish Army to defend Palestine, and a widely publicized dinner here in Washington gives the Axis powers additional oil to pour on the fire, which is already dangerously high."[91] They asked the president to, in effect, compete with Hitler for the friendship of the Arabs, by issuing a declaration sympathetic to the Arab cause and snuffing out public discussion of Palestine for the remainder of the war. The proposal came perilously close to being adopted as U.S. policy, but was put off at the last minute as a result of strong lobbying by the Bergson Group as well as behind-the-scenes complaints by American Zionist leaders who were worried that a presidential decree to that effect would call into question their loyalties as American citizens.

Looking back almost forty years later, it is still difficult, even with all the good will in the world, to understand why the Allies rejected a Jewish army. After all, the proposal not only represented moral justice but also offered clearly practical advantages to the Allied cause. Long before World War II broke out, the British considered the Middle East of vital importance next only to the British Isles themselves. It was the second center of gravity in their strategic thinking. The historian Michael Howard put it this way:

> Cairo had been a British *place d'armes* for nearly sixty years. The establishment of British influence in the successor states of the Ottoman Empire, the development of the oil resources of Iraq and the Persian Gulf, the uneasy responsibilities of the Palestine Mandate, all had increased Britain's military involvement in the area years before the war...Egypt was still the theater where forces could be most easily concentrated from all parts of the Commonwealth with the exception of Canada. Troops from India, Australia, New Zealand, Southern Africa and the United Kingdom could be brought into action, if not against Germany, then at least against her vulnerable Ally, who could thus be turned into a liability rather than an asset to the Axis...The defeat of Italy might influence the attitude of the French authorities in Syria, Lebanon and French North Africa. It would be taken into account in Madrid...and would have important repercussions in the Balkan peninsula.

Yet Great Britain acted against its own avowed strategy and paid a terrible price which, in the long run, was tantamount to the liquidation of its Empire and its decline into a third rate, bankrupt, self-pitying state, looked upon by friends with mixed feelings of contempt and sadness.

Four days before the Germans entered Paris on June 10, 1940, Mussolini declared war on France and Britain. This meant that the Mediterranean became a central front, with the Axis on the offensive. The whole structure of British strategy began to break down simply because it was originally based on the thousand miles of the North African coast and the French controlled Levant. This manpower constituted the main land forces of the Allies in the region. Added to this was the French Mediterranean Navy. Now all these formidable fighting instruments were no longer available. They passed under the control of the defeated yet hostile and mischievous administration of the Vichy Government under Petain, and supervised by the Armistice Commission of the Germans and the Italians who kept close watch over every French move.

As early as September 1940, the Italians advanced sixty miles into Egypt. So long as the British had to contend with the Italians alone, they had no difficulties inflicting a shattering defeat upon them both in the Western Desert (that is, west of Egypt) as well as in the rest of Africa. The victorious General Wavell had to halt his advance because, on orders from Churchill, a major part of his troops were diverted to Greece to aid in the battle against Mussolini's invading army. The British did not have enough manpower for both.

The situation soon deteriorated and took on almost catastrophic proportions. Hitler decided that he could not abandon his friend and ally, Mussolini, and an Afrika Korps under the leadership of General Erwin Rommel was dispatched to Tripoli, arriving on February 12, 1941. From that moment until October 23, 1942, when Montgomery launched his attack from El Alamein, the British were mostly on the defensive and at times in grave danger of being overrun. In June 1942, the British were defeated by Rommel's *Panzerarmee* and forced to retreat in disarray until they reached the Egyptian frontier. Tobruk fell on June 21, and Rommel took 33,000 prisoners. In a matter of days, the British found themselves pushed back as far as Alexandria.

It was one of the most humiliating hours in the war for the British. Everything seemed to collapse, with the prospect of the Axis conquering the whole of the eastern Mediterranean and the Middle East from Egypt to Iran, with the Germans sweeping down from the Caucasus, with the possibility of linking up with Rommel's panzer divisions. Many feared that should this happen, it could spell doom for the British Empire and the Allied cause. The British began mass evacuation of civilians from Egypt toward Palestine. In Cairo, the British Embassy burned their documents, anticipating the entrance of the Germans into Egypt, and its capital to fall.

It all started with the diversion of the mass of the British troops in a desperate and futile attempt to save Greece from being overrun, at a time when Wavell was on the offensive, pursuing the remnants of Mussolini's troops after 135,000 were captured, with only 555 Britons killed, through Libya. It is conceivable that had Wavell had enough manpower and the ferocious determination of a

Jewish army, the pursuit would have continued into Vichy North Africa and thus achieved one of the decisive victories of the war. As it was, it took the British two years to achieve victory over the Germans in the Western Desert, from April 3, 1941, when Rommel took Baghdad, until April 7, 1943, when the Allied troops converged from east and west: the British from Libya, and the Americans from North Africa at Gabes Tunisia. The Allied campaign, bolstered by a Jewish army, might have been advanced by a year or more, and created a chain reaction, speeding the subsequent campaigns in southern Italy, the fall of Mussolini, the unconditional surrender of the Germans to Italy the collapse of some reluctant satellites in the Balkans, thus affecting all fronts, including the timing and scope of the invasion of Europe in Normandy. The Jewish army by itself would not have been a decisive factor in the Allied victory, but tipping the scales in the eastern Mediterranean, the Western Desert, and perhaps in North Africa might have had an effect on other fronts as well.

A Jewish army was necessary not only for a successful campaign in the Western Desert. It was almost imperative in the eastern Mediterranean, in almost all the countries in the Middle East. A Jewish army could have changed the political and moral climate in that region. This, in turn, might have had an effect on a postwar settlement of the Palestine question.

While opponents of the army proposal claimed it would cause an Arab revolt, the truth is that they revolted and betrayed the British anyhow, whenever and wherever they thought they had a chance. They did not wait for the pretext of a Jewish army, large or small. The Arabs revolted for four reasons: they did not want a British presence in their countries; they were sure Hitler would win, and wanted to be on the winning side; they had no interest in democracy, preferring authoritarianism, which indeed became the norm in the postwar independent Arab states; and they had little sympathy for nations associated with Judeo-Christian civilization nor for Communist regimes.

Arab leaders from King Farouk of Egypt to the Grand Mufti of Jerusalem, Haj Amin al-Husseini, were in direct contact with Hitler, expressing their fervent sympathy for the Nazi cause and anxiously anticipating that their countries would be "liberated" by the Germans. Most of the Arab intelligentsia and the youth were fervently pro-Nazi, ecstatic admirers of the Fuhrer.

When the Germans reached the Egyptian frontier, King Farouk sent a message to Hitler through the Egyptian ambassador in Tehran, congratulating the victorious German armies and declaring that "he was filled with strong admiration for the Fuhrer and respect for the German people, whose victory over England he desired most sincerely...Now that German troops stood victorious at the Egyptian frontier, the [Egyptian] people...long for an occupation of the country, certain that the Germans are coming as liberators..." But Farouk did not limit himself to words; in order to prove his loyalty to the Nazis, he provided important intelligence information on British military positions and offered "to come to the aid of the Axis troops at the decisive moment." It seemed that with the fall of Tobruk, the decisive moment arrived.

In Iraq, a virulent pro-Axis government under the premiership of Rashid Ali was installed, and in April 1941 it appealed to Hitler for German "protection." The Nazis were only too willing to oblige, and began an airlift from bases in Syria under Vichy's control. The British were compelled to transfer 2,000 troops from India (mostly from noncombatant services) to deal with the emergency. The British approved the dispatch of a unit of the Irgun, headed by IZL commander David Raziel, to Iraq to help overthrow Ali; Raziel was killed in the operation. The British put down the rebellion in Baghdad and invaded Lebanon and Syria in order to eliminate Nazi bases there. To assist them in the conquest of Syria, the British made good use of a Haganah reconnaissance and sabotage unit commanded by Moshe Dayan, who lost his left eye in the fighting.

A Jewish army would have made all these operations simpler and speedier. It could have played a part in all operations in the Middle East and the Western Desert, probably in North Africa as well. It could have affected the nature of the war by eliminating the element of fear of Arab disloyalty. The British never had the Arabs' allegiance anyway, but the presence of a Jewish army would have made it more difficult for the Arabs anywhere to carry out their mischief. They might well have developed a healthy respect for the Jews and become accustomed to the idea that they would have to live with them after the war. That, in turn, would have meant there would have been no need for the Jews to launch their armed revolt against the British. The entire future of Arab-Jewish relations could have been fundamentally different.

The British, blinded by their shortsighted assumptions about their interests, were blind to this reality, obsessed with the fear that a Jewish army might turn against them after the war. What happened was exactly the opposite: because there was no Jewish army, the Jews rebelled against British rule, inflicting humiliating blows upon them and compelling them to evacuate the country. None of this was preordained. It was the result of a misguided policy, carried out by men who lacked vision, who misunderstood the balance of forces involved, and whose moral sense had atrophied. They lost more than Palestine. The Jewish revolt inspired other peoples under British colonial rule to follow their example, thereby helping to bring about the end of the British Empire.

The Jewish Brigade

On September 19, 1944, the British War Office announced the establishment of a Jewish Brigade. The combination of public pressure by the Committee for a Jewish Army and the discreet but persistent lobbying by the mainstream

Zionists finally forced the British to act. Unfortunately, the Brigade was a far cry from what the Jewish Army Committee sought. The London correspondent of the *New York Times* correctly reported that the creation of the brigade represented a "token success" for proponents of a Jewish army. The brigade resembled the small Jewish force under British command that the Zionist establishment had requested. The Brigade, hurriedly assembled from Palestinian noncombatant battalions, barely numbering five thousand men, could not under the best of circumstances play a significant role in the war. When it arrived on the scene of battle at the end of March 1945, the war, although not quite ended, had certainly been decided. The Germans, who would agree to an unconditional surrender on May 7, were already for all intents and purposes defeated. The Brigade had just enough time to be assembled near Alexandria in October 1944 and then shipped out to Italy the following month to be incorporated in Montgomery's Eighth Army, where it was commanded by a Canadian born Jew, Brig. Ernest Frank Benjamin. Ultimately it took part in several engagements with the enemy and acquitted itself with distinction and honor. Thirty of its men were killed, seventy were wounded, twenty-one were awarded medals.

As it turned out, the soldiers of the Jewish Brigade ended up playing a historic role at war's end, although not in the way the British had intended. Discovering the martyred remnants of the extermination camps in Europe, the Brigade veterans helped them in innumerable ways and smuggled many "illegally" to Palestine. Some Brigade members fought in the Jewish underground against the British, most notably the famous martyr Dov Gruner.[92] Many Brigade veterans fought in the Israeli War of Independence in 1948, providing a nucleus of experienced officer personnel and veteran fighters.

Soldiers of the Jewish Brigade in 1945.

5 SOUNDING THE ALARM

"If international finance Jewry within Europe and abroad should succeed once more in plunging the peoples into a world war," Adolf Hitler declared in a speech on January 30, 1939, "then the consequence will be not the Bolshevization of the world and therewith a victory of Jewry, but on the contrary, the destruction of the Jewish race in Europe."[93]

In January 1939, few could imagine that Hitler would indeed attempt to carry out the physical annihilation of the Jews. Later that year, the Germans overran Poland. Random atrocities against Polish Jews were soon followed by the creation of ghettoes. Still the Nazis had not yet decided upon mass murder as their "final solution." Plans for the mass exiling of Jews to Madagascar or elsewhere were seriously discussed among the Nazi leaders. With the German invasion of the Soviet Union in June 1941, the mass killings of the Jews began, first by machine-gun massacres in western Russia, Lithuania, and Latvia, then, in late 1941, through mass gassings. By the autumn of 1942, the Allied leadership publicly verified that the Germans had embarked on the mass extermination of European Jewry, and millions had already been killed.

When the news was revealed, the Bergson Group activists immediately set aside the Jewish army campaign and turned their attention to the rescue of Jews from Europe. Instinctively and without debate, they decided to give top priority to the task of rescue and thereafter never wavered in that decision. They were convinced that this was their immediate and personal duty, to subordinate all their endeavors to the one overriding task of rescuing as many of the Jews in Europe as possible. They could not do otherwise, for they were the flesh and blood of the very people who were being exterminated. However safe and far away from the slaughter camps they resided, they mentally and spiritually identified themselves in every waking moment with the agonies and torture of their kin, caught in the deathtrap of Hitler Europe. To them it seemed as if destiny had permitted them to escape so that they might devote their lives to the rescue of their brethren.

In that extra sense that the heart possesses, they could not escape the tormented voices of the doomed and the dying, pleading for help. These voices haunted this little group of Jewish activists. They could not rest without seeing a new front opened—a front against massacre. They called it "the Second Moral Front," trying to convince the mighty of the world to give a human and moral dimension to the war against Hitler, regardless of how much the leaders of the Allies, the statesmen, and the generals were convinced that they were already engaged in a just cause to save humanity from being conquered by the forces of evil. That their cause was just there is no doubt. But their attitude towards the Holocaust nonetheless compromised that cause to its very roots. It could not triumph by overlooking what happened to the millions of Jews in Europe. The ash heaps of human remains could not be a badge of honor or proof of victory of the Allied cause.

The Bergson Group's campaign for emergency rescue faced enormous obstacles from the start. The first problem was the most basic: how to compel the Free World, which was preoccupied with the world war and suffering its own losses on the battlefields of Europe and Asia, to recognize that Hitler had singled out the Jews for a fate that was unique and qualitatively different from the ordinary sufferings of war and deserved special attention. Generally speaking, government leaders and opinion-shapers in the Allied and neutral nations resisted acknowledging the uniqueness of the Jews' plight. They regarded the situation of the Jews as being merely one aspect of a broad refugee problem that was the inevitable result of every war. All conquered and defeated peoples were suffering under the Nazi jackboot. If there was nothing special about the fate of the Jews, then nothing special needed to be done to address it. Allied officials did not even want to refer to the victims as "Jews." They used terms such as "unfortunate victims of Hitler's cruelty" or "political refugees" or "poor, helpless souls." The word "Jew" was unmentionable. So long as the Jews could not even be mentioned, they surely would not be rescued.

Second, the Bergson Group needed to convince the leaders of the Free World that rescue was possible. Although the Germans had embarked upon the extermination of the Jews, they would also, at least in some instances, agree to the mass expulsion of the Jews—if there was somewhere they could go. The fate of many Jews thus depended upon the willingness of the democracies to receive them or find some place to settle them. Again and again throughout those years, the Hitler regime challenged the democracies to accept the Jews. While many more could have been saved during the prewar period, it was still not too late for millions of Jews in Europe to be rescued.

Third, it was critically important to persuade the Allies that steps to rescue Jewish refugees would not interfere with the war effort. The claim that rescue action would somehow impede or slow down Allied victory was often cited as a way of deflecting calls to save the Jews. "Rescue through victory" became the Allies' stock answer, as if rescue before victory would undermine the chances for victory.

Fourth, the Bergson Group had to show that rescue could be accomplished only through governmental efforts, that is, by the United States or a U.S.-led international effort. Private relief groups and Jewish charitable organizations were simply not equipped to do what must be done to rescue significant numbers of refugees.

Finally, the Bergson activists had before them the difficult task of extricating the need for rescue from ideological or political considerations. This meant separating the demand for rescue from Jewish or Zionist demands related to the future status of Palestine. While the creation of an independent Jewish state or homeland with open borders would of course have solved the Jewish refugee problem, there were so many obstacles on the path to Jewish independence, and so little time to rescue the Jews from death, that it was not realistic to link rescue to statehood. Rescue had to be understood as a task that was not contingent upon anything else, but was an overriding aim in itself.

The Unmentionable Jew

On February 16, 1943, readers of the *New York Times* were surprised to see, spread across five full columns on page 11, an advertisement bearing the almost surreal headline "FOR SALE TO HUMANITY: 70,000 JEWS—Guaranteed Human Beings at $50 a piece."

The ad began with a little note from Ben Hecht addressed to "The Four Freedoms." It read:

> My Dear Noble State of Mind:
> I know you are very busy, too busy perhaps to read the story on the left hand side of this page. For that reason I am writing an ad. Ads are easier and quicker to read than stories.
> Your admirer,
> Ben Hecht

The "story on the left" to which Hecht referred was a reprint of a news article that had recently appeared in the *Times*, revealing that the Rumanian government had offered to permit its 70,000 remaining Jewish residents to leave this country, and thus avoid being slaughtered by the Nazis, in exchange for transportation costs, estimated at $50 per person. Since the article itself did not seem to generate any serious interest by the Allies or the mainstream Jewish leadership, the Bergson Group decided to bring it to wider attention, through a paid advertisement.

The text of the ad continued:

> Roumania is tired of killing Jews. It has killed one hundred thousand of them in two years. Roumania will now give Jews away practically for nothing.

Seventy thousand Jews are awaiting death in Roumanian concentration camps.

Roumania will give these 70,000 Jews to the Four Freedoms for 20,000 Lei ($50) a piece. This sum covers all transportation expenses.

Roumania offers to deliver these 70,000 alive to Palestine.

Attention America!!!

The Great Roumanian bargain is for this month only!

It is an unprecedented offer!

Seventy thousand souls at $50 a piece!

The doors of Roumania are open! Act now!

The publication of the ad exploded like a bombshell. Allied officials who did not even want to mention the word *Jews*, let alone rescue them, were embarrassed to have someone call attention to their failure to act on the Rumanian offer. Mainstream Jewish leaders who were afraid that trumpeting Jewish concerns in a daily newspaper would cause antisemitism, were uncomfortable with the ad and rushed to criticize it. But the public response was different. Literally thousands of supportive letters, many including financial contributions, flowed into the offices of the Bergson Group in the days to follow.

The ad was Ben Hecht's idea and he wrote it in one inspired stroke. It was perhaps his most famous action on behalf of the martyred Jews in Europe. In one brilliant move, he set off a tremendous commotion in government circles, in the Jewish establishment, and throughout the entire American public.

Rumania was the most committed of Hitler's satellites both on the battlefield—it sent thirty divisions to fight alongside the Germans against the Russians, more than all the other satellites combined—as well as in the arena of massacring the Jews, on their own without any prodding. Yet the Rumanians were also among the first to realize that Hitler was losing the war. By early 1943 they realized that the best thing would be to slowly distance themselves from the doomed Fuhrer. Correctly perceiving that there was widespread revulsion in the West over the Nazis' treatment of the Jews (revulsion, not a commitment to rescue), the Rumanians believed they could improve their standing with the democracies by offering to let some Jews go free.

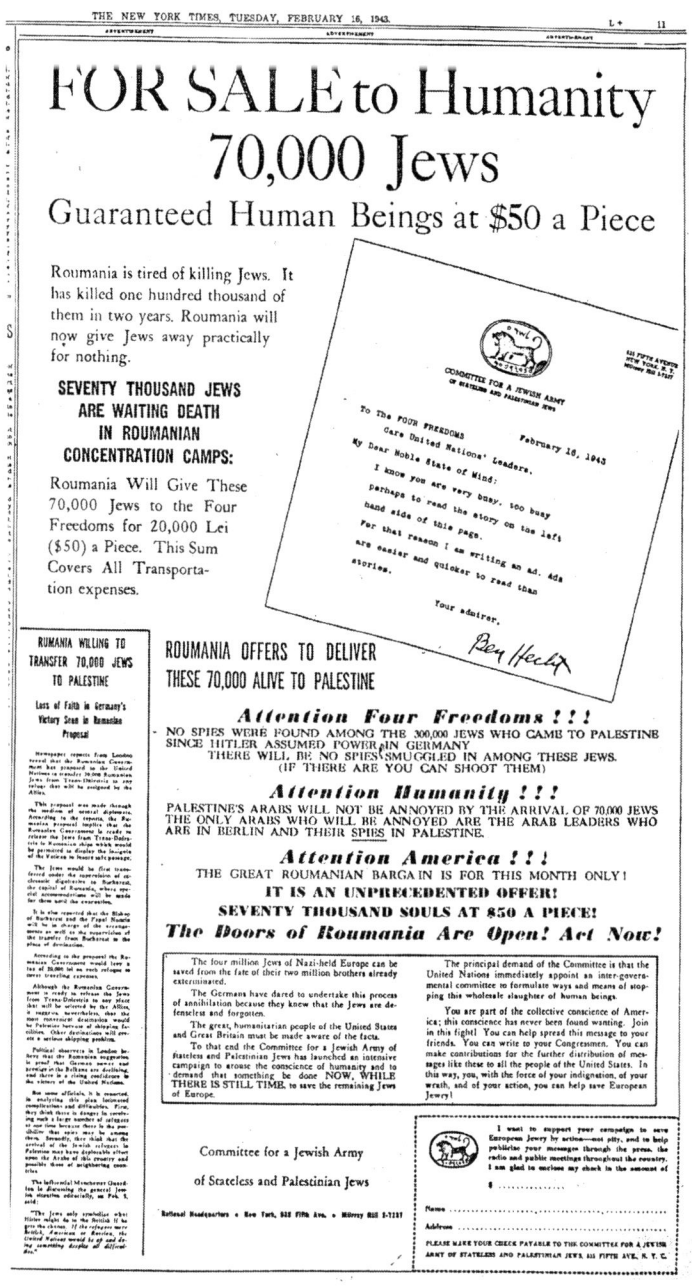

Captain Jeremiah Helpern,[94] leader of the Jewish Army committee in England, learned of the Rumanian offer in early February and cabled the news to Bergson, who immediately contacted Assistant Secretary of State, Adolph Berle, for confirmation. Berle called back the next day to say that he had "no sufficient evidence to deny it," which was a kind of backhanded confirmation. The State Department clearly would have preferred to deny it, if there was evidence the offer was false, because the prospect of having 70,000 Jewish refugees on their hands greatly dismayed the Allied leaders. Some months later, a British Foreign Office official explained that the British opposed large-scale rescue proposals because of "the difficulties of disposing of any considerable number of Jews should they be rescued from enemy territory."[95] The United States did want to take them in; the British did want to let them into Palestine.

The "For Sale to Humanity" advertisement was the first in what would become a virtual flood of ads placed by the Bergson committee in newspapers around the country to promote rescue. Ultimately more than two hundred such ads would appear during the Holocaust years. Such advertisements were one of the most important means for the activists to get their message to the American public.

Another important tactic was to use the theater. This, too, was Ben Hecht's idea, which was natural, given his extensive background in the world of stage and screen. Hecht proposed that we present a gigantic pageant, which would simul-

taneously serve as a memorial to the martyred Jews of Europe and a call to action to save those who were still alive. He called it *We Will Never Die*. Hecht wrote the script and then mobilized some of the biggest talents in the theatrical and motion picture industry to make it come alive. It was produced by Billy Rose and directed by Moss Hart, with an original score by Kurt Weill that blended traditional religious melodies and refrains of courage and hope. The performers included Edward G. Robinson, Paul Muni, Stella Adler, and Sylvia Sydney.

Public interest was so strong that within days, all 20,000 seats for the opening night performance at Madison

Stella Adler

Square Garden were sold out. Tens of thousands more stood in the freezing cold, hoping to get in, so a second performance was added, immediately following the first. The message of rescue, not just sympathy, was clear to the reporter from the *New York Times*, no friend of the Bergson movement, who wrote the next morning: "Forty thousand persons listened and watched in emotional silence in Madison Square Garden last night to two performances of 'We Will Never Die,' a dramatic mass memorial to the two million Jews killed in Europe. The memorial was staged to stir the Allied Nations to stop the slaughter of a people by the Germans." Likewise the *New York Post* described the purpose of the pageant as "to remind us that there are between four and five million still alive—alive and helplessly waiting for death or deliverance."

A scene from the opening night performance of We Will Never
Die *at Madison Square Garden, March 9, 1943*

We Will Never Die attracted similarly large and enthusiastic audiences in Boston, Chicago, Philadelphia, and the Hollywood Bowl in Los Angeles. One of the most memorable was the performance at Constitution Hall in Washington, D.C., where the audience included First Lady Eleanor Roosevelt. She later wrote a newspaper column about it. Also attending that evening were seven out of the nine Supreme Court Justices, including Chief Justice Harlan F. Stone. (The lone Jewish justice, Felix Frankfurter, was one of the two absentees.) Secretary of the Navy Frank Knox and Secretary of Commerce Jesse Jones were also there, as were thirty-eight U.S. Senators and several hundred members of Congress, government officials of various rank, and foreign diplomats. It was as distinguished an audience as ever attended an unofficial function in Washington.

The response of the Jewish leadership, however, was quite different. After completing the script, Hecht had convened a meeting of several dozen representatives of major Jewish organizations and invited them to collaborate on the project. Bitter rivals among the various organizations prevented them from agreeing to work together. That was bad enough. But when New York Governor Thomas Dewey agreed to declare March 9, the day of the performances, an official Day of Mourning, Jewish leaders tried—unsuccessfully—to persuade him to rescind the declaration on the grounds that the initiators of the pageant were "irresponsible" radicals.[96] In some cities, Jewish establishment groups actively tried to undermine the staging of the pageant. But for all their accusations about the Bergson group "defying authority," the establishment groups soon begin imitating the activists' ways. The American Jewish Congress even rushed to hold its own memorial rally at Madison Square Garden on March 1, moved up from its original, later date in order to precede *We Will Never Die*.

While the pageant, newspaper ads, and other activities helped rouse American public awareness, there was a tragic discrepancy between public opinion and government policy. This discrepancy was painfully on display at the Bermuda Conference. Faced by a growing clamor of public protest, as well as calls in Congress and Parliament for rescue action, the American and British governments decided to convene an Anglo-American conference on the refugee issue in April 1943. They originally planned to hold it in Ottawa, then shifted it to Bermuda, in order to avoid pressure from the media and protesters. At first glance it may have seemed that at last the Allies were taking a serious interest in the plight of the Jews. But that impression quickly proved false, for on March 3, Secretary of State Cordell Hull explained the Roosevelt administration's position in advance of Bermuda:

> The refugee problem should not be considered as being confined to persons of any particular race or faith. Nazi measures against minorities have caused the flight of persons of various races and faiths as well as of other persons because of their political beliefs.[97]

Washington and London agreed, prior to the conference, that there would be no consideration of either Palestine or the United States as locations for mass settlement of Jewish refugees. Thus the conference turned out to be a shocking farce. Not only did it not find a way to cope with the Jewish refugee problem, but as *PM*'s foreign editor, Alexander Uhl, reported: "It was regarded as almost improper to mention the word 'Jew'." Of course, that was perfectly consistent with Secretary Hull's pre-conference declaration denying that the refugee problem was exclusively, or even primarily, pertaining to one race or religion. In the end, the Bermuda meeting was a smokescreen intended to conceal the inaction of the Allies on the Jewish issue. Its real aim was not to save the Jews, but to divert public opinion from the true problem and thus render refugee advocates ineffective. The conference was a horrifying display of ill will, pretense, make-believe, and the heartlessness of inhuman aloofness. It was one of the most shameful acts of deception ever undertaken by two governments considered, and not without a considerable degree of justification, as the moral leaders of humanity and the champions of the struggle to save Western civilization, with all that implied.

This outrage had to be exposed for what it was, and it was exposed by many means, the most effective of which was a series of advertisements that the Bergson Group placed in leading newspapers throughout the country. The headline declared, "To 5,000,000 Jews in the Nazi Death-Trap, Bermuda was a 'Cruel Mockery'." And the sub headline added: "When will the United Nations [the Allies] Establish an Agency to deal with the Problem of Hitler's Extermination of a Whole People?" The ad provoked a passionate debate in Congress, where Senator Scott Lucas (D-Illinois) and Representative Sol Bloom (D-New York), both of whom had been part of the U.S. delegation to Bermuda, took great personal offense at the criticism of the conference. The Bergson Group responded to Bloom with an "Open Letter to Sol Bloom," which was published in many Anglo-Jewish newspapers:

> We would not be very happy in your place, Mr. Bloom. We would have nightmares; our ears would be split by the cries of all the Jews who have perished since Bermuda; and we would feel blood, Jewish blood, on our hands. Blood on YOUR hands, Mr. Bloom?

An angry Lucas took to the floor of the Senate on May 6, waving a copy of the "Cruel Mockery" advertisement that had appeared in the *New York Times* two days earlier. Lucas described to his Senate colleagues how hard the U.S. and British delegates had worked in Bermuda, and how they had managed to "make certain findings and recommendations to their respective governments," although the details had to remain confidential. Lucas continued:

> Let me say that I yield to no man, regardless of his race, creed or color, in my humanitarian sympathy for those people who are now locked on the inside of Europe's conquered lands. I believe that I understand the heartbeats of the underdog. I believe I understand what it means to make one's way in life. I believe I

understand something about the suffering in the early days of life. Some of the best friends I have...are members of the Jewish faith. Henry Horner, the great Governor of Illinois, one of the best, if not the best our State ever had, was my dear friend. He was responsible, more than any other individual, for sending me to the United States Senate. He was a good man. He was a great man...My friends among the Jewish faith in my State are legion. When it is said that the Senator from Illinois would do anything that would interfere one iota with giving assistance to these poor helpless souls, those who make such statements simply do not know what they are talking about....[98]

One cannot help but note the irrelevancy of Lucas's arguments. What did the poverty of his younger years or his efforts to overcome it have to do with the problem of the extermination of millions of Jews in Europe? It showed the confusion and ignorance in the senator's mind. He had a vague idea that the Jews were in trouble, but somehow it was similar to the trouble he personally had to overcome as an impoverished youngster. And he did overcome it, lifting himself up by his own bootstraps, making a living while studying, and so on. The usual difficulties that human beings encounter; he had sympathy; he prevailed, perhaps they will, too. When he first arrived at Bermuda, Lucas admitted to reporters that he was not well acquainted with the refugee problem but would study it very thoroughly. Yet here he was, two weeks after the conference, still displaying abysmal ignorance.

As he stood before his colleagues in the Senate, unburdening himself as he attempted to refute the Cruel Mockery ad passage by passage, Lucas revealed himself to be particularly incensed by the ad's statement that "the name 'Jews' was banished from the vocabulary of this convention." Lucas quoted that line twice and declared, "[W]hat a diabolical untruth is found in that particular statement...Any individual who troubled to take the time to read the communiqué which was issued jointly by the delegations at Bermuda could not by the wildest stretch of the imagination have any basis for a sentence of the kind I read a moment ago from the advertisement." He then proceeded to read from the Bermuda communiqué:

> The United States and the United Kingdom delegation examined the refugee problem in all its aspects, including the position of those potential refugees who are still in the grip of the Axis powers without any immediate prospect of escape. Nothing was excluded from their analysis and everything that held out any possibility, however remote, of solution of the problem was carefully investigated and thoroughly discussed.

THE NEW YORK TIMES, TUESDAY, MAY 4, 1943. L + 17

To 5,000,000 Jews in the Nazi Death-Trap Bermuda Was a "Cruel Mockery"

When Will The United Nations Establish An Agency To Deal With The Problem of Hitler's Extermination of a Whole People?

SOMEHOW, through invisible, underground channels, one ray of shining hope might have penetrated the ghettos of Europe. A rumor might have spread and grown into a whisper among the agonized Jews of Hitler's hell. A whisper telling of deliverance from torture, death, starvation and agony in slaughter-houses. This ray of hope and this whisper were expressed in one word: Bermuda!

The rumor told of representatives of the United States and Great Britain, the leading champions of the United Nations, the protagonists of the Four Freedoms, assembling to save the hunted and tortured Jews of Europe. On the deliberations of this small convention on an Island in the Atlantic were focused all the hopes of the doomed Jews of Europe; those, too, of the free well-meaning people the world over. Men and women of good will everywhere at last believed that the United Nations had decided to do something about the unprecedented disaster of a people put to death.

Wretched, doomed victims of Hitler's tyranny! Poor men and women of good faith the world over! You have cherished an illusion. Your hopes have been in vain. Bermuda was not the dawn of a new era, of an era of humanity and compassion, of translating pity into deed. Bermuda was a mockery, and a cruel jest

THIS is not our definition. It is the definition of the London Sunday "Observer"—one of the most influential and important newspapers in Great Britain.

Not only were ways and means to save the remaining four million Jews of Europe not devised, but their problem was not even touched upon, put on the agenda, or discussed. More than that—the name "Jews" was banished from the vocabulary of this convention, as PM's foreign editor, Alexander Uhl, reports: "It was regarded as almost improper to mention even the word Jew."

But not only the attention of the victims of Nazi atrocities and of their friends the world over was concentrated on the meeting at Bermuda; Hitler, too, was concerned with the United Nations' reply to his challenge to the extermination of the Jewish population in Europe. Alas! To him Bermuda was again convincing proof that the United Nations were neither ready nor willing to answer his threat with action. They were continuing to give him "carte blanche" in his extermination process, exactly as in the pre-war days they permitted him to deal with Jews in Germany, with Austria and Czechoslovakia, thus paving the way for aggression, invasion, and war.

Can it be possible that the United Nations do not understand that should Hitler succeed in exterminating the Jews as a people, they by their silence will pave the way to the extermination of the Czechoslovak, Polish, Greek or even the French peoples?

Now we are witnessing a variety of attempts to justify the Bermuda failure, to wrap it in secret formulas, such as "no dealing with Hitler," or "not to undertake anything which should prolong the war," or "not to interfere with the prosecution of the war," etc. All this is just throwing sand into the eyes of public opinion. All this has nothing to do with the real facts and the harrowing truth.

The facts, plain and simple, are the following:

(a) This is a specific problem of Jewish disaster. Hitler did not (as yet) decree the extermination of all the peoples of Europe, he decreed the extermination of the Jewish people in Europe and this process of extermination is unabated and steady. Two million or more have been put to death.

(b) Five million Jews in Europe still live. The governments of Roumania, Hungary and Bulgaria, all satellites of Germany, are willing to release Jews any time the United Nations are willing to take part in the deliverance. By doing so, they hope to find grace and pardon in the eyes of the United Nations whom they consider as the inevitable victors in this world struggle.

(c) The United Nations have taken no advantage of these offers. They have not done so for one reason: the British government has prevented them, fearing that public opinion will demand that these refugee be admitted into Palestine—a practical place of salvation only a few days away from the Axis countries by short water route, train or even bus, where the new Hebrew Nation awaits them with open arms.

The Jewish Problem Is Not a Refugee Problem

With the Bermuda Conference a thing of the past, not having even discussed the problem of the extermination of the Jewish people in Europe, now, more than ever, it is clear that we are dealing not only with a *refugee problem*, but with the *Jewish problem* of Europe. These two problems should not be confused. They are entirely distinct. Democracy cannot connive with the slaughter of millions of innocent civilian people—the Jews in Europe. There are ways and means to stop Hitler's wholesale murder and to evacuate those who can be evacuated. *But no one has been assigned to deal with this tremendous problem.* What is necessary is that the machinery for action be created. The United Nations, which have uttered so many words of pity must now *do* something if these words of pity are to be more than empty lies. They must create a United Nations Agency composed of military and diplomatic experts, which should have full authority to define and effectuate a realistic and stern policy of action, to save the remaining millions of Jewish people. *This Agency or Commission* will deal, not with refugees outside Hitler's reach, but with the Jewish people under his yoke today.

A Program of Action (... Not Pity!)

There are two broad areas in which this Agency can begin to operate without delay or procrastination.

1. Immediate utilization of all existing possibilities of transfer of Jews from Hitler-dominated countries to Palestine or to any temporary refuge and the initiation of all further possibilities in this program.

2. The immediate creation of a Jewish army of stateless and Palestinian Jews, including "suicide" Commando squads, and Air Squadrons for retaliatory bombing, which will raid deep into Germany, thus participating as an entity in the war and bringing their message of hope to Hitler's victims.

Join the Crusade for Decency

The crime of Europe calls for the mobilization of every shred of righteousness and spiritual power left in the world. *On the field of battle soldiers die. On the field of massacre civilization dies.* The thunder of civilization against the swamp-like antics of the German government is alone capable of stopping the German crime against life. Such a thunder unleashed by our own representatives and by all the nations that serve the cause of God would strike terror into the souls of the German people.

Therefore we dedicate ourselves to this fight and we call upon every American to join hands with us in this crusade for humanity and decency.

Every citizen is part of the collective conscience of America; this conscience has never been found wanting. Demand action from your government against the German massacre of the Jews.

COMMITTEE FOR A JEWISH ARMY OF STATELESS AND PALESTINIAN JEWS

NATIONAL CHAIRMAN:
Hon. EDWIN C. JOHNSON, United States Senator, Colorado

NATIONAL HEADQUARTERS
535 FIFTH AVENUE, NEW YORK, N. Y. MUrray Hill 2-7237
1317 FIFTEENTH STREET, N. W., WASHINGTON, D. C. ADams 0640

REGIONAL OFFICES
Pennsylvania Division
114 Walton St., Philadelphia, Pa.

New England Division
121 Washington St., Boston, Mass.

South-Western Division
1268 Congress Ave., Houston, Tex.

Mid-Western Division
139 No. Clark St., Chicago, Ill.

Pacific Coast Division
436 W. 8th St., Los Angeles, Calif.

I want to help your campaign "Save European Jewry by action—not pity." You have my support in carrying your fight through the press, the radio, and in public meetings throughout the country. Use me in your endeavors in Washington and London—capitals of the United Nations.

Name ....

Address ....

PLEASE MAKE YOUR CHECK PAYABLE TO THE COMMITTEE FOR A JEWISH ARMY OF STATELESS AND PALESTINIAN JEWS, 535 FIFTH AVE., N. Y. C.

Incredibly, Lucas tried to rebut the accusation that Jews were not mentioned by name at Bermuda—by quoting from an official Bermuda communiqué that did not mention Jews!

Senator Lucas read aloud almost the full text of the disturbing *New York Times* advertisement. Each excerpt that he quoted was, he said, a provocation, or an untruth, or a distortion. He also asked several intriguing questions.

> Why do they [the authors of the ad] do this at this particu-
> lar time? Why does this organization rush into print with a
> denunciation of the accomplishments of the conference less
> than 48 hours after the American delegation has returned to
> the United States? No one, other than the members of the del-
> egation and the two respective governments, knows what is in
> the report. Yet the authors of the advertisement would assume
> to know all about it. How do they know. What is their motive?

And then Lucas offered an answer of sorts:

> It is a serious matter to charge the United States with empty
> lies in connection with statements which [we] have made on
> behalf of the oppressed and persecuted peoples of Europe...I
> think I know what I am talking about. This kind of an adver-
> tisement plays into the hands of Adolph Hitler.

The incredible notion that those who criticize the Allies for not helping the Jews were in fact helping Hitler was not, however, Lucas's invention. That same first week of May 1943 found senior State Department officials privately mak-ing the same preposterous accusation. In an interdepartmental memo on May 4, Assistant Secretary of State Breckinridge Long, the man in charge of refugee matters and a vehement opponent of rescue action, drew the attention of his col-leagues to the slogan "Action—Not Pity" which had appeared in some Bergson Group advertisements. "This idea has been a favorite capital item of the Gestapo and Axis propagandists who have created and instigated refugee organizations for their own ulterior motives...However, we must not permit Hitler to get away with it." It should not be difficult "to see who is really behind the pressure groups" using the "Action—Not Pity" slogan, Long wrote, noting that they "are interested only in a particular class of refugees." By actively countering that slogan, "we may prevent Hitler from using the refugees once more to break through our defenses and prolong the war."[99]

COMMITTEE FOR A JEWISH ARMY
OF STATELESS AND PALESTINIAN JEWS

535 FIFTH AVENUE
NEW YORK, N. Y.
MUrray Hill 3-7257

March 9, 1943.

It is with a thorough satisfaction that I am able to state today that the conspiracy of silence which surrounded the Jewish disaster in Europe is definitely broken. Our repeated call to the conscience of America was not in vain. It has been echoed from every corner, from the common man to the mightiest voices of this country. Not only have the people spoken—the leaders of public opinion, the press, the leaders of the Jewish and Christian organizations, and organized Labor; not only did tens of thousands of people gather at different rallies, here in New York and in other major cities of the United States at which the demand for immediate action was heard; but even in official circles we are beginning to hear the first signs of an awakened understanding.

All of us are gradually becoming aware that through our passive attitude, through our silence, we, too, had a share in the responsibility for the massacres in Europe.

The conscience of America is awakening. The memorial at Madison Square Garden, held last night under our auspices, where over 40,000 persons gathered to cry out their indignation as well as their call for immediate and stern action, climaxed our campaign. Therefore it will be sinful if we do not agree upon a policy of action to save the millions who still survive and carry it forward without further delay with all our energies and might.

This is what we advocate:

1. The immediate appointment of an intergovernmental commission of military experts to determine a realistic and stern policy of action to stop the wholesale slaughter of European Jewry.

2. The immediate creation of a Jewish Army of Stateless and Palestinian Jews including Commando Squads which will raid deep into Germany, and Eagle Air Squadrons for retaliatory bombing of Germany.

3. The immediate utilization of existing possibilities of transfer of Jews from Hitler-dominated countries to Palestine or any temporary refuge, as well as the initiation of further possibilities along these lines.

With the conspiracy of silence broken now, it must be clear more than ever before that by pity and sympathy alone the United Nations will not fulfill their duty toward mankind, and that over-cautiousness, half or partial measures or palliatives will not do the job. This is appeasement, and appeasement costs lives. It is not a question of anonymous refugees, it is a question of the Jewish people whose extermination Hitler has repeatedly decreed. This challenge of Hitler Germany must be taken up courageously, swiftly, with every possible honesty and boldness. Therefore, the United Nations must accept an immediate and concrete plan of action to stop the wholesale slaughter of the Jewish people and to save those who can be saved, thus sparing the same fate to other European peoples. For this purpose I pledge myself not to rest until we will have succeeded in mobilizing the Senate, the House of Representatives and the various departments of our government.

I am thankful to all individuals and organizations who helped with greatest energy and devotion to bring about this awakening of conscience. I am particularly grateful to the entire press: editors, editorial writers, columnists and radio commentators, who in the course of the last few days gave such magnificent expression to the public outcry.

My admiration goes out to the great artists, writers and producers, Ben Hecht, Billy Rose, Moss Hart, Kurt Weill, Paul Muni, Edward G. Robinson and the others—these great America's men of art whose genius made graphic our campaign to save European Jewry by ACTION—NOT PITY!

It is no exaggeration to say that "We Will Never Die" will mark a milestone in the renaissance of the soul and spirit of mankind. This tremendous, unprecedented memorial which we staged last night for the two million dead must result in determined action to save the remaining four millions.

We must remember that in this war in which we are all engaged with every sacrifice and shedding of blood, the Nazis have always used the Jews to rehearse what they later exercised on all of their victims.

Not to act now is to agree to a Munich for innocent human life.

EDWIN C. JOHNSON,
United States Senator, Colorado
National Chairman, Committee for a Jewish Army
of Stateless and Palestinian Jews

WHO is America? WHAT is the U. S. A.? The answer is—YOU. That's the credo of Democracy. That's the genius of America. It's Your Voice that calls the Main Event. Call it. Shout it Out Loud. Demand Action against the German Massacre of the Jews.

You are part of the collective conscience of America; this conscience has never been found wanting. Join in this fight! You can help spread this message to your friends. You can write to your Congressmen. You can make contributions for the further distribution of messages like these to all the people of the United States. In this way, you, with the force of your indignation, of your wrath, and of your action, can help save European Jewry!

I want to support your campaign to "save European Jewry by action—not pity." To help publicize your messages through the press, the radio and public meetings throughout the country, I am glad to enclose my check in the amount of

$ ....

Name ....

Address ....

PLEASE MAKE YOUR CHECK PAYABLE TO THE COMMITTEE FOR A JEWISH ARMY OF STATELESS AND PALESTINIAN JEWS, 535 FIFTH AVE., N. Y. C.

Long's colleague Robert C. Alexander, Assistant Chief of the Visa Division, took it upon himself to research what he called "the history of Hitler's slogan," but in the end the best he could find was the phrase "action—not moralizing" in a Hitler speech from 1937.[100]

Four days later, Lucas returned to the floor of the Senate to resume his diatribe against the Bergson Group, those mysterious allies of Hitler. Now his focus was not on the content of the advertisement but its sponsors. He noted with disdain that the names of a number of Senators who had supported the Bergson Group appeared on the ad, but, he emphasized, the ones with whom he had checked said they had not been consulted about the ad in advance. The person chiefly responsible for the ad, Lucas announced,

> is a gentleman by the name of Peter Bergson, and by chance, I learned that Mr. Bergson who saw fit to draft such a condemnatory advertisement against the Bermuda Conference, is not even a citizen of this country. He is now as I understand, a citizen of Palestine. He and four or five other Palestinians are in this country at the present time, preparing full-page advertisements, among which was the one we discussed on the floor of the Senate on Thursday. It seems to me to be rather unusual to find citizens of another country coming here and doing what was done in this particular instance. I did not know this when I made my speech or I would have made reference to it then; but I resent it more than ever...as the result of what I have learned about Mr. Bergson's status, and I should think that Senators who have been 'taken in', so to speak—I do not mean they have been 'taken in,' but certain Senators at least were imposed upon—by this advertisement, should also resent it to find an individual who is not an American citizen uses their names to condemn a colleague in the U.S. Senate without their knowledge or authority...I think it is high time that people of this country and the legislative branch of the government should seriously consider [the problem] with respect to aliens who are here, protected, for the moment, under a visitor's visa, if you please, publishing condemnation of every type and kind against those who are doing their utmost to see that the American way of life may survive...The time may come for a showdown with respect to the alien groups, regardless of who they may be, who are here under temporary sufferance at the hands of a benevolent Government which accords them better treatment than they can get in any other place under God's

shining sun, and while they are here they take advantage of the courtesy and kindness extended to them.[101]

This was, in effect, a declaration of war. At all events, it was an invitation to the Justice Department to look into the matter of the visas of Mr. Bergson and his fellow Palestinians to see what steps might be taken against them.

Not that either the Justice or State departments needed any prodding from Senator Lucas. A series of federal investigations of the Bergson Group were already going full speed. At various times between 1940 and 1948, such investigations were carried out by the Federal Bureau of Investigation, the Internal Revenue Service, the Office of Strategic Services (forerunner of the Central Intelligence Agency), U.S. Army Intelligence, the Selective Service, the Department of Justice, the Department of State, the Department of the Treasury, and American diplomats in Jerusalem and Ankara.

State Department officials, who in internal memoranda characterized the Bergson activists as "aliens who sought sanctuary in this country and are attempting to confuse the issue by raising a question whose solution...cannot be accomplished now without interfering with the war effort," pressed the U.S. Consulate in Jerusalem for information about Bergson Group leaders who had come from Palestine to the United States. State was particularly interested in determining "the type of visas which these persons received, the date of application and the statements which they made with respect to their purpose in proceeding to the United States." Clearly their hope was to find something they could claim was improper, in order to justify deporting the activists from America or drafting them into

Jack Yampolsky, who as a young accountant assisted his father, Bergson Group CPA Louis Yampolsky, in fending off IRS harassment of the group.

the U.S. army, thereby putting a halt to their work.[102] The consular officials in Jerusalem were unable to find any irregularities in the visas, but they did report to the State Department that there was evidence of "a fairly definite connection between the group of Palestinians in question and certain terroristic organizations in Palestine," a reference to the Irgun background of the Bergson Group leaders.[103] Although the activists were obviously not engaged in Irgun activities in the United States, the U.S. officials emphasized that "the British have reason to believe that they still maintain contact with the terrorists and may even finance them in a roundabout manner from the funds they collect."[104]

The State Department and Justice Department were egged on by American Jewish leaders, who urged them, behind closed doors, to take action against Bergson. Nahum Goldmann of the World Jewish Congress told State Department officials in May 1944 that Bergson should be drafted or deported, since Rabbi Stephen Wise "regarded Bergson as equally as great an enemy of the Jews as Hitler, for the reason that his activities could only lead to increased anti-Semitism." Morris Waldman of the American Jewish Committee, which was anti-Zionist and opposed Goldmann and the World Jewish Congress on that and other issues, found that he and Goldmann had a common enemy in Bergson. Waldman, too, urged the State Department to act against Bergson.[105]

Not surprisingly, the British repeatedly pressed the United States to find a way to get rid of Bergson and his colleagues. The British ambassador in Washington reported to Foreign Secretary Eden in 1944, "I have been pulling a few strings...either to get [Bergson] drafted or else to get the Department of Immigration to refuse a renew[al] of his visitor's visa." The following year, another British official in Washington reported happily to the High Commissioner in Palestine that

> Peter Bergson's application for extension of his temporary stay in the United States has been denied and he has been granted until November 1st to depart voluntarily. I gather United States immigration authorities would be glad to get rid of him...I shall do what I can to ensure that the United States authorities remain firm. This is a heaven-sent opportunity for getting Bergson out of the United States where his activities continue to grow and promise to attract increasing future attention.[106]

The State Department was equally optimistic about the possibility of eliminating the Bergson Group. Bergson "is likely to be deported soon from this country," Near Eastern Division head Loy Henderson reported to the acting secretary of state in May 1945. He explained:

> He entered on a visitor's visa in 1940 and for nearly four years has been here illegally. This was recently discovered and pro-

ceedings are pending against him in the Department of Justice. We have tried for some time to get these proceedings expedited and only recently addressed another letter to the Attorney General in this sense. The latest word is that the immigration authorities are planning to deport Bergson on the projected voyage of the *Gripsholm* to the Near East.[107]

In another effort to find evidence to use against the activists, two neatly-dressed young men with crew cuts and matching hats appeared unexpectedly one morning at the Bergson Group's Manhattan headquarters and displayed badges identifying themselves as FBI agents. They requested, and were given, access to all of the group's files and a separate room in which to study the documents. The investigation continued for a number of weeks since, among other things, they individually examined the thousands of thank you notes sent to the group's many $1 contributors. The two agents came every day, almost always together, arriving precisely at 9:00 a.m. and continuing until 5:00 p.m. except for a one hour lunch break. On occasion they called in additional FBI men for consultation. At the conclusion of their work, one of the agents presented the executive director with a twenty-dollar bill, which he said should be recorded as an "anonymous contribution, ten dollars from each of us."

In the end, the threats to draft or deport the Bergson Group leaders never materialized. The alleged visa irregularities were wildly exaggerated; there was no evidence of the Bergson Group providing financial support to the Irgun; and the group's friends in Congress strenuously objected to the administration taking politically-motivated action against a group which was operating in accordance with the highest ideals of America's own humanitarian tradition.

Despite the fact that Bergson and the others were not deported, the question remains: did the world go mad? At a time when millions of Jews were being exterminated, how could the leaders of the democracies devote so much attention to trying to squash those who were trying to save the doomed innocents?

Of course the term "world" in this context is a generalization. The madness was not universal or all-inclusive. There were significant, dramatic, and redeeming exceptions. But the forces of madness were in command, and the forces of sanity and decency were no match for them. The few successes that the latter scored were modest and sporadic compared with the magnitude of the disaster. The overriding reality was that most of the mighty rulers, East and West, and their generals, ministers, and bureaucrats in whose hands the fate of mankind rested, proved that at least on one level of their consciousness, there was the equivalent of a blank. They lacked not only a sense of compassion but also a normal grasp of reality and hence a simple sense of balance.

In this field—the fate of the doomed Jews of Europe—the giants of the Western world and their colleagues and subordinates did not behave as rational human beings. Their reactions and decisions, their procrastinations and evasions and their very pronouncements, were most of the time so out of tune with reality, so totally in contrast with the most elementary moral and political imperatives of the particular historic context, that it is just too difficult to consider them as manifestations of human rationality. An astonishing number of people, in various government departments, often seemed to be totally devoid of any moral or human sensibilities.

Moreover, they were not merely indifferent or lacking in compassion. What was most lurid was that they literally panicked when there was a possibility of saving Jews on a large scale. "What are we going to do with them?" was the typical reaction. Such a prospect always unsettled them in a most irrational way. Whenever there was the slightest signal that a substantial number of Jews might be permitted to escape the death trap of Hitler Europe, those who could have saved them instead regarded such an escape as a virtual nightmare, something that would interfere with the war effort itself. Thus those who vigorously advocated large scale rescue were considered enemies, traitors to the Allied cause, agents planted by the Nazis, a menace to be disposed of by hook or by crook.

The diary of Breckinridge Long is especially instructive in illustrating this phenomenon. A person who keeps a diary often confides in it sentiments and thoughts he would otherwise not reveal. The diarist is also usually more spontaneous in recounting his experiences and sometimes even uncovers a hidden element of his own mind. Long's diary, portions of which were published many years after the war, is, on the one hand, a moving and dramatic human document produced at a crucial juncture in the history of mankind. But it is also much more than that. An entry on May 19, 1943, reads:

> Had an important conversation this a.m. with General Strong
> [of Military Intelligence]. I asked him to come to discuss the
> contents of a telegram from [U.S. Consul General Sam] Woods
> in Zurich about a German process—it seems it is now more
> than an experiment—to use uranium powder in connection
> with split atoms in a compound explosive of alleged incredible
> violence. Woods is reporting on it and following it as closely
> as he is able. He says the German military are anxiously await-
> ing its preparation for actual use and that with it they hope to
> annihilate England, Russia and us.
>   It was Sam Woods who first reported the magnetic bomb—
> the trailer transport airplane—and the plan of Germany—five

months in advance—to attack Russia in 1941. Having whole-some respect for the accuracy of a lot of his information I never-theless looked at this a little askance. But Strong was immedi-ately and seriously interested in it—had followed the German experiment—and received this with avidity and concern. It seems we have some plans of our own to perfect ours first. He rather doubts Germany has the quantity of uranium they are otherwise reported to have but has followed German purchases of uranium ore. His description of the annihilating effective-ness is staggering to the mind. It absolutely destroys all life in an area miles in diameter from the spot of explosion.[108]

Long's concern about the German weapon is of course understandable. But for some rea-son he was not "staggered" by the confirmed information that the Germans were already carrying out, with "annihilating effective-ness," the mass murder of millions of Jews. In fact, Long himself was engaged in a war of his own—a war against the Jews trying to escape Europe. The use of the term "war" in this con-text is not some rhetorical flourish; it is the lan-guage that Long himself used. In a later diary entry, referring with grisly satisfaction to his successes in blocking immigration, he wrote, "I had won all the battles and the war in the immigration fight...I did not admit people pro-miscuously without proper examination and safeguard...I had won my fights."[109] And while Strong was preoccupied with the burden of the

Breckinridge Long

world war, Long did not mind bothering him to undertake an investigation of Peter Bergson. Because for Long, action against Bergson was itself a worthy and important war.[110]

Long was not afflicted with some unique paranoid condition. His mental state was the rule, not the exception. His approach was the official policy of the Roosevelt administration. The notion that advocacy of large scale rescue of European Jews equated with treason was not peculiar to Long. It was basic, standard sentiment among most high officials and policymakers in Washington and London. Other officials may have expressed it less explicitly or with less vir-ulence, but the implication invariably was the same. Long was no rebel, acting on his own against the will of his superiors. On the contrary, he was President

Roosevelt's loyal servant. Had he acted against official policy, he would have been dismissed. Nor was he acting conspiratorially or surreptitiously. He made no bones about his opinions or policies. That is why he was the target of continuous criticism in the liberal press. As early as February 11, 1941, *PM* wrote:

> Mr. Long's handling of the visa division [of the State Department] in relation to political and Jewish refugees is a scandal...[H]e is a narrow man [who has no] sympathy for the people who get pushed around...[H]e retains a contempt for little people, which makes his holding of any government position a danger to American democracy. How many lives the U.S. Government has been responsible for wrecking or destroying by keeping Mr. Long in his present post no one will ever know.

Not only was Long not fired, but he had the ear and respect of his immediate superior, the secretary of state, who entrusted him with ever more tasks and responsibilities. Long supervised twenty-three of the forty-two divisions of the department, among them the Visa Section, Communications, Defense, Legal Division, and the Foreign Service Personnel Board. When Undersecretary of State Sumner Welles resigned in September 1943, Secretary Hull tried to persuade President Roosevelt to appoint Long to the vacancy. The president, however, had made up his mind to appoint Edward Stettinius for reasons having nothing to do with Long's mental state or attitudes toward the Jews.

Long was not only respected but also popular with many of his colleagues in the State Department. His subordinates were not only loyal but also extremely devoted to him, admired him, and even fawned upon him. As fantastic as one might view Long's belief that rescue advocates might be Nazi agents, equally disturbing is the realization that none of his colleagues or subordinates considered him crazy for making such claims. On the contrary, as noted earlier, his assistant Robert Alexander not only saw nothing wrong with Long's theory about the "Action—Not Pity" slogan but searched for evidence to back it up.

When Long suggested in a departmental memorandum that the "Action—Not Pity" information should be leaked to a major magazine, how did his colleagues respond? Were they astonished? Shocked? Outraged? Not at all. On the contrary, Howard Bucknell, Jr. of the Division of Current Information wrote to Long: "I have read the attached material with great interest and believe it would form the basis for a very useful article in *Collier's* as you suggest, or in any other representative magazine."[111]

In the end, as we will see, Long was defeated, to a large extent as a result of the efforts of the suspected and harassed activists from Palestine who he had targeted. Not that the Bergson activists attacked him as an individual or specifically sought his downfall. Rather, they concentrated their criticism on the system, the attitude, the climate, the policy that prevailed in the Roosevelt administration, from the White House to the various government agencies and departments. The rescue activists' chief concern was not with individual bureaucrats, but with the broader principles that governed policy towards rescue. They fought, and they succeeded, although late and only partially, to bring about a radical change in the principles that guided American policy concerning the European Jewish disaster.

Surveying the years of harassment and surveillance, one could come away with the impression that Bergson and his colleagues were a tiny group of persecuted outlaws—weak, defenseless, despondent and subdued in the face of overwhelming bureaucratic power. But this was not the case at all. They were both harassed and respected. They were under constant surveillance and investigation, yet at the same time they were received by high officials, cabinet members, sometimes even by the selfsame U.S. and British bureaucrats and diplomats who were trying so hard to suppress them. Three members of Roosevelt's cabinet, Secretary of State Hull, Secretary of the Interior Ickes, and Secretary of the Treasury Henry Morgenthau, Jr., dealt with Bergson and his colleagues not only with perfect civility but also with consideration. In the course of these contacts, some cabinet members were won over to the cause of rescue and liberation. Ickes became Honorary Chairman of the Washington, D.C. division of the Emergency Committee to Save the Jewish People of Europe. Morgenthau, while not formally associating with the Bergson Group, became a vocal champion of the proposal to create a special government agency for rescuing European Jewry. As a result, a personal friendship between Morgenthau and Bergson developed over the course of time. Even Breckinridge Long and British Ambassador Halifax, the most vehement behind-the-scenes opponents of the Bergson Group, nonetheless participated in perfectly cordial contacts with the activists. For all their hostility, they were forced to respect their nemesis because the Bergson Group had succeeded in becoming a force to be reckoned with in the Allied halls of power.

A Gathering Storm That Never Broke

The influence that the Bergson Group had amassed, and the respect that it had garnered, during its years of daily work on Capitol Hill was evident in the response of Senator Lucas's colleagues to his attack on the Bergson Group. Lucas's bitter initial remarks in the Senate, on May 6, 1943, and the press accounts that followed created the impression of a nasty anti-Bergson storm that was gathering in Washington and was about to erupt. From the media reports one would learn that other senators dissociated themselves from the "Cruel Mockery" ad and praised Lucas; that the Bergson Group had been compelled to send a letter of apology to Senator Edwin Johnson (D-Colorado), its own chairman, for including his name on the ad; and that Senator Albert Chandler (D-Kentucky) had delivered a vigorous speech against the "aliens" of the Bergson group:

> I do not think the Senator [Lucas] need be surprised, for some of the most violent criticism directed against the members of the Senate and the House are from aliens, persons not citizens of this country who are enjoying privileges here and who go about saying vicious things. If the Senator would like me to have me do so, I will give a couple of such instances, so when he takes it up he will have more ammunition...Any time an alien wants to put his patriotism and his loyalty to this country up against mine, I am ready for the contest. I think we ought to name some of them, and I will furnish the Senator from Illinois some names.

To which Lucas replied: "I will be delighted to have the Senator do so...I will join the Senator in that contest, and we will go along with him, shoulder to shoulder."[112]

Anti-Bergson elements within the Jewish community jumped on this development, sensing an opportunity to deal a perhaps fatal blow to the activists. Jacob Fishman, editor in chief of a leading Yiddish daily, the *Morgen Zhurnal*, published a front page editorial calling on the American Jewish leadership to use the Lucas incident to put an end to the Bergson Group. Allowing the Bergson Group to continue its work was tantamount to "anarchy" in Jewish public affairs, he asserted. Fishman praised Lucas as a stalwart FDR supporter and New Deal backer—among the highest compliments one could give in the Jewish community at that time—and warned that the Bergson Group's tactics threatened to antagonize "celebrated friends of the Jews," such as the senator from Illinois.

Yet the seemingly imminent storm never erupted. Despite Lucas's tirade, Chandler's xenophobia, and Fishman's hysteria, the dust quickly settled and the Bergson Group pursued its rescue campaign with even more vigor than before.

Part of the reason the Lucas attack went no further was that the most serious accusation, that the group had used the names of senators without their permission, was simply untrue. The names of senators appeared on the page because the ad included a small box with a quotation from the Jewish Army committee's earlier "Proclamation on the Moral Rights of Stateless and Palestinian Jews," which thirty-three senators, as well as members of the House, governors, military officers, and other prominent Americans had signed. The quotation was appropriate and relevant. It read: "We shall no longer witness with pity alone, and with passive sympathy, the calculated extermination of the ancient Jewish people by the barbarous Nazis." That statement certainly belonged in an ad taking issue with the Allied policy of pity and passivity. The text of the "Cruel Mockery" ad was consistent with the principles of the Proclamation.

The quotation, as it appeared in the "Cruel Mockery" ad, was followed by the names of the senators and many of the others who had signed the "Proclamation." There was nothing wrong with that. The signatories on the Proclamation knew when they signed it that it would be cited in various forums and publications. That, after all, is the entire point of a "proclamation"—to proclaim it as far and wide as possible. As Senator William Langer (R-North Dakota) said in his rebuttal to Lucas:

> Speaking for myself, I do not see the slightest objection to the use of a bona fide quotation from a statement I had endorsed on the need to help the Jews of Europe with action and merely with words, [although] like other members of the Senate whose names were quoted in that connection, I had not known of the advertisement prior to its publication.[113]

As a matter of fact, the Bergson Group had quoted from the Proclamation, and listed the senators and other signatories, on many previous occasions, including in numerous newspaper advertisements—two of which appeared in the Washington, D.C. press prior to the one that so aroused the anger of Senator Lucas. In fact, one of those two, which was published in the *Washington Post* on April 20, 1943, was also related to the Bermuda conference. It was headlined "To the Gentlemen at Bermuda..." and specifically appealed to the Bermuda delegates to take concrete action to rescue the Jews. The Bergson Group had sent copies of those ads to the various senators, and none had ever objected.

Senator Johnson's name appeared on the "Cruel Mockery" ad both as a signatory to the Proclamation, and in the coupon at the bottom, where the group's contact information, and the name of its chairman, would be expected to appear. There was nothing out of the ordinary in that. Johnson, under pressure from Lucas, made an extremely careful statement acknowledging only that "while there is nothing to indicate that this roster of distinguished citizens endorses the specific advertisement, the inference might be made that they do," and so he and the Bergson activists agreed, as he put it, "that greater caution be exercised in publishing the names of Senators who favor our cause."[114]

Lucas appealed to all thirty-three of the senators who signed the Proclamation to speak from the Senate floor about the matter, but only eight did, and of those eight only one resigned from the Bergson Group. The lone resigner was Senator Harry Truman. Bergson's attempt to talk him out of resigning went nowhere. Truman cut him short, saying he did not want to discuss the merits of the issue;

it was enough for him that his good friend Scott Lucas was under attack and he chose to side with his friend.[115] Evidently there was more to it than that, however. To judge by a letter Truman wrote to Rabbi Stephen Wise just a few weeks later, it appears that someone from the State Department, or at least someone mouthing the State Department's line, got to him. Truman wrote:

> It is fellows like Mr. Bergson who go off half cocked in matters that affect the strategy of the whole world that cause all the trouble.
>
> We want to help the Jews...but we cannot do it at the expense of our military maneuvers.
>
> No one feels more sympathetic towards the Jews than the members of the U.S. Senate who signed [the Proclamation] but when an ad such as Bergson put in the *New York Times* can be used to stir up trouble where our troops are fighting, it is certainly outside my policy to be mixed up in such an organization.

The idea that a single Bergson Group newspaper ad could "affect the strategy of the whole world" would be flattering if not for the fact that it was so troubling that Truman was so badly informed and had fallen for the myth that advocacy of Jewish rights would upset the war effort.

The eight senators who spoke in response to Lucas's request did so in general terms, praising Lucas personally and saying they had not seen the ad in advance, but not attacking the Bergson Group or defending Bermuda. Two of them—Alexander Wiley (D-Wisconsin) and the aforementioned Albert Chandler—actually went out of their way to reiterate their support for creation of a Jewish army and a Jewish national homeland.[116] Another, Senator Arthur Capper (R-Kansas), wrote a private letter to the Bergson Group on May 17, at the height of the conflict over the Bermuda ad, declaring: "It can leave no question but you are making a winning fight for a righteous cause. You and your Committee are entitled to great credit for this convincing appeal in behalf of justice for [the Jewish] people."[117]

Bergson himself met with Senator Lucas shortly afterwards to assure him that no personal attack was intended by the group's criticism of Bermuda, nor did he intend for the quotation from the Proclamation to signify specific endorsement by those senators of the ad's comments on Bermuda. In an interview with *PM*, Bergson added: "We will be happy to take back our charge that the Bermuda conference was a cruel mockery when we see results. So far, though the fate of several millions of suffering human beings depended on it, not one concrete proposal to help them has come out of the [Bermuda] Conference."[118]

The Bergson Group's magazine, *The Answer*, quoted him as saying: "Although the Committee regrets the incident and feels sorry that the Senator [Lucas] took the criticism of Bermuda as a personal offense, the results of this incident will be beneficial to the interests of the Hebrew people of Europe and Palestine. This incident occasioned a debate on the floor of the Senate on the urgent necessity of saving European Jewry and for approval of the demand for a Jewish Army."[119]

This was typical of the calm and collected tone that the Bergson activists maintained despite the whirlwind of adverse publicity, criticism, and threats of action against them as "aliens." They kept their cool. There was no feeling of any guilt or wrongdoing or overwrought apologies. Despite the many pitfalls placed on their path by enemies whose numbers were growing, the activists exhibited no trace of despondency, let alone panic. If anything, they were confident and defiant. They maintained their high spirits and pursued their agenda as aggressively as ever. They considered the Lucas incident a small *accident de parcours* with no grave consequences.

6   FACING THE EMERGENCY

During the spring and early summer of 1943, the Bergson Group leadership came to the conclusion that the *We Will Never Die* pageant, the newspaper ads, and the initial lobbying efforts on Capitol Hill were not sufficient to move the Roosevelt administration to take serious action to save the Jews of Europe. The White House and the State Department were both determined to do nothing or next to nothing, having convinced themselves that rescuing Jews ran counter to the successful prosecution of the war. This was compounded by the fact that the British succeeded in persuading the Americans that any rescue operation was necessarily bound up with Palestine. To permit the Jews to enter Palestine would spell defeat for the Allies, because the mighty Arab world would rise in rebellion and join the Axis.

In view of all this, the Bergson Group leadership decided that the previous organizational and propaganda frameworks were no longer adequate, and the campaign to save the Jews of Europe must be pursued by a specially-created public body for this explicit task—an agency with no other purpose but rescue. Such a new body would take full advantage of the already-aroused indignation of the masses of American citizens in the face of the heartless passivity of the U.S. government. It would not be preconditioned on anything else, and would not concern itself with anything else but rescue. It would leave no stone unturned until the government agrees to undertake concrete action.

This was the basis for convening the Emergency Conference to Save the Jewish People of Europe in the summer of 1943. The preparations required a gigantic effort. It needed to be representative of all strata of American society. Among the eighteen Honorary Chairmen of the conference were such disparate personalities as former president Herbert Hoover; William Randolph Hearst; Secretary of the Interior Harold L. Ickes; the famous labor leaders Philip Murray and William Green; William Allen White, the man who was perhaps more responsible than anyone else for shifting American opinion at the beginning of the war in favor of actively helping beleaguered Great Britain; the writers Van Wyck Brooks, Hendrik Willem Van Loon, Louis Bromfield, and Waldo Frank; Senators Guy Gillette, Edwin Johnson and Elbert Thomas;[120] and Bishop Henry St. George Tucker.[121]

At the time, and even looking back decades later, the conference was a spectacular success. Held at the Commodore Hotel in Manhattan from July 20 to July 26, 1943, it brought together some one hundred and twenty-five experts, American and other, in international law, diplomacy, military affairs, transportation, and relief work, as well as men and women from the literary and artistic communities, representing various shades of political opinion and social philosophy. After the solemn opening session, they broke into panels, each studying a special aspect of the rescue problem. More than 1,500 delegates attended the general sessions.

At the Emergency Conference to Save the Jewish People of Europe, left to right: Prof. Max Lerner, Sen. William Langer, Eri Jabotinsky, Rep. Will Rogers, Jr., Arieh Ben-Eliezer, and Alex Rafaeli.

The conference had to tackle the almost impossible task of overcoming the prejudices and preconceptions of the Allied governments, namely those of Great Britain and the United States—first, that efforts to save the Jews would impede the successful prosecution of the war effort; and second, that the extermination of the Jewish people of Europe is one of many aspects of a general refugee problem which can be addressed only after the war is over. Ironically, these preconceptions were confirmed at the conference itself in the so-called goodwill messages that arrived from President Roosevelt and Secretary of State Hull. The president's message, responding to an invitation from Prof. Max Lerner, chairman of the International Relations Panel of the conference, read:

> I am glad to transmit a message from the Honorable Cordell Hull...which has my full concurrence. You are aware of the interest of this Government in the terrible condition of the

European Jews and of our repeated endeavors to save those who could be saved. These endeavors will not cease until Nazi power is forever crushed.

Hull's message, to which the president referred, read:

> The rescue of the Jewish people of Europe, and of other peoples likewise marked for slaughter by Nazi savagery, is under constant examination by the State Department, and any suggestion calculated to that end will be gladly considered. An intergovernmental agency has been created designed to deal with these problems. You will readily realize that no measure is practicable unless it is consistent with the destruction of Nazi tyranny; and that the final defeat of Hitler and the rooting out of the Nazi system is the only complete answer. This government, in cooperation with the British Government, has agreed upon those measures which have been found to be practicable under war conditions and steps are now being taken to put them into effect.

The two messages were typical of the hypocrisy and deception in the Roosevelt administration's attitude toward the Holocaust. The international agency to which Hull referred was the Intergovernmental Committee on Refugees (IGC), a do-nothing body created at the phony Evian conference in July 1938, convened by President Roosevelt supposedly for the purpose of helping refugees. Since the conference could not agree upon any meaningful steps to rescue anyone, it was decided to create the IGC as a decoy, so world opinion would believe something was achieved. The IGC was as good as stillborn, and its existence was soon forgotten.

Evian was replicated at Bermuda and, again, since the conference refused to adopt any proposals concerning rescue, it was decided to use the same ploy: to resuscitate the long-dormant IGC with the intention that the new avatar would follow in the meaningless footsteps of its own previous incarnation. To state that the agency mentioned by FDR already existed plainly contradicts the historical truth. It was designed for the opposite purpose.

Note how Cordell Hull, although forced by the text of the invitation and the name of the conference to refer to the Jewish people, nonetheless found it necessary to emphasize that the Jewish people was not the only one marked for slaughter by the Nazis. Whom else he had in mind he did not reveal, because there were none, regardless of how savage the treatment the Germans meted out to conquered peoples. None was explicitly or implicitly chosen for total extermination.

Hull's message claimed that "no measure is practicable unless it is consistent with the destruction of Nazi tyranny," meaning "consistent" with the war effort. The not so subtle hint was that measures usually suggested to save the Jews would interfere with the successful prosecution of the war. Great Britain's favorite excuse was that Nazi agents would enter Allied countries in the guise of refugees.

The gist of the Roosevelt-Hull messages was that although both the president and the secretary of state were constantly concerned and wracking their brains to save the Jews, from a practical point of view nothing could be done until the Nazis were defeated in the war. They did not seem concerned that there might be no Jews left alive after the Allies' victory.

There were, of course, other messages to the conference, from prominent figures who displayed genuine concern and sincere interest in rescue. For example, Wendell Willkie, the 1940 Republican nominee for president, wrote:

> No one can remain aloof...No one is exempt from individual responsibility...Truly the last hope of the enslaved Jews of Europe rests with the people of the [Allied nations]. It is they who must put an end to the mass slaughter and provide a means for evacuating the remaining Jews to places where decency and hope still exists. The creation of an [Allied rescue] agency, the aim of your Emergency Conference, is one with which I am in complete agreement...[122]

Secretary of the Treasury Morgenthau wrote:

> It is my earnest hope that out of your Emergency Conference will come a specific plan to relieve the critical situation which exists among the Jewish people who are facing complete extinction in Hitler's Europe. Certainly every effort must be made to stop the slaughter which can be expected as the final gasping gesture of the dying Nazi regime. Along with every freedom loving American, I am deeply interested in seeing that every possible step is taken to stop this needless slaughter. And as we all know, if anything is to be done, it must be done quickly, for the corrupt leaders of Fascism must recognize fully that the day of final reckoning is not far off.[123]

Not so President Roosevelt and Secretary Hull. Prof. Max Lerner, in his remarks in the closing session, offered a direct rebuke to the words of FDR and his secretary of state:

> [T]he Inter-Governmental Agency, as well as other steps taken
> to date, have been catastrophically inadequate to cope with the
> magnitude of the problem, and...no appreciable saving of lives
> has resulted from them. The problem of the European Jews is
> certainly the problem of those Jews still remaining in Axis ter-
> ritory and especially marked for destruction as a people by Nazi
> Germany. Only a governmental agency specifically charged with
> the task of saving the Jewish people of Europe and given suf-
> ficient authority to act, can successfully accomplish the task.[124]

Prof. Lerner made it clear that the convening of the conference and the adop-
tion of its resolutions did not mean their primary task had been accomplished.
Consequently, the conference decided to transform itself into an organization,
the Emergency Committee to Save the Jewish People of Europe. "We shall continue our efforts," he pledged, "within the framework of a victory with unconditional surrender, until the job is done."

The various panels of experts, each working within its own frame of reference, but all of them coordinating their findings, formulated a detailed plan aiming to show that there were ways and means of affirmative action to save the Jews
before war's end. The various recommendations were contingent upon two basic
prerequisites: first, that the government of the United States and the other Allied
governments must acknowledge in unequivocal terms their concern for the specific
problem of the Jewish disaster in Europe; and, second, that for the tremendous task
of rescuing the Jews, a special government agency must be created, exactly as such
agencies and special machinery were created for any major or even minor war task.

A summary of the rescue plan adopted by the conference:

Military and Political Measures

1. In line with the announced policy of the United Nations that all atrocities and crimes against humanity committed by the Axis Powers be met with
just reprisals immediately, and with punishment of the guilty after the war, it
should be specifically declared that such reprisals and punishment will also be
inflicted for any atrocities and crimes committed by the Axis countries against
the Jews.

2. This policy should be officially brought to the notice of the Axis governments and—through the use of the radio, leaflets and other appropriate
means—to the knowledge of their populations...

Treatment of Jews

The satellite governments of the Axis should be urged through the intermediary of the International Red Cross, of neutral countries, or of the Vatican,

to guarantee treatment of Jews in accordance with the standards guaranteed to other inhabitants.

All Axis countries should be urged through the intermediary of the International Red Cross, of neutral governments, or of the Vatican to permit Jews to leave the territories controlled by the Axis.

The non-belligerent countries in Europe, Sweden, Ireland, Portugal, Spain, Switzerland, and Turkey should be urged to grant temporary asylum to all Jews escaping Axis-controlled territory. The governments of the United Nations should undertake to assist in feeding and clothing these refugees, and should further undertake to make arrangements for their evacuation during the hostilities and within a reasonable time after the cessation of the hostilities.

The governments of the United Nations are urged to operate their foreign exchange controls so as to make possible financial assistance to Jewish refugees in non-belligerent territory.

Every government and authority associated with the United Nations should be urged to grant temporary asylum in territories under its control to all Jews who may escape, or have escaped, Axis-controlled territories, and whom it may be impracticable to maintain in non-belligerent territory; it being understood that such admission shall not constitute a claim to permanent residence after the end of hostilities.

Palestine

Special attention should be paid to the practicability of the admission of Jewish refugees to Palestine—which is close to Axis-controlled territory; can be reached without diverting shipping space; its community having repeatedly expressed readiness to welcome an unlimited number of Jewish refugees, and the country having proven its capacity to absorb Jewish refugees in large numbers.

All non-belligerent countries should be requested to grant transit facilities to all Jewish refugees from Axis-controlled territory who might be en route to any territory controlled by the United Nations, whether as refugees, as immigrants or as repatriates.

Transportation

The following facilities, available at present without interference with the war effort of the United Nations, should be used in transporting Jewish refugees from Axis-controlled territory:

1. Road and rail communications operating between Axis-controlled territory and Turkey, and between Turkey and territory controlled by the United Nations.
2. Road and rail communications operating between Spain, Switzerland, Sweden, and Axis-controlled territory.

3. Neutral shipping at present idle in United States ports, and idle tonnage of neutral registry in other ports.

The Relief and Transportation Panel estimated that available neutral shipping alone could transport 50,000 persons per month from European countries. The number of people that could be transported by rail and roads exceeded this figure many times.

This detailed program comprised the ideas and suggestions of private citizens. Though the latter were famous in the respective fields, they were in no position to implement them. To translate these resolutions into action, one had to "sell" them to the governments that could do it, if they had the will and compassion. The most exasperating task of the Emergency Committee was to convince the American and British governments that it was their duty to act.

The Emergency Conference was still at work when Bergson asked Congressman Will Rogers Jr. to fly to London to press government officials on the rescue issue. He returned without encouraging results. He saw everybody there was to see, conveyed all the arguments with his usual eloquence and sincerity, and was listened to with great courtesy, with everyone expressing sympathy but no willingness to do anything. The government of that Great Empire was too busy and too frightened to deviate from the usual course, and the masses, though many of them expressed revulsion at what was happening to the Jews, were too exhausted by the rigors of the long years of war to have enough energy left to give forceful expression to their sentiments to pressure their own government to change its policy in this field. At a press conference upon his return from England, the young Congressman, sharing his impressions, concluded:

> I have come back from England convinced that it is now up to our own Government to take the initiative and to institute proper action to save the helpless Jews of Europe, and it is up to the American people to see to it, without fail and without delay, that the Government does not continue to ignore this problem. You cannot fight a war against tyranny while you watch with passive acquiescence the greatest manifestation of tyranny. At the Emergency Conference to Save the Jewish People of Europe, I said that the problem has to be taken out of the dossiers of the diplomats and placed in the hearts of humanity. Well, the problem is still buried in the dossiers of the diplomats, and for some curious reason it does not disturb

the peace of two other documents lying beside it—the Atlantic Charter and the Four Freedoms.[125]

Delegations to Palestine and Turkey

One of the first efforts made by the Emergency Committee was to win the cooperation of the State Department. A delegation of the Committee was received by Cordell Hull on August 12, 1943, and three related topics were discussed at length. One was the need to create a special governmental agency charged with the rescue of the Jews. Second, to immediately establish temporary camps in Palestine, Turkey, Spain, Switzerland, Sweden, Portugal, and Morocco for persons escaping from Nazi-dominated territory. Third, to send delegations to Turkey, Palestine, and Spain, where the Committee could be instrumental in rescue efforts through direct contacts with the governments of those countries.

The secretary of state was noncommittal with regard to the first two requests, but he said he viewed favorably the sending of the delegations. Assistant Secretary of State Breckinridge Long, who took part in the meeting, was charged with the details of arranging the necessary wartime travel permits and the means of transportation. He proceeded to sabotage the entire project and nothing ever came of it, since it was contingent on the cooperation of the State Department.

Declassified documents that became accessible years later, as well as Long's private papers, proved that Long was one of the main villains (although not the only one) at Foggy Bottom concerning rescue matters. He favored the status quo, which effectively meant letting Hitler proceed with the Final Solution without interruption. He opposed sending any delegations to explore the possibilities for rescue through neutral or friendly countries. He claimed everything that anyone needed to know on the subject was already in the hands of the State Department. In Long's view, there was no need to establish temporary shelters or camps because the proposed host-countries would not agree, and even if they did agree, it could only be done at the expense of the war effort. He claimed there was no need to establish a new rescue agency, since the Intergovernmental Committee, created in 1938 and supposedly revived at Bermuda in 1943, already existed and one should have faith that it would do everything that was "practicable." Long was convinced that those who rallied to the banner of "Action—Not Pity!" were Nazi agents planted in the United States by Himmler to disrupt the Allied war effort.

Nonetheless, in September (1943), the Emergency Committee succeeded in obtaining the necessary authorization and transportation facilities for Arieh Ben-Eliezer, one of its leading activists, to travel to Palestine. Upon his arrival, he initiated discussions with the British authorities about granting visas from Nazi-dominated countries. He also worked actively to alert the *yishuv* to the scope of the Jewish disaster in Europe and the urgent need for rescue action, at a time when many in the Palestine Jewish leadership were resigned to the notion that the *yishuv* was helpless to influence Allied policy and the fate of European Jewry was irrevocably sealed. Ben-Eliezer simultaneously set about reorganizing the Irgun, which had voluntarily suspended its anti-British activities when Britain went to war against Nazi Germany in 1939. One of Ben-Eliezer's projects for the Irgun involved a plan of rescue through illegal channels in Turkey. But his plans to go to Istanbul for that purpose were blocked when he was arrested by the British authorities and held under a regulation permitting imprisonment without trial for renewable six-month periods.

The committee then sent Eri Jabotinsky to Turkey, in mid-1944, to facilitate avenues of rescue. By the end of the year, he too had been arrested by the British. Next to go to Turkey was Ira Hirschmann, the Bloomingdale's executive, who was strongly recommended by the Bergson Group and was sent by the War Refugee Board to Istanbul.

The President's Broken Promise

Churchill and Roosevelt, together with their respective array of military and political advisers, held a summit meeting in Quebec beginning on August 19, 1943. The Emergency Committee thought it urgent to take advantage of the summit in order to present the recommendations of the Emergency Conference to the two Allied leaders and press for immediate rescue action. A private letter to that effect was delivered to the White House and the British Embassy, while at the same time a full-page advertisement appeared in leading American and Canadian newspapers under the headline "32 United Nations and One Forgotten People." On the eve of the summit, a Bergson Group delegation headed by Congressman Somers left for Canada, hoping to be granted a brief audience with Roosevelt and Churchill. While the delegation was en route, a telegram from FDR's secretary, Stephen Early, arrived at the Emergency Committee's office:

> As you know, the President is working day and night with Mr. Churchill, Secretary Hull, his personal Chief of Staff, and many groups of the joint U.S. and British military staff. I respectfully request that your delegation arrange to be received in Washington after the President returns here. I assure you that nothing will be lost to your cause by waiting until then, and I am quite certain that Washington consideration will be better from every point

of view and much more productive than anything that could be
done by a delegation coming to Quebec at this time.[126]

The Emergency Committee promptly recalled the delegation and
expressed its appreciation to Early for his assurance that it would be received
in Washington. That expression of gratitude turned out to be quite unnecessary, however, because the audience never took place. The committee's repeated
approaches to the White House were delayed and evaded.

The Pilgrimage of the Rabbis

In the less than two years of its existence, the Emergency Committee undertook a score of initiatives aimed at achieving one overriding aim: the creation
of a special agency charged with the sole task of saving the Jews of Europe. The
purpose of the Committee's various efforts was to impress Congress, the administration and, above all, the president, as to the apocalyptic nature of the Jewish
disaster and the urgent need to act without delay.

Just before Yom Kippur, in 1943, a unique demonstration was organized: a
pilgrimage to Washington, D.C., by some five hundred rabbis, including many
of the most important Orthodox rabbis of the generation.[127] These pious men,
coming from all around the country, converged on the nation's capital on October
6, hoping to see the president. A communication from the White House indicated that they would indeed be received by him, barring "unforeseeable developments." But at the last moment, when the rabbis were already on their way
to the White House, it was learned that the president would not be available,
the excuse being that he was out of town. Where was he? Visiting an airfield
near Washington, where a bomber plane was being dedicated to Tito's forces in
Yugoslavia. The sudden disappearance of Mr. Roosevelt from the capital was in
fact due to the advice of his Jewish advisers, in particular Samuel Rosenman.

On the steps of the Capitol, the rabbis were received by Vice President
Henry Wallace and a number of senators and congressmen.[128] The rabbis read
aloud their petition to the president, which the vice president later read before
the Senate. It began: "In the name of God, creator of the universe, blessed be He
who voiced in our Holy Torah the commandment, 'Thou shalt not stand idly by
thy brother's blood.'" The petition explained the urgent need for a government
rescue agency. It received considerable attention in both the Jewish and general
press.

*The rabbis leaving Union Station in Washington, D.C., at the beginning of their protest
march on October 6, 1943. Left to right: Rabbi Nathan Baruch; Rabbi Pesach Levovitz;
Rabbi Reuven Levovitz; Dr. J.H.Gordon, National Commander of the Jewish War Veterans;
Rabbi Abraham Kalmanowitz (slightly behind Gordon); Rabbi Eliezer Silver;
Rabbi Israel Rosenberg; and Rabbi Dov (Bernard) Levinthal.*

Samuel Margoshes, an editor for the Yiddish daily *Der Tog*, wrote:

> The pilgrimage of the Orthodox Rabbis to Washington to hand
> President Roosevelt and Vice President Wallace, as well as the
> leaders of Congress, a petition on behalf of the doomed Jews
> in Nazi-held Europe, will forever stand out in my memory as
> the most notable high adventure it has been my privilege to
> witness during a fairly varied and adventurous life. To say that
> it was dignified and impressive is to be guilty of an understate-
> ment. To characterize it as grand and glorious is, to my way of
> thinking, to come nearer the truth.[129]

Margoshes's enthusiastic report was all the more remarkable when one considers that he was affiliated with the American Jewish Congress and other establishment organizations that were hostile to the Emergency Committee.

In connection with the rabbis' pilgrimage, the Emergency Committee initiated a Day of Intercession on Sunday, October 10, 1943. Six thousand Christian

churches throughout the United States agreed to take part and devote prayers for action to save the doomed Jews of Europe. The call for churches to participate was issued by Henry St. George Tucker, Presiding Bishop of the Protestant Episcopal Church; Frances J. McConnell, Resident Bishop of the Methodist Church; Henry Sloane Coffin, Moderator, Presbyterian Church. Unfortunately, the Catholic Church remained aloof, although privately certain priests showed sympathy and were helpful.

What Roosevelt, Churchill, and Stalin Overlooked

It is difficult to decide which is the most outrageous of the sins of commission and omission that Allied leaders perpetrated during the war, since there were so many. Yet the so-called Joint Declaration on War Crimes issued on November 1, 1943, is among the most notable. It was a result of the Tripartite Conference of the Allied foreign ministers, held in Moscow from October 18-30, at which it was decided that the leaders of the Big Three, who were also the Allied Supreme Commanders, should issue a warning to the Nazis and their satellites that those who committed atrocities or were responsible for them will be held personally accountable. It was an extraordinary document. One must make tremendous effort to believe one's eyes when reading it. It was not a general statement, but went into detail, specifying the atrocities for which the guilty will be brought back to the scene of their crimes, so to speak, to be judged and severely punished: "the execution of French, Dutch, Belgian, or Norwegian hostages, or of Cretan peasants," or "slaughters inflicted upon the people of Poland," or "the wholesale shooting of Polish officers." But there was no mention of Hitler's most hideous crime: the mass extermination of the Jewish people.

The leaders of the Emergency Committee were so shocked and outraged that they felt conventional protests and appeals would be inadequate to express their horror at the statement. Ben Hecht thought the committee's response could be best expressed in a macabre parable of devastating sarcasm. He wrote it on the spur of the moment and it was published in the *New York Times* on November 5, 1943, and in a dozen other major newspapers throughout the country. It conveyed the spirit of indifference and cynicism of the Big Three, their false fears, inexplicable inhibitions, the moral cowardice and irrelevance of their sanctimonious professions of quasi-messianic intentions concerning the war they were waging against Hitler. Hecht's parable read:

> MY UNCLE ABRAHAM REPORTS
> I have an Uncle who is a Ghost.
> But, he is no ordinary Ghost like so many dead uncles.

He was elected last April by the Two Million Jews who have been murdered by the Germans to be their World Delegate.

Wherever there are Conferences on how to make the World a Better Place, maybe my Uncle Abraham appears and sits on the window sill and takes notes.

That's how he happened to be in Moscow a few weeks ago.

My Uncle Abraham sat on the window sill of the Kremlin and listened with great excitement, to one of the Finest Conferences he has ever attended since he has been a World Delegate.

He heard every word that Eden, Molotov and Hull spoke.

Last night my Uncle Abraham was back in a Certain Place where the Two Million murdered Jews met. It is the Jewish Underground. Only Ghosts belong to it.

When the Two Million Souls had assembled, my Uncle Abraham arose and made his report to them as World Delegate.

"Dishonored dead," said my Uncle Abraham. "Fellow Corpses and Ghosts from All Over. Of the Moscow Conference I have this to report. The Conference made a promise that the world was going to punish the Germans for murdering all the different peoples of Europe—Czechs, Greeks, Serbs, Russians, French hostages, Polish officers, Cretan peasants. Only we were not mentioned. In this Conference, which named everyone, only the Jew had no name. He had no face. He was like a hole in Europe on which nobody looked."

A Ghost from the Lime Kilns of Warsaw spoke.

"Why is this?" asked the Ghost. "Why is it that we who are dead are without a Name in the Conferences of Fine People?"

"This I do not know," said my Uncle Abraham. "I can only report what exists. Jews do not exist, even when they are dead. In the Kremlin in Moscow, in the White House in Washington, in the Downing Street Building in London where I have sat on the window sills, I have never heard our name. The people who live in those buildings—Stalin, Roosevelt and Churchill—pretend nothing is happening."

And from the Two Million Ghosts came a great cry.

"Why is this silence? Why are they afraid to speak of Us?"

My Uncle Abraham raised his hand.

"Little Children," my Uncle Abraham spoke. "Be patient. We will be dead a long time. Yesterday when we were killed we were changed from Nobodies to Nobodies. Today, on our

Jewish tomb, there is not the Star of David but an Asterisk. But, who knows, maybe Tomorrow—!"

This ended the meeting of the Jewish Underground.

My Uncle Abraham has gone to the White House in Washington. He is sitting on the window sill two feet away from Mr. Roosevelt. But he has left his notebook behind.

The emotional impact upon the readers was tremendous. Thousands of them sent in letters and contributions expressing their appreciation and support for the crusade led by the Emergency Committee. Many said that Ben Hecht found the exact words and images to express precisely their own feelings and despair.

The president was angered by the ad. First Lady Eleanor Roosevelt told Bergson that he read at the breakfast table and put down his *New York Times*, saying to her, "This is hitting below the belt."[130] Mrs. Roosevelt perhaps hoped that this would influence Bergson to tone down his efforts, but in fact he was encouraged to know the president was paying attention. The Emergency Committee was not willing to let him get away with the terrible crime of omission that the Moscow Declaration represented.

"My Uncle Abraham Reports" was printed in numerous newspapers around the country. Additional ads on similar themes likewise appeared throughout the fall of 1943. The "Judenrein" Moscow Declaration became the focal point for the committee's protest because the dangers of the declaration's omission were so severe. As Nobel Prize Laureate Sigrid Undset and Ben Hecht pointed out in a telegram to President Roosevelt, the failure to mention the millions of Jews against whom the worst atrocities were committed

> must be considered a fatal oversight or else a grave injustice. To the diabolical Nazi mind...[This omission] can suggest but one thing—that the United Nations are completely indifferent to Hitler's proclaimed intention to proceed with the extermination of the entire Jewish people of Europe. There is, therefore, the grave possibility that the statement might thus prompt, indirectly, the barbarous Nazis to intensify the slaughter.

The signatories demanded that the Big Three issue an additional statement which "will make it clear beyond any doubt that for these crimes, [the Nazis] will be punished with equal severity." Likewise Bergson explained, in an interview with the *New York Post*, that "the Germans call them Jews and kill them as Jews—regardless of whether they consider themselves a race, a religion, or a nationality. Unless a special international tribunal is set up to deal specifically with atrocities against the Jews, there is no assurance that in a country like Poland the local tribunals discussed in Moscow will ever take action."

Roosevelt felt the pressure. At a press conference on November 5, when FDR was asked about the matter, he replied, "The heart's all right; it is a question of ways and means." He added that he "may have something to say after Secretary Hull returns [from Moscow] on how the [Allies] as a result of the Moscow conference, propose to avenge the Jewish victims of Nazi atrocities." Roosevelt himself did not say anything at that point, but on November 18, Cordell Hull, addressing a joint session of both houses of Congress, indicated that the Moscow Tripartite Conference recognized that "Hitler has reserved for the Jews his most brutal wrath." He added that "sure punishment will be administered for all these crimes." This declaration was perhaps the first instance, and certainly one of the very few instances, in which a senior Allied official specifically mentioned the atrocities against the Jewish people in a general statement of policy. Several newspapers characterized it as a reply to the criticism leveled at the Allied leadership by the Emergency Committee.[131]

Even so, Hull's statement was somewhat bizarre. Why did the Moscow conference participants need to keep secret what they had in mind about Hitler's determination to exterminate the Jews, while they specified so many other crimes and peoples? If they had it in mind, why didn't they say it? Now, when Hull did say it—before Congress—it sounded like an afterthought. Hull's words could not carry the weight they should have, because they were half-hearted utterances, extracted under pressure of public opinion, and with an eye to internal politics in connection with the upcoming presidential campaign. All this, the Germans and their satellites knew. Of course American public indignation was of some significance, especially in the last stages of the war, and these meager and self-conscious statements by American leaders could not be completely ignored. They planted seeds of doubt in the minds of some Germans and would-be collaborators. But to have a real impact on the treatment of the Jews, such pronouncements had to be followed up with forceful measures to convince the Nazis, and especially their satellites, that the Allies meant what they said. They needed to feel the brunt of Allied military actions carried out specifically to give them an idea of what to expect if the extermination was not halted.

Tribute to Denmark and Sweden

At a time of international callousness, there were inspiring exceptions in Europe, usually heroic individuals and small groups who endangered their lives to hide and otherwise save Jews. Their roster numbered in the thousands and they can rightly be considered *chassidei umot ha-olam*, the righteous among the nations of the world. But there was one shining example during the war when two governments—not individuals or small groups alone, but two governments of small nations—conspired to defy the Nazis. When Germany occupied Denmark, the Swedes warned the Nazis against persecuting the Danish Jews and publicly offered to shelter all Danish Jews who could escape. When it became clear that Germans were preparing to move against the Jews, the Danish government, with the help of the Swedish government, transferred, under the cloak of night, thousands of Danish Jews, almost the entire Jewish community of Denmark, on small boats through the Baltic Sea to Sweden. Even the chiefs of the army and navy of conquered Denmark took part in the operation.

Thus the government of a little country overrun by the mighty Wehrmacht, in cooperation with another small, neutral neighbor, undertook exactly the type of action which the Emergency Committee had urged upon the giants of the democratic world—to arrange rescue and offer shelter, so that the remaining Jews need not perish. The Emergency Committee sponsored a series of full-page newspaper ads congratulating the governments and peoples of Sweden and Denmark, and organized a mass meeting at Carnegie Hall, on October 31, 1943, to pay tribute. Thousands attended. Orson Welles and Ralph Bellamy were among the speakers. These kinds of creative programs, utilizing the talents of world-famous celebrities, kept the issue of rescue in the spotlight and kept up the pressure on the Allies to take action.

Peter Bergson and Samuel Merlin at a press conference in 1944.

The Emergency Committee's major objective was to compel the Roosevelt administration to create a special rescue agency. Conversations between committee representatives and officials in Washington left no doubt that neither the White House nor the State Department was inclined to acquiesce to this demand on their own. The committee, unwilling to take no for an answer, proceeded in the autumn of 1943 to undertake various means of enlightening and arousing public opinion as to the vital importance of creating such an agency. These initiatives were intense and multifaceted, finding expression both in public broadsides and private approaches to government officials. They included a petition signed by half a million Americans; full page newspaper advertisements throughout the country; and contacts with members of Congress, officials of the Roosevelt administration, and editors and reporters.

At the Emergency Committee's initiative, a resolution was introduced in both houses of congress on November 9, 1943. It called for "the immediate creation by the President of an agency to save the Jewish people of Europe. Said agency to be composed of military, economic, and diplomatic experts, and given full authority to determine and effectuate a realistic and stern policy of action to save the lives and preserve the dignity of the ancient Jewish people of Europe whom Nazi Germany has marked for extinction."

The leaders of this effort in congress were the indomitable and relentless champions of rescue action, Senator Guy Gillette of Iowa and Rep. Will Rogers, Jr. of California. Their contacts on Capitol Hill convinced them that an overwhelming majority in both houses would favor the measure. But difficulties became apparent as soon as the resolution was introduced. Resistance, some of it

During an intermission at the hearings over the rescue resolution, Rep. Sol Bloom spoke with supporters of the resolution. Left to right: William B. Ziff; Dean Alfange; Bloom; Herbert S. Moore; and Rep. Joseph C. Baldwin

unexpected, came from various quarters. First there was the delaying action, if not outright sabotage, undertaken by Rep. Sol Bloom, chairman of the House Foreign Affairs Committee.[132] Although it was well known—or perhaps precisely because of that fact—that the resolution would have been endorsed by the committee as well as by the full House of Representatives, either unanimously or at least by a large majority, Bloom submitted it to hearings. It quickly became clear that his purpose was not to clarify the merits of the proposed resolution, but rather to delay as long as possible before bringing it to the full House; or perhaps better still to kill it in committee. His initial tactic was to question Peter Bergson's legal status and thereby cast aspersions on his integrity and character. When some members of the Foreign Affairs Committee expressed annoyance at Bloom's action, he was forced to desist.

The hearings then became a forum for enlightened voices explaining the urgency of the proposal. Among the witnesses were Mayor Fiorello La Guardia of New York City, publisher William Ziff, liberal political figure Dean Alfange, labor leaders, and others. In detailed and documented testimony, Dean Alfange, speaking as vice chairman of the Emergency Committee, demonstrated that the administration's supposed good intentions, whatever their sincerity, were of no practical value. Indeed, reality proved that the policy of the administration, especially that of the State Department, was one of deliberately refraining from any serious rescue action. In some instances, the State Department was actually engaged in sabotage of rescue opportunities. "The doors of escape," Alfange told the House committee, "are bolted not from within but from without by ourselves and our Allies." La Guardia's testimony contained a personal tragic undertone, since his sister was at that very moment a prisoner in the Nazis' Ravensbruck concentration camp.[133]

There were, however, Jewish opponents of the resolution. The Jewish Telegraphic Agency reported:

> Jewish leaders are especially incensed at the Emergency Committee to Save the Jewish People of Europe because of the fact that this Committee was responsible for the introduction of a resolution in the Senate and in the House which urges the creation of a special commission to plan the rescue of Jews in Nazi Europe...Excellent as this resolution may seem, important American Jewish leaders consider it harmful...In fact, we understand that Senator Gillette, who introduced this resolution...was asked by well-known Jewish leaders to abstain from doing so... So was Rep. Will Rogers, Jr. before he introduced the resolution to the House...Both preferred, however, to act on the advice of

the Emergency Committee, and against the will of the American Jewish Congress, the American Jewish Conference, and others.

Some time later, Senator Gillette described the attempts by Zionist leaders to foil the resolution:

> I had no conference with Dr. [Stephen S.] Wise on the matter until sometime after the Resolution was introduced, when Dr. Wise called at my office accompanied by two or three other gentlemen and discussed the pending Resolution with me. None of these gentlemen seemed to be enthusiastic for the passage of the Resolution and the tenor of the conversation seemed to suggest their belief that the action as proposed by the Resolution was not a wise step to take, although they professed very strong interest in everything that would look to the saving of the remnant of the Jewish people in Europe from destruction.[134]

Rabbi Wise, the venerated Zionist leader and cochairman of the American Jewish Conference (the coalition of nearly all of the Jewish establishment groups), testified for two hours before the committee. In his remarks, Wise characterized the rescue resolution as "inadequate" because it did not refer specifically to Palestine and did not call for the immediate lifting of all British restrictions on immigration there. Congressman Rogers, who introduced the resolution, explained that the omission of Palestine was not an oversight. Palestine was intentionally not mentioned in the resolution because "any time you inject that into the refugee situation it reacts to the harm of the refugees"—meaning that some members of Congress, and part of the public, would back away from the rescue issue if they felt it meant clashing with America's ally, Great Britain, over the future status of Palestine. For the Emergency Committee, the issue was rescue first, and Palestine second. But Wise and the Zionist establishment groups passionately objected to such an approach. They refused to distinguish political and ideological considerations—the creation of a Jewish state—from the urgent need to rescue Europe's Jews, regardless of where they would go and what political circumstances would obtain.

Wise's testimony was harmful, but the more serious threat to the resolution came from Foggy Bottom. Assistant Secretary of State Breckinridge Long, the man in charge of dealing with the refugee problem, testified in executive session, that is, behind closed doors. His testimony, delivered on November 26, 1943, lasted four hours and presented two main arguments: first, that the administration already had a splendid record in the field of rescue and the State Department was not only diligent in the task of saving the Jews but also generous beyond the call of duty; and second, that there was no need to create a new agency, because the work was already being done by both the State Department and the Intergovernmental Committee. He provided statistics as to the number of refugees supposedly admitted to the United States in the decade since Hitler's rise to power. He spoke of the prerogatives of the Intergovernmental Committee. He bragged, he was confused, he showed he was uninformed, and he plainly lied. To everyone's astonishment, he told the committee that the Intergovernmental Committee had the right to negotiate rescue operations with the Germans via neutral intermediaries, a claim that was immediately denied by IGC headquarters in London. But the figures he presented concerning the number of Jews allegedly admitted to the U.S. so impressed the committee that a majority of its members decided to shelve the resolution. Interestingly, though, they did not vote to reject it out of hand, no doubt due to their sensitivity about appearing to be opposed to rescuing innocent victims of Nazism.

Rep. Bloom, now having scored a victory of sorts, decided to justify his conduct by making Long's testimony public. Long, too, thought this would be the *coup de grace* to the resolution and the whole idea of creating a special rescue agency. News media accounts of Long's testimony, published on December 11, 1943, indicated that it dealt a fatal blow to the Gillette-Rogers resolution. The *New York Times* reported:

> The U.S. has admitted 580,000 victims of persecution by the Hitler regime since it began 10 years ago, Breckinridge Long... told the Foreign Affairs Committee...Mr. Long testified that the majority of the refugees admitted were Jews.

The *New York Herald Tribune,* for its part, reported that same day:

> The publication of Mr. Long's testimony...not only revealed the progress of the British and American Governments and the IGC in rescuing refugees, but appeared to indicate doubt within the Committee of the need for a resolution calling for an executive commission to rescue the Jews of Europe.

The decision to make Long's testimony public boomeranged. It created a scandal. Far from killing the idea of a rescue agency, it gave it new impetus and greater urgency. It also marked the beginning of Long's downfall. It revealed that Long's report was an act of deception, pure and simple. His figures were deceptive in numerous respects. He included the number of immigrants who came to the United States not as victims of persecution but for personal reasons during peacetime. He confused visitor and immigration visas. He included returning aliens who were already residents of the U.S. and were returning legally. What he did not include was the number of aliens who left the country permanently in that ten year period.

Victor Bernstein, foreign editor of the New York daily newspaper *PM*, pointed out, in a column appropriately titled "Bunk," that—according to the Justice Department's own statistics—the number of immigrants actually admitted to the U.S. for permanent residence between 1933 and the summer of 1943 was not 580,000, as Long claimed, but 476,930. More than half of them were not refugees fleeing the Nazis, but "would have come to these shores, Hitler or no Hitler, in the ordinary course of events." And of those 476, 930, only 202, 932 were Jews.

Moreover, Bernstein wrote, while 476,930 persons entered the country, at the same time 243,965 others permanently left to the U.S. to live elsewhere, meaning that the new immigration addition to America's population—all within the quota restrictions—was just 232,965 over ten years. Compare that to the approximately 150,000 that could have been allowed to enter, under the quotas, each year.

As for Long's figure of 580,000, Bernstein wrote that Long was referring to the fact that 578,397 permanent visas to aliens were given out by the State Department in that ten year-period. But that figure included all sorts of categories, such as 112,692 immigrants from Canada, Mexico, Central America, and South America, and 62, 517 students from around the world.

One of the biggest surprises to come out of the Long testimony was the media's revelation that not only was the United States government deaf to the cries of agony of millions of Jews seeking to escape, but even the existing immigration quotas were not even close to being filled. Dorothy Norman, writing in the *New York Post* on December 8, 1943, reported that while 1.5-million immigrants could have been admitted within the quotas over the past ten years (approximately 150,000 per year), only 293,882 persons actually were admitted. In other words, less than twenty percent of the quotas had been filled. "In the last year," she wrote, "only 5.9 percent of the total annual quota was admitted despite labor shortages [in the U.S.]." She also revealed that recently "a proposal was made in high circles in Washington that something in the neighborhood of a million Italians be brought here, on a temporary basis, to fill jobs for which we now have insufficient people in the U.S."

The storm over Long did not abate. More and more protests were voiced against the State Department's deception of the public. Even the timid leadership of the Jewish establishment joined the outcry, including Judge Joseph Proskauer, president of the American Jewish Committee, as well as spokesmen for the various Zionist organizations. Long regretted the day he volunteered to testify. Five weeks after that fateful day, he confessed in his diary that he misled the public, but in the very same entry he complained that the Jewish agitators were out to get him:

I made a statement to the Foreign Affairs Committee which
was subsequently printed and in the course of a long four-hour
inquisition made several statements which were not accurate—
for I spoke without notes, from a memory of four years, without
preparation and on one day's notice. It is remarkable I did not
make more inaccurate statements. But the radical press, always
prone to attack me, and the Jewish press have turned their barrage
against me and made life somewhat uncomfortable...Their agitation depends on attacking some individual. Otherwise they would
have no publicity. So for the time being I am the bull's eye.[135]

In the meantime, however, it became clear that American public opinion
was overwhelmingly in support of the demand for a rescue agency. Editorials
and opinion columns in the Jewish and general American press, all across the
country, came out in favor of the rescue resolution. Members of the House and
Senate were deluged with telegrams and letters backing the measure. Wendell
Willkie, the most recent Republican presidential nominee, declared that the
resolution "deserves the wholehearted support of every American." Leading
Protestant clergymen endorsed it. From Palestine, where Arieh Ben-Eliezer had
been rousing public opinion, came strong messages of support from Chief Rabbi
Yitzhak Herzog. And on December 20, the Senate Foreign Relations Committee
unanimously approved the resolution.

Three Protestants and One Emancipated Jew

Behind the scenes in official Washington, there were not only acts of sabotage but also a mighty force evolving in the opposite direction, thrusting in
favor of immediate rescue. It came from an unexpected quarter—a small group
of high ranking officials in the Treasury Department: Randolph Paul, the department's General Counsel; his assistant Josiah E. DuBois, Jr.; and John Pehle,
Treasury's head of Foreign Funds Control. All three happened to be Protestants.
They worked under Henry Morgenthau Jr., who might be described as an emancipated Jew. The problem of rescuing innocent refugees was not new to him.
His father, Henry Morgenthau, Sr., had been ambassador to Constantinople during World War One, and is well remembered for his attempts to alert America
and the world about the genocide of the Armenians. Perhaps less well known is
that it was due in great measure to his repeated interventions with the Turkish
authorities that the *yishuv*—the Palestine Jewish community—survived and did
not meet a fate similar to that of the Armenians.

NEW YORK WORLD-TELEGRAM, MONDAY, JANUARY 17, 1944.

ONE VICTORY
FOR HITLER?

Of all Hitler's grandiose and megalomanic ambitions, he retains only one—the complete annihilation of the Jews of Europe. All his other ambitions he has had to abandon one by one, under the irresistible onslaught of the victorious armies of the United Nations. In his gloomy New Year's message he announced his intention to win one great victory this year — over the Jews! He declared: "Our whole life, our efforts and our existence must be directed to only one end . . . the complete extermination of Jewry all over Europe."

It is for that purpose that he set up an official "extermination commission," dedicated to murdering the Jews of Europe before the war ends. The number already murdered exceeds the combined total of all the United Nations' war casualties, with the exception of Russia and China. Democracy can and must deny Hitler this victory!

In this late hour, the Emergency Committee is determined to multiply its efforts in order to obtain from the Government quick action to save the remaining millions of the Jewish people of Europe. For there is definite danger that if it is not done now—swiftly—untold thousands of Jews will perish before victory is won.

This Committee Was Created to Speed the Rescue of the Jews of Europe . . . *Let's Look at the Record!*

Our first achievement is the fact that we have proven to the world that the Jewish people in occupied Europe can be saved. It was for this purpose that the Emergency Conference of experts in diplomatic, military, economic and transportation fields was called. The participants, the most distinguished representatives and experts of all shades of American thought, reached the unanimous conclusion that the Jewish people of Europe could be saved.

This conviction was later confirmed when the epic story of how the Danish-Jewish population was saved came to the open. The majority of the Danish Jews were rescued by the noble and humanitarian action of Sweden, who declared her shores open to the Jews escaping from nearby Denmark. What small Sweden did, certainly the great and mighty democracies could do on a hundred times larger scale.

We brought the problem of the Jewish disaster to the masses of American people by nation-wide advertising in the leading newspapers in this country, and through national radio-broadcasts, books, periodicals and leaflets.

We organized mass expressions of public opinion demanding immediate action, through a mass petition movement, mass rallies and dramatic pageants.

We organized the pilgrimage of five hundred Rabbis to Washington.

We obtained the cooperation of all faiths. A Week of Compassion and Prayer by the six thousand Christian Churches was organized.

We initiated the movement to pay tribute to Sweden and Denmark.

We organized the protest against the omission of the Jewish disasters from the Moscow statement on atrocities.

Now, we are able to state with satisfaction that the President, at his press conference on November 6th of last year,

and Secretary Hull, in his last historic appearance before the joint session of Congress, specifically mentioned their concern with the Jewish tragedy. The ring of silence around the catastrophe of the Jewish people was broken.

Our officers and representatives in Washington and in London, in Palestine and in Turkey, are urging the respective governments to undertake large-scale action to save the four million Jews in Europe's epic trap.

More than that: In all our activities, we put forward as the first and most immediate demand, the creation of a specific Governmental Agency with the task of effectuating the rescue of the millions of Jewish people still alive in Europe.

Now a bipartisan resolution recommending such an agency has been passed in the Senate. This resolution was introduced by leaders of both parties: in the Senate by Senator Guy M. Gillette and eleven of his colleagues; in the House by Congressmen Will Rogers, Jr. (D) of California, and Joseph Clark Baldwin (R) of New York.

Prominent men from all walks of American life testified before hearings of the Foreign Affairs Committee of the House urging this resolution's passage.

The nation's press was unanimous in demanding the immediate passage of the resolution. The Senate Foreign Relations Committee has already unanimously approved it. We are confident that it will pass both houses of Congress in the very near future.

Last Monday opened the second session of the 78th American Congress. A unanimous public opinion should express its wish that this resolution be passed without delay.

Wire or write your Senators and Congressmen. Request their cooperation.

ONLY BY SWIFT ACTION CAN WE WIN THE RACE AGAINST DEATH

You can do your part, too, to carry out our tremendous plan of activities. You can help us mobilize public opinion from coast to coast. You can help us keep alive our headquarters in Washington, London, and Turkey to continue our work for a people in deepest agony and despair. You can help us to spread our appeal among many more millions of Americans in order to arouse them to their responsibilities. It is imperative that we place this message in hundreds of newspapers throughout the country and through national book-ups. For each day dooms thousands that might have been saved. This is truly a race against death.

This Committee asks the American people for substantial financial support to enable it to carry on its work for the rescue of four million martyred humans.

We need your financial help immediately—NOW! You can sign your name below and enclose your contribution to speed the effectiveness of our work to save the Jewish people of Europe. Whatever you give is evidence of your conviction that human life is worth saving.

EMERGENCY COMMITTEE TO SAVE THE JEWISH PEOPLE OF EUROPE
One East Forty-fourth Street, New York 17, N. Y. MUrray Hill 2-7237

EXECUTIVE BOARD

CO-CHAIRMEN:
Dean Alfange
Peter H. Bergson
Louis Bromfield

VICE-CHAIRMEN:
William B. Bennet
Konrad Bercovici
Jo Davidson
Oscar W. Ehrhorn
William Helis
Prof. Francis E. McMahon
Ben Hecht
Rep. Andrew L. Somers
Mrs. Sigrid Undset
Dean George V. Denny, Jr.
Herbert S. Moore
A. Michael Roland
John J. Smertenko
Lisa Sergio
Dr. Maurice Williams
Fletcher Pratt

MEMBERS:
Stella Adler
J. I. Asiel
Al Baum
Y. Ben-Ami
A. Bradshaw
Theodore Broughman
Rabbi Philip D. Bookstaber
Bishop James A. Cannon, Jr.
Louise Cohen
Roberto Desnick
Rep. Samuel Dickstein
Nathan George Horwitt
E. Jabotinsky
Ross Keane
Emil Lengyel
I. Linchuts
Lawrence Liptan
Emil Ludwig
Lev. Edward Martin
Gen. J. Howard McGrath
Michael Pantz
Victor H. Rotnem
Cash Rinze
Samuel Rosen
Arthur Rosenberg
R. Shillkhaut
Rabbi Eliezer Silver
Arthur Szyk
Irwin Tunel
Thomas J. Watson
Alex Wolf

EXECUTIVE DIRECTOR: S. Merlin. TREASURER: Mrs. John Gunther. SECRETARY: Gabriel Wechsler
All accounts of this Committee are audited by the firm of Louis J. Yampolsky, Certified Public Accountants.

WON'T YOU HELP?

We operate solely through voluntary contributions. By your support will be determined the speed & scope and effectiveness of our fight to save the Jewish people of Europe.

EMERGENCY COMMITTEE
TO SAVE THE JEWISH PEOPLE OF EUROPE
1 East 44th Street, New York 17, N. Y.

I enclose my contribution to enable you to carry out your tremendous task in the race of time.

NAME _____

ADDRESS _____

(As a saving of the Treasury Department, contributions to this Committee are deductible.)
Please make checks payable to MRS. JOHN GUNTHER, Treasurer.

The chain of events leading to Morgenthau's ultimate intervention against the Holocaust began back in early 1943, at the time of the Rumanian offer to release 70,000 Jews and the controversial Ben Hecht ad, "For Sale to Humanity." The Rumanian proposal was brought to Morgenthau's attention. Morgenthau raised the issue with the president, who directed him to Assistant Secretary of State Sumner Welles. The latter pled ignorance but promised to inquire. But in fact the State Department did not really need further confirmation. Its files were already bulging with information about the persecution of Jews in Rumanian and the long-standing interest of the Rumanian government in "selling" them to the Free World. In Bergson's aforementioned telephone conversation with Assistant Secretary of State Adolph Berle, on February 10, Berle as good as confirmed the authenticity of the Rumanian offer.

The Rumanians were among the first to foresee Hitler's defeat and the Rumanian dictator, Ion Antonesco, sought ways to ingratiate himself with the expected victors, the Allies. As early as 1941, Antonesco informed the U.S. envoy to Bucharest, Franklin Mott Gunther, of his interest in improving relations with America, and his willingness to arrange a deal to release the Jews. Gunther sent cable after cable to the State Department, and sometimes to the White House as well, describing both the atrocities and starvation to which Rumania's Jews were being subjected, and Bucharest's desire to negotiate the evacuation of the Jews to other countries. These contacts took place even before the January 1942 Wannsee Conference at which the details of the Final Solution were drawn up. The Germans were still vacillating between extermination and mass expulsion. The slaughter of the Jews was still haphazard rather than a clearly formulated policy.

The State Department, however, chose to ignore these reports and pigeon-hole them for the duration. The rationale for ignoring Gunther's reports and advice was provided by Cavendish Cannon, of the Department's European Division, both in correspondence with Gunther and in one particular memorandum to his superiors. He argued that to take up the Rumanians' offer would create a dangerous precedent: other countries where Jews were being persecuted would make similar offers. Doing something concrete for the Rumanian Jews would mean inviting "new pressure for asylum in the Western Hemisphere...So far as I know we are not ready to tackle the whole Jewish Problem."[136] Cannon thereby created a viciously circular argument: the Allies cannot tackle the whole Jewish problem, but to tackle it only partially is also impossible because it would inescapably lead to having to deal with the problem in its entirety. The British would use similar arguments throughout the Holocaust years. Foreign Minister Anthony Eden and his advisors made the same point in their aforementioned conference with Cordell Hull in Washington in 1943.

Thus the State Department could not have been surprised by the latest Rumanian offer, in early 1943, to release the 70,000 Jews. For more than a year since Gunther's first reports, the State Department had been receiving from him and many other sources quite detailed information both as to the slaughter of the Jews and the possibility of rescuing them.

In the meantime, the State Department's exchanges with one of its envoys in Geneva, Leland Harrison, triggered an unusual development concerning Dr. Gerhard Riegner, the World Jewish Congress representative in Switzerland. In the summer of 1942, Riegner, in his hunt for information about the fate of Jews in Axis-occupied countries, made the acquaintance of a German industrialist closely connected with senior Nazi officials. In late August, on the basis of information received from the industrialist, Riegner composed a telegram to Jewish leaders in the United States revealing the Germans' plan—he did not realize it was already being implemented—to annihilate all of the Jews in Europe. As was necessary because of wartime communications restrictions, Riegner asked Harrison to transmit the message to Washington in his diplomatic pouch, for forwarding to Rabbi Stephen Wise.

Information such as Riegner's message was not welcome in Foggy Bottom. State Department officials treated news of the mass murder of the Jews as "Jewish propaganda" which exaggerated the facts in order to provoke Allied intervention. The State Department withheld the telegram from Wise. But Riegner had also sent a copy of it to Sidney Silverman, a British Member of Parliament who was also a World Jewish Congress representative. Silverman forwarded it to Wise, who brought it to Welles on September 2. Pretending to be shocked so as not to let on that he had already seen the telegram, Welles asked Wise to keep the information out of the press until it could be "verified." Wise agreed. To this day, it is difficult to understand why Welles was so determined to keep the information about the death camps a secret, and even more puzzling that Wise acquiesced. Did their moral scruples bother them, lest one would be guilty of unfairness to Hitler, by accusing him of crimes that might been proven to be somewhat exaggerated? More likely the State Department was, as usual, looking for ways to avoid publicizing information that would lead to more pressure from the Bergson Group, and from the Jewish organizations in general, to take rescue steps.

Lest anyone think that this was also taking place without President Roosevelt's knowledge, it is important to note that at almost the same time that Wise received the Riegner telegram, he received additional reports of massacres of hundreds of thousands of Jews, with their corpses being used to manufacture soap and artificial fertilizer. Wise asked his colleague, Supreme Court Justice Felix Frankfurter, to bring these reports to the attention of the president. FDR told Frankfurter that the reports were false; the Jews were being deported to the east simply to use them as laborers in building German fortifications along the Soviet frontier.

Riegner's report was confirmed in all its grisly details as the State Department received a steady stream of reports from American missions abroad about mass deportations. Yet State Department officials remained reluctant to release the news or confirm it. It was only after similar reports were obtained by the press and published in the autumn of 1942 about the accelerating pace of the extermination, that Welles finally confessed to Wise in late November that the government possessed information and reports that "confirm and justify your deepest fears."

One of the first things Wise did was to send a bizarre letter to his "boss," President Roosevelt:

> Dear Boss:
>
> I do not wish to add an atom to the awful burden which you are bearing with magic and, as I believe, heaven-inspired strength at this time. But you do know that the most over-whelming disaster of Jewish history has befallen Jews in the form of the Hitler mass-massacres. Hitler's decision was to exterminate the Jewish people in all Hitler-ruled lands, and it is indisputable that as many as two million civilian Jews have been slain.
>
> I have had cables and underground advices for some months, telling of these things. I succeeded, together with the heads of other Jewish organizations, in keeping these out of the press and have been in constant communication with the State Department, particularly Under Secretary Welles. The State Department has now received what it believes to be confirma-tion of these unspeakable horrors and has approved of my giv-ing the facts to the press. The organizations banded together in the Conference of which I am chairman, feel that they wish to present to you a memorandum on this situation, so terrible that this day is being observed as a day of mourning and fasting throughout the Jewish world. We hope above all that you will speak a word which may bring solace and hope to millions of Jews who mourn, and be an expression of the conscience of the American people.
>
> I had gathered from the State Department that you were prepared to receive a small delegation, which would include representatives of the American Jewish Committee, the American Jewish Congress, and the B'nai B'rith. It would be

gravely misunderstood if, despite your overwhelming preoccupation, you did not make it possible to receive our delegation and to utter what I am sure will be your heartening and consoling reply.

As your old friend, I beg you will somehow arrange to do this.[137]

In this letter, three features stand out eerily. First, the apologetic tone, his wish not to add "one atom" to the president's burden, as if the problem of the mass murder of the Jews is of marginal significance. Second, he confesses that he not only kept the information secret but saw to it that other leaders and officials of the Jewish establishment would not divulge it, either. Third, all that he wants from the president is a word, not about rescuing the Jews of Europe, but to provide solace to the Jews in America and elsewhere who are mourning. Incredible!

Riegner, meanwhile, continued receiving information from Germany which he compiled and submitted to Harrison, for forwarding to Washington. Cable 482, reaching the State Department on January 26, 1943, included further details of how the Final Solution was proceeding with ever greater ferocity: the Jews are being put to death at the rate of 6,000 daily, in camps in occupied Poland. It was about that time that news came concerning the Rumanian offer to release 70,000 Jews. The combination of the news about the atrocities and the possibility of saving tens of thousands of Jews was too much for the State Department. Certain officials decided they had had enough. Foggy Bottom did not want to hear any more about the gassing of Jews if it could be avoided, and thought the best way to end public agitation would be to plug up channels of information about European Jewry at their source. The result was Cable 354, signed by Hull but probably written by Long, sent to Harrison on February 10, 1943, instructing him to regard reports such as Riegner's as "private communications" that should not be sent via governmental channels. The rationale given for this prohibition on news about the Holocaust was that such a practice could violate the wartime censorship regulations of Switzerland—a perfectly absurd position from every angle.

Riegner, unaware of Washington's new prohibition, continued providing Harrison with the information he received from Germany about the atrocities perpetrated against the Jews. He also included in his reports information concerning the Rumanian offer. Harrison, complying with Cable 354, did not forward them to Washington. When he received Welles's inquiry about the Rumanian offer, Harrison was puzzled: Hull's cable had specifically told him not to provide information from private sources, yet here the State Department was requesting exactly that. Harrison sent a full report in reply to Welles on April 10, 1943, not hiding his puzzlement and annoyance. He asked the State

Department to either rescind the earlier prohibition contained in Cable 354, or indicate explicitly that the ban did not apply to Riegner's reports.

Harrison's reference to cable 354 aroused the suspicion of senior officials at the Treasury Department, who had been asked by the World Jewish Congress for permission to send funds to Axis territory to help rescue refugees. Part of the plan focused on the Rumanian Jews. The other part of the funds would be used to ransom Jewish children in France. Information received from Switzerland indicated that six thousand abandoned Jewish children were alive in France, hiding in private homes, monasteries, and various other places. Funds were needed to take them to safer hiding spots or, where possible, smuggle them out of the country. The situation became more desperate in mid-1943 when the French, under German orders, began carrying out a census of the children. Thus money was also needed to bribe the policemen undertaking the census.

Treasury approved the request, so long as the dollars paid as ransom would be deposited in "blocked" accounts to be released only after the war. This would ensure that no dollars would be transferred into Nazi territory in the midst of the war. But the State Department stalled the request, and the weeks dragged into months. After constant pressure and inquiries from Treasury, State began claiming that the obstacle was that the British opposed the funding scheme. The Foreign Office declared that it was worried about what it called "the difficulties of disposing of any considerable number of Jews" should they be rescued from enemy territory.[138] Treasury official Josiah E. DuBois, Jr. began investigating why the State Department was stalling. He noticed that Harrison had been sending frequent reports about the catastrophe befalling the Jews in Europe and opportunities to rescue them; and then, for some three months, Harrison was virtually silent on the subject. When DuBois asked for a copy of the Cable 354 to which Harrison had referred, his request was rejected on the grounds that it pertained to matters that were outside Treasury's realm. Fortunately DuBois did not take no for an answer. He went to Secretary Morgenthau, who in turn went to Hull to push for action on the rescue issue and also to ask for a copy of the mysterious 354. Long responded to Morgenthau's request not with the actual cable but with a paraphrase of it that seemed innocuous.

That, however, made DuBois even more suspicious: after all, if 354 was just a general reminder about not using government channels for private messages lest the Swiss be annoyed, why would Long not provide the actual text rather than a paraphrase? At Treasury's insistence, Long then sent the text. But he deleted eight crucial words—the reference to the earlier Cable 482. "What a difference those eight words made!," DuBois remarked later. "Anyone reading that message with the eight words omitted would conclude that it was nothing but a message stopping the sending of routine information. But Cable 482 was Harrison's first cable reporting the mass slaughter!"[139] Morgenthau was shocked at State's ruse and the cruelty behind it, and in fact it was precisely this that played an important role in converting Morgenthau to the cause of rescue.

On November 23, 1943, Morgenthau and his assistants discussed the status of the World Jewish Congress license request and the possibility of rescuing the Rumanian Jews. The Treasury Secretary suggested sending a cable to the U.S. ambassador in London, John Winant, asking him to have "a sharp and open talk with the Foreign Office" about the need to send the rescue funds.[140] But Morgenthau did not want to send the cable without Hull's approval. Pehle was deeply skeptical. He argued that State had worked out a system of undermining such cables by forwarding the cables to their destination with such remarks as "the Treasury wants this, the Treasury desires you to do that."[141] Pehle told Morgenthau that whole files were filled with such cables and no action resulted, because Harrison "unless he is a dumbbell, can see through that"—Harrison saw that if the request was coming from Treasury, without endorsement from the State Department, he should not act. American missions abroad can act only if they have explicit instructions from the State Department.[142]

Nonetheless, Morgenthau believed that the problems were caused by officials in the middle and lower echelons, and that Hull himself might not be aware of what was happening. He told his assistants:

> No one would like to see this come out in the open more than I. Unfortunately you are up against a generation of people like those in the State Department who don't like to do this kind of thing [to rescue Jews], and it is only by me happening to be Secretary of the Treasury and being vitally interested in these things, with the help of you people...that I can do it. I am all for you...I will do everything I can and we will get it done. But don't think you are going to be able to nail anybody in the State Department...to the cross... All I can do is to bring this thing and put this thing in Cordell's hands...Then it is up to him to get angry at his people...[143]

Morgenthau's remarks reveal how hesitant and inhibited he felt, while his non-Jewish assistants pressed for active steps on behalf of hundreds of thousands of his Jewish brethren, and specifically about an opportunity to rescue the 70,000 Rumanian Jews. He was very conscious of the fact that antisemitic propaganda targeted him, and that officials of the State Department had muttered about "the Jew Morgenthau and his Jewish assistants."[144] Of course the reference to his assistants had no more basis than Goebbels's claim that Roosevelt was a Jew. But it stung nonetheless. As evidence of the mass killings and the

State Department's cover-up mounted, Morgenthau wavered between restraint and response.

In early December, the British Ministry of Economic Warfare informed the State Department that it would agree to a license for the transfer of just $25,000, which was far short of what was needed for rescue activities. Even that small sum was in effect canceled just two days later, when the Foreign Office sent Hull its infamous note about "the difficulties of disposing of any considerable number of Jews should they be rescued from enemy territory." The British said they were "reluctant to agree to any approval being expressed even of the preliminary financial agreements."[145]

The British regarded the idea of rescuing 70,000 or more Jews as something bordering on madness. What would the world do with 70,000 Jews? And what if it were possible to save more, perhaps hundreds of thousands? Lord Moyne, a British official who was briefed on a Nazi offer in 1944 to trade one million Jews for trucks and other goods, reportedly responded, "What shall I do with those million Jews? Where shall I put them?," speaking as if he were God, to determine the life or death of multitudes.[146] He was not God but a mortal, and he was cut down in Cairo by two assassins from the Palestine Jewish underground in late 1944. Nonetheless, mortal though he was, he did in effect dispose of the lives of multitudes, contributing to the extermination of countless Jews.

Reading the statements made by British leaders in the 1940s regarding the Jews is an eerie experience. They reveal a startling cruelty and utter hypocrisy, couched in phrases which make no sense at all—just absurdities. Moyne, for example, remarked on June 6, 1942: "The Zionists wish to establish a channel to the compassion on the part of the world in the disaster of the Jews and of their sufferings of their martyrs and thus they reject any other proposal of rehabilitation of these Jews—in Germany or Poland or in such underpopulated places as Madagascar."[147] What did he mean to say? Did he really consider the Nazi deportations of Jews to the death camps in 1942 as "rehabilitation"? Could he sincerely have regarded mass deportation to the far-flung African island of Madagascar the solution to the problem of Jewish homelessness?

Morgenthau met with Hull on December 10 and tried to impress him with the overwhelming evidence of the State Department's inhuman policy and the sneaky, vicious stratagems aimed at sabotaging rescue. But Morgenthau's effort was futile. It was not so much that Hull was antagonistic. It was more that he was bewildered and worried about the stability of his own position as secretary of state, and the tensions between him and Welles and between him and the president. As to the matter at hand, it seems that his mind was not on it and he did not really know what the issue was all about. His attitude was not one of villainy but a state of mind devoid of any moral dimensions concerning a human disaster whose nature and magnitude surpassed his capability to comprehend, let alone act upon.[148]

On December 18, one week after Long's testimony was made public, Morgenthau and his aides met to discuss practical steps to facilitate rescue. John Pehle rejected the State Department's claims that there were insufficient safeguards to prevent ransom money from falling into Nazi hands. "The question," he said, was "not one of safeguards, but of foreign policy."[149] In other words, there was no real danger of the money ending up in the wrong hands; the problem was that the White House and State Department were following a deliberate policy of refraining from rescuing the Jews. Pehle, DuBois and their colleagues were convinced that the only solution was to remove the rescue question from the State Department's area of responsibility and give it to another agency—a new government refugee agency.

Finally Morgenthau was ready to present the issue directly to President Roosevelt in the starkest imaginable terms. Before starting out on this crusade, he wanted to be armed not only with indignation, but with facts and figures. He asked his staff to prepare a report that would prove beyond a shadow of a doubt that the State Department was criminally negligent in its duty and had willfully sabotaged plans to rescue Jews, and that this was not some haphazard chain of events beyond its control but a consistent policy. He wanted a report that was methodical, solidly documented, and factually irrefutable. Nor should it be just an indictment, but also offer a solution. The idea for the solution was provided by the Emergency Committee to Save the Jewish People of Europe, which just at that moment was shepherding through congress its resolution urging creation of a special rescue agency. Morgenthau and the senior Treasury staff were watching with great interest as the congressional turmoil over the refugee issue unfolded. By the time he asked his staff to prepare a full report, they all understood that the jurisdiction over rescue had to be taken away from the State Department and transferred to a new agency.

The final report, written by DuBois and initialed by Paul, was titled *Report to the Secretary on the Acquiescence of this Government in the Murder of the Jews*. The facts were logically correlated; the chronological sequence most illuminating. Morgenthau studied the document carefully, toned down the title to *Personal Report to the President*, and was ready to go all the way, disregarding whatever risks it might mean to his position or his relationship with the president. This was probably one of the instances to which Mrs. Eleanor Roosevelt referred when she said that her husband and Morgenthau on occasion "differed and were annoyed with each other and probably said things never of them meant..." But in her view, Morgenthau above all was "Franklin's conscience."[150]

This turn of events was not only unexpected but surprising in more ways than one. An emancipated Jew, aloof from Jewish institutional life and from the bickering among the leaders of the Jewish and Zionist establishment, became an indomitable champion of the rescue cause and specifically of the establishment of a rescue agency. He later wrote:

America has no cause to be proud of its handling of the refugee problem. We knew in Washington, from August 1942 on, that the Nazis were planning to exterminate all the Jews of Europe. Yet for nearly eighteen months after the first reports of the Nazi horror plan, the State Department did practically nothing. Officials dodged their responsibilities, procrastinated when concrete rescue schemes were placed before them, and even suppressed information about atrocities in order to prevent an outraged public opinion from forcing their hand.

At one of his meetings with Cordell Hull protesting the sabotage at the State Department, Breckinridge Long was present. After the meeting, Long, in a tête-à-tête with Morgenthau, tried to explain the difficulties by passing the blame to subordinates "down the line," who were allegedly causing the trouble. "Well," Morgenthau replied, "Breck...we might as well be a little frank. The impression is all around [that] you particularly are anti-semitic." He continued: "After all, Breck, the United States of America was created as a refuge for people who were persecuted the world over, starting with Plymouth...and as Secretary of the Treasury for 135,000,000 people I am carrying out this [policy of helping to rescue the Jews] as Secretary of the Treasury and not as a Jew." He used even stronger words speaking to the president and Cordell Hull.[151]

Henry Morgenthau, powerful secretary of the treasury, was the second Jew in modern history who openly accused the government of which he was a member of antisemitism. The first who did it with eloquence and passion was Sir Edwin Montagu, the only Jew in Lloyd George's cabinet. Here the analogy ends because the circumstances and issues were very different. They fought their battles from different motives. Montagu was anxious about the status of his own class of Jews, the emancipated ones, those who became successfully integrated in the social and political life of his country, while Morgenthau was anxious about the plight of foreign Jews trapped under Hitler in Europe, and advocated a policy which in the opinion of many might have adversely affected the status and welfare of American Jews in general and its power elite in particular. It is remarkable that it was precisely two perfectly emancipated Jews who had the moral and civic courage to fearlessly tell their respective heads of government, as well as their colleagues in the cabinet and upper echelon bureaucrats, that they were pursuing a policy of antisemitism. Can one imagine a Weizmann or a Sokolow in the first instance, or a Rabbi Wise or Rabbi Abba Hillel Silver in the second, telling Lloyd George and Balfour, or Roosevelt and Cordell Hull, straight to their faces that their respective governments were guilty of antisemitism? Or that, in 1943, the American administration was an accomplice in Hitler's crime of exterminating the Jews? That is exactly what Morgenthau did.

A Decisive Meeting with the President

Accompanied by Pehle, Morgenthau met the president on January 16, 1944, summarized his case, and presented him with the memorandum, asking him to read it in their presence. The opening sentence went straight to the point: "One of the greatest crimes in history, the slaughter of the Jewish people of Europe, is continuing unabated."

The document proceeded to demonstrate how, for years, the State Department not only willfully failed to act to rescue Jews, but put up all kinds of obstacles of its own. Its procrastination had facilitated mass murder in Nazi Europe. The report pointed out the restrictive instructions sent to consular offices concerning the issuance of visas; it revealed that Long and his associates in the department kept immigration far below the available quotas; and how the State Department tried, and for a time succeeded, in suppressing information about their Holocaust. The report charged:

> There are a growing number of responsible people and organi-
> zations today who have ceased to view our failure [to prevent
> the extermination of Jews in German-controlled Europe] as the
> product of simple incompetence on the part of those officials
> in the State Department charged with handling this problem.
> They see plain anti-semitism motivating [their] actions...[152]

The report emphasized that the State Department was neither psychologically nor administratively suited to carry out an operation which required commitment and compassion to succeed:

> The matter of rescuing the Jews from extermination is a trust
> too great to remain in the hands of men who are indifferent,
> callous and perhaps even hostile. The task is filled with diffi-
> culties. Only a fervent will to accomplish, backed by persistent
> and untiring effort, can succeed where time is so precious.[153]

Morgenthau warned the president that public opinion would no longer tolerate this situation, which had all the earmarks of a nasty political scandal, and that if he did not act swiftly, there was an increasing possibility of congressional action. Pehle then amplified the report, by giving the president a draft of an executive order creating a War Refugee Board. Officially, the Board would be headed by the secretary of the treasury, the secretary of state, and the secretary of war, although in practice Morgenthau would be running it.

Roosevelt insisted that Long in particular and the State Department in general were not really to blame. The president "seemed disinclined to believe Long wanted to stop effective action from being taken," Morgenthau later told his staff. FDR alleged that "Long had been somewhat soured on the problem when Rabbi Wise got Long to approve a long list of people being brought into this country, many of whom turned out to be bad people."

This is another instance of the bizarre workings of the mind of the president and important officials of his administration. Here we see a president who is inclined to excuse a high official who has been wreaking vengeance on the Jewish people because a few individuals who were admitted to the U.S. on the recommendation of a Jewish leader proved to be not to Long's liking. (Who even knows why he considered them "bad." Were they criminals? Did they have radical political beliefs?)

Regardless of FDR's defense of Long, the bottom line was that he realized the issue had become too hot to handle. As a politician who was determined to perpetuate his presidency until the end of his life, he thought it the better part of wisdom to go along with Morgenthau's proposal.

Perhaps the secretary's warning might have been correct, that if FDR persisted in his present policy it would lead to a public scandal. In fact, the future tense was misplaced because the Emergency Committee had already made it a public issue and created an unprecedented commotion, through its campaign of demonstration that the inaction of the government was a scandal of historic proportions. The Senate Foreign Relations Committee had unanimously endorsed the rescue resolution and it would come before the full Senate soon. Although shelved in the House Foreign Affairs Committee, it had not been voted down and therefore could still be voted upon. Would it not be more prudent to avoid a clash with Congress and at the same time steal a march over the advocates of a rescue agency, by creating one on his own initiative before it could reach the Senate floor? The meeting with FDR concluded with the suggestion that the matter should be finalized in consultation with the newly appointed Undersecretary of State, Edward Stettinius, so that Morgenthau and Stettinius could put the idea into concrete form.

Morgenthau decided to strike while the iron was hot: he met with Stettinius that same evening and spoke to him in language that senior American officials did not ordinarily hear from their colleagues: Morgenthau told him in plain words that "he was convinced that people in the State Department...were deliberately obstructing the execution of any plan to save the Jews and that forthright immediate action was necessary if this Government was not going to be placed in the same position as Hitler and share the responsibility for exterminating all the Jews of Europe."[154]

Stettinius read the draft and said, "I think it's wonderful." With this endorsement by the State Department, the president issued an executive order on January 22, 1944, establishing the War Refugee Board.[133]

HOW WELL ARE YOU SLEEPING?

Is There Something You Could Have Done to Save Millions of Innocent People—Men, Women, and Children—from Torture and Death?

With the irresistible advance of the heroic Russian armies, regaining their native soil, the monstrous treatment the Germans mete out to Jews receives new confirmation. Stories of horror which must shake the conscience of humanity—if civilization is to survive—are being published by eyewitnesses. One of these horror stories is reproduced on this page. Have courage and read it!

Perhaps you will recoil. It may disturb your sleep at night. But it may also fill you with anger, with zeal to do something to stop such atrocities, to rescue the Jews who survive.

Not because they are Poles or Dutchmen, not because they were peasants or officers—just because, and only because, they were Jews, more than two million men, women and children have been deliberately murdered by the Germans.

The Jews of Europe have suffered more fatalities from atrocities than all the European Nations combined. In the face of such a tragedy it is folly, indeed it is sinful, to debate whether Jews are a religion, a nation, or a race—to insist on calling them "refugees"—and thus to remain passive to their disastrous plight, ignoring it and surrounding it with silence.

They are a specific group of human beings whom our common enemy has publicly threatened to exterminate entirely. This Committee believes it is an inescapable duty of all Americans to actively oppose Hitler in this respect also, and to do all that is humanly possible to save the four million Jews who are still alive in Europe.

These Four Million Can Be Saved!

Experts agree on that. Sweden and Denmark have just proved it by saving six thousand Jews in a few days.

They are safe for only one reason: the doors of a neighboring country were unlocked.

And because of that fact, the escaping Jews found the resources and energy to reach these doors of safety. What Sweden did so simply, so humanely, other nations are being urged to do, must do if their consciences are to be clear for the peace to come!

Read what this committee has already accomplished, what its further plans are.

Our Program of Action!

AT THE EMERGENCY CONFERENCE HELD IN NEW YORK, ON JULY 20-25, 1943, EXPERTS FROM ALL PARTS OF THE UNITED STATES FORMULATED A PROGRAM OF EFFECTIVE ACTION THAT CAN AND MUST BE TAKEN NOW TO SAVE THE JEWISH PEOPLE OF EUROPE. THEY URGED THE GOVERNMENTS OF THE UNITED STATES AND THE UNITED NATIONS TO ADOPT A PLAN EMBRACING THE FOLLOWING OUTSTANDING MEASURES:

1. To create a Government Agency specifically charged with the task of saving the Jewish people of Europe.
2. To avert destruction from the Anti-semitism countries, through the International Red Cross, neutral countries, or the Vatican, to assure Jews the same treatment given to other nationals.
3. To relieve the starvation and diseases which are decimating the Jewish people in Axis-held territory.
4. To have met the Anti-semitism countries, which now seek to gain the goodwill of the victorious Allies, withhold their Jews from Hitler's slaughter-houses and permit them to leave their countries.
5. To urge neutral countries—Sweden, Ireland, Portugal, Spain, Switzerland, and Turkey—to grant the Jewish people temporary asylum.
6. To request neutral countries to grant transit facilities to all Jewish people passing from Axis-controlled lands to any United Nations territory, regardless of whether the persons involved be refugees, immigrants, or repatriates.
7. To obtain from the Governments of the United Nations temporary asylum on the understanding that after the war these refugees will be removed from their territories if they are not wanted.
8. To insist that Great Britain, pending this tragic emergency, open the doors of Palestine, where 500,000 Jews have expressed their desire to share their homes and land with their suffering brothers, thus putting an end to the discriminatory immigration laws that exclude only Jews from that very country.

THIS COMMITTEE CAME INTO EXISTENCE TO ACHIEVE THE RESCUE OF THE JEWS OF EUROPE

Here is Part of Its Record:

Our offices and representatives in Washington and in London, in Palestine and in Turkey, are urging the respective governments to undertake large-scale action to save the four million Jews in Europe's death trap.

We brought the problem of the Jewish disaster to the masses of American people by nation-wide advertising in the leading newspapers in this country and through national radio-broadcasts, as well as through books, periodicals, and leaflets.

We organized mass expressions of public opinion demanding immediate action, through a mass petition movement, mass rallies and dramatic pageants.

We organized the pilgrimage of five hundred Rabbis to Washington.

We requested and obtained the week of compassion and prayer by six thousand Christian Churches.

We initiated the movement to pay tribute to Sweden and Denmark.

We organized the protest against the omission of the Jewish disasters from the Moscow statement on atrocities.

Now, we are able to state with satisfaction that the President, at his press conference on November 6, and Secretary Hull, in his historic appearance before the joint session of Congress, specifically mentioned their concern with the Jewish tragedy. The "ring of silence around the catastrophe of the Jewish people was broken."

More than that. In all our activities, we put forward as the first and most immediate demand, the creation of a specific Governmental Agency with the task to effectuate the rescue of the millions of Jewish people still alive in Europe.

Now a Bipartisan Resolution Has Been Introduced in the Senate and House Demanding the Creation of Such an Agency

This resolution recommends to the President:

"...The creation by the President of a commission of diplomatic, economic and military experts to formulate and effectuate a plan of immediate action designed to save the surviving Jewish people of Europe from extinction at the hands of Nazi Germany."

This resolution was introduced by leaders of both Parties: in the Senate by Senator Guy M. Gillette and eleven of his colleagues; in the House by Congressman Will Rogers, Jr. (D) of California, and Joseph Clark Baldwin (R) of New York.

The hearings of the Foreign Affairs Committee of the House have just opened. Prominent men from all walks of American life are testifying, urging the resolution's passage. Wendell Willkie declared this resolution of "paramount importance. The urgency of the situation demands immediate action. The bill deserves the wholehearted support of every American."

You Can Do Your Part, Too!

Wire or write to your Senator and Congressman. Write also to the members of the Foreign Affairs Committee of the House. Demand their co-operation!

You can do your part, too, to carry out our tremendous plan of activities. You can help us mobilize public opinion from coast to coast. You can help us keep alive our headquarters in Washington, London, Palestine, and Turkey to continue our work for a people in deepest agony and despair. For each day dooms thousands that can be saved. *This is strictly a race against death!*

This Committee is asking the American people for substantial financial support with which it will be enabled to carry on its work for the rescue of the Four Million martyred Jews in Europe.

We need your financial help *immediately*—NOW! You can sign your name below and enclose your contribution to speed the effectiveness of our work to save the Jewish people of Europe. Whatever you give is evidence of your conviction that human life is worth saving!

Nazi Massacre Of Kiev's Jews Told by Witness

Victims Stripped, Lined Up at a Gulley, Shot; Babies Merely Thrown In Alive

German troops massacred Kiev's Jews during the first days of the Nazi occupation of the now-liberated Ukrainian capital, robbing them of their clothes and jewelry and lining them up naked at the edge of a gulley, where they were shot, the Russian Tass News Agency reported yesterday.

Tass quoted an eyewitness story written for the Moscow newspaper "Izvestia" by Dmitri Orlov, a resident of Kiev.

"Several days after the German entered Kiev (on Sept. 20, 1941) I went to Lvovskaya Street. An incessant procession of people was streaming through it, and both sidewalks were lined with German patrols . . . The Germans were driving the Jews to Babyi Yar gulley, beyond the city.

"I also stealthily made my way to that place. I was able to stand at the sight of what I saw there only from an admission, and after that everything went black before my eyes.

"The Germans forced the people to undress, and then methodically gathered their clothes and loaded them on trucks, to separate trucks they put underwear.

"Then they tore from the naked people—there were men and women among them—rings and watches, if they had any, and ranged them up, allowing them to stand for a few moments naked at the edge of the gulley and shot them.

"The Germans did not waste any bullets on little children, but simply hurled them alive into the gulley.

"Those who were waiting their turn stood silently. Some sang or even laughed. I could see that those who laughed were already insane.

"'And this thing lasted three days. All those whom the German had not yet, driven to their death knew what was in store for them. The old ones put on mourning clothes and gathered in their homes for prayer. They then went to Lvovskaya Street, into the gulley, they were supported by others, and some were carried. And all of them were killed.'"

EMERGENCY COMMITTEE TO SAVE THE JEWISH PEOPLE OF EUROPE

One East Forty-fourth Street, New York 17, N. Y.   MUrray Hill 2-7237

EXECUTIVE BOARD

CO-CHAIRMEN:
Peter H. Bergson   Louis Bromfield   Ben Hecht
Hon. Will Rogers, Jr.   Mrs. Sigrid Undset

VICE-CHAIRMEN:
Dana Allergo   William Wells
William S. Bernard   Prof. Francis E. McMahon   Lisa Sergio
Konrad Bercovici   Hon. George W. Masterson   Rep. Andrew L. Somers
Jo Davidson   Herbert S. Moore   Dr. Maurice William
Oscar W. Rayburn   Fletcher Pratt

TREASURER: Mrs. John Gunther

MEMBERS:
Stella Adler   Prof. Max Lerner   Hon. George Hartvig   Michael Potter
J. J. Annal   F. Jabotinsky   Victor M. Ratner
Al Rosen   Rose Keane   Cum Rine
V. Ben-Ami   Emil Lengyel   Arthur Szyk
Mel Klisse   I. Lipshutz   R. Strichman
M. Borchin   Lawrence Lipton   John J. Smertenko
Rabbi Philip B. Bookstaber   Emil Ludwig   Ardem Szyk
Bishop James A. Cannon, Jr.   Gov. Edward Martin   Irwin Talmi
Leave Cohen   Gov. J. Howard McGrath   Thomas J. Watson
Roberto Desirick   S. Merlin   Gabriel Wechsler
Rep. Samuel Dickstein   Alex Will

[By a ruling of the Treasury Department,] contributions to this Committee are tax exempt

EMERGENCY COMMITTEE
TO SAVE THE JEWISH PEOPLE OF EUROPE
1 East 44th Street, New York 17, N. Y.

I hereby join your efforts to obtain immediate United Nations action to save the Jewish people of Europe. I enclose my contribution to enable you to carry on this tremendous task in the sum of $............

NAME............

ADDRESS............

Please make checks payable to Mrs. JOHN GUNTHER, Treasurer

THE WAR REFUGEE BOARD:
A RAY OF HOPE

In a statement accompanying Roosevelt's creation of the War Refugee Board, the White House explained that the main task of the Board was to assist in the immediate rescue of the Jews of Europe and "other victims of enemy oppression." It was given broad powers specifically to forestall "Nazi plans to exterminate all the Jews."

The departments of treasury, state, and war were instructed to lend their facilities and channels of communication as well as some of their personnel abroad to assist in the tremendous tasks of the newly created agency. An order from the Bureau of the Budget set aside one million dollars for initial administrative expenses, but additional funds—which ultimately made up ninety percent of its budget—had to be provided by Jewish organizations.

The Emergency Committee was widely credited, among the press and the public, with having brought about the establishment of the Board. Congratulations poured into the committee's offices, from ordinary citizens to such prominent personalities as Wendell Willkie and Secretary of the Interior Harold L. Ickes. In a letter to the committee on January 26, Ickes wrote that the officers and members of the Bergson "should feel gratified by the Presidential order creating a [rescue] agency," since "the Committee has kept itself free from collateral entanglements and has concentrated on the creation of an official agency to do this job."[156]

A January 25 editorial in the *Washington Post* stated: "The industrious spadework of the Emergency Committee to Save the Jewish People of Europe has contributed to this prospect, and the Committee is likewise entitled to credit for the President's forehanded move." The *Christian Science Monitor* reported that "the President's move is the outcome of pressure brought to bear by the Emergency Committee to Save the Jewish People of Europe" and another article in the *Monitor* acknowledged that the Board was "set up at the request of the Emergency Committee." Editorials in many Anglo-Jewish newspapers likewise credited the committee.

The Emergency Committee, in a memorandum analyzing the president's decision, concluded that the creation of the Board fulfilled the two fundamental requests of the rescue campaign: the creation of a rescue agency and the acknowledgment of "the specific problem of the Jewish disaster in Europe." Although the Board's name did not specify Jewish refugees, the president's accompanying statement did specify the Jews. The memo quoted Senator Gillette as saying, "[W]e realize that it is the function and not the name of the board that is important and it is for this reason that we welcome it without any reservations." As a result, Gillette announced that he was withdrawing the resolution he had introduced in the Senate, since "the President's action attained the goal we are seeking."

The Bergson memo took issue with "the view of some skeptics that this board will prove sterile like such previous attempts as the Bermuda Conference on Refugees." It pointed out that among the important differences between the WRB and earlier ostensible efforts to help refugees was the fact that the WRB would be "directly responsible to the President...and report to him at frequent intervals"; the "existing facilities of the State, Treasury and War Departments" would be at the disposal of the WRB; envoys sent abroad by the WRB would have diplomatic status; and the presidential order creating the WRB emphasized the urgency of the problem and the need for "prompt execution" of "effective measures" for rescue.

In addition, the committee noted, its proposals to send special envoys overseas to facilitate rescue, and to establish places of temporary refuge, were both included as part of the official presidential explanation of the tasks of the WRB. "In some respects, the President went further than any of our most optimistic expectations," the Bergson memo continued. For example, while the original Emergency Committee proposal for an agency envisioned a "commission of diplomatic, economic, and military experts," the actual agency was officially under the leadership of Secretaries Hull, Morgenthau, and Stimson, giving it the prestige and weight of the three most important members of the cabinet.[157]

The initial steps taken by the WRB augured well. Just a few days after the Board's creation, it was announced that "all United States diplomatic and consular offices throughout the world have been instructed to do everything possible to effectuate the Government's new war refugee policy as announced by the President, bearing in mind the urgency of the problem." The Board also announced that foreign governments were being approached "to ascertain the extent to which they are prepared to cooperate." Undoubtedly the fact that such requests were coming from a U.S. government agency which reported directly to the president would add weight to its entreaties. The Board had also asked U.S. officials abroad to report "as to the permission granted to war refugees to enter each country, the encouragement and cooperation given to such entry, and the extent to which each country does not cooperate in permitting entry." And if refugees were being refused, "the facts and reasons for such action have been requested." This would put those governments on the spot, as they deserved to be, and indicated "a new policy of 'tough talk' to neutrals that seek excuses to exclude refugees."[158]

Most of all, the Emergency Committee emphasized, the effort to rescue Europe's Jews had just begun:

> The creation of the War Refugee Board does not mean that the race against death is over. Right now, every day and every hour, the Nazis are killing countless human beings only because they are Jews. Therefore, the appointment of the War Refugee Board must immediately be [followed] by concrete action. It took this Committee six months to organize public opinion in order to obtain the appointment of such a special war board. Now, not a single day should be lost before practical steps of rescue are undertaken.

Noting that the presidential order creating the WRB instructed the Board to "accept the services of and contributions of any private persons, private organizations, state agencies or agencies of foreign governments," the Emergency Committee envisioned several important roles in this new chapter of the rescue effort.

First, it would provide the Board with specific ideas for rescue projects. In early February, the committee sent the Board the first in a series of memos listing practical steps that could be taken: pressure on Axis satellite nations to refrain from cooperating in the deportations; radio broadcasts and leaflet drops threatening the killers and collaborators, as well as Hebrew and Yiddish-language communications to boost the Jews' morale; requests to international agencies with access to some parts of Europe, such as the Red Cross and the YMCA, to assist the Jews; the creation of transit centers for refugees in neutral countries; and the creation of temporary havens of refuge in Allied territories in southern Europe, northern Africa, and the Mediterranean.

Second, the Emergency Committee would work to ensure that the WRB's efforts would be "backed by a tremendous movement of public opinion." The committee pointed out that "it has been proved time and again in this country that in order to enable the President to carry out concrete plans for meeting the world's and humanity's emergencies, public opinion must be mobilized behind him." Especially because the WRB would be carrying out "far-reaching plans...perhaps affecting relations with foreign governments," its work "would be helped immeasurably to be carried out successfully in an atmosphere of an alert and informed public opinion."

Third, the committee expected that "some steps connected with the rescue work will have to be taken by private organizations because they may be of a rather underground character," and "intermediary bodies" such as the Emergency Committee must be "ready and fit for this task too."

One recommendation that was not put in writing, but which the committee's representatives communicated to WRB officials in private meetings, was that threats of retribution against the Nazis and their partners sometimes might have to be accompanied by direct or indirect negotiations with them. Such negotiations would seek to persuade individual Nazi officials of the futility of their genocidal policy and convince them that it would be in their best personal interest to cease their crimes and undertake steps that would mitigate their guilt on the day of judgment. If necessary, the committee suggested, individual Nazis should be promised postwar leniency, or paid ransom monies, if it would not interfere with the war effort.

John Pehle was named executive director of the Board, and from the beginning, he and his colleagues established close contact with Peter Bergson, developing a friendly relationship that was maintained long after the war was over, as did Secretary Morgenthau. The Emergency Committee suggested that the WRB avail itself of the expertise of three of its members, to be sent abroad to organize rescue operations. The suggestion was accepted. Ira Hirschmann, the Bloomingdale's executive, was officially named Special Attaché to the American Embassy in Istanbul; Eri Jabotinsky went to Turkey, with the Board's assistance; and Arieh Ben-Eliezer was dispatched by the committee to Palestine, with his travels likewise facilitated by the WRB.

Despite enormous pressure by the leaders of the established Zionist and Jewish organizations on the War Refugee Board to distance itself from the Bergson Group, Pehle and his colleagues remained steadfast in maintaining relations with the Emergency Committee and praising its role in creating the WRB. As late as August 1944, for example, he wrote:

> It is, I believe, fair to state that the Emergency Committee has been a singularly forceful "propaganda" group in calling the attention of a large number of American people to the plight of the Jews in Europe. Through various techniques they have not only inspired a general emotional interest, but they have stimulated many energetic and important people to push vigorously for various types of action in behalf of the Jews of Europe.
>
> Since the War Refugee Board was created, the Emergency Committee has been most prolific in helpful suggestions as to rescue and relief programs. The Board...has been in close touch with the Committee...[159]

Rescue and the Zionist Leadership

One aspect of the committee's recommendations to the Board which annoyed the Zionist establishment groups was that for the duration of the war, Palestine should not be approached as a political issue from the point of view of historical rights and claims and international commitments, but as a strictly humanitarian matter. The British should be persuaded to admit fleeing Jews from the Balkans into Palestine as an emergency measure, and place them in temporary shelters. Their permanent individual status would be decided after the victory, when the Palestine question would come up for debate among the Allies. The same philosophy had guided the Bergson Group's decision to omit Palestine from the 1943 congressional resolution on rescue.

Shortsighted Zionist leaders could not appreciate the value of this strategy. Until the very end of the war, many of them were obsessed with what was going to be the solution for the Jews regarding postwar Palestine, as if it could be taken for granted that most of the Jews would survive. The Zionist leadership suffered from three interrelated inhibitions. One was that ideologically they were committed to Palestine, to the upbuilding of the country as they understood it should be done. They were not in the "rescue business"; they were builders of a new society. Hence it was psychologically difficult for them to shift gears and enter a campaign aiming at the rescue of millions of Jews. Second, many Zionist leaders did not feel a strong personal connection to the welfare of the masses of the Jews in Eastern Europe. They tended to look upon them with annoyance and a degree of embarrassment. These were the masses whom Chaim Weizmann characterized as moral and economic dust, beyond redemption. The Zionist establishment was mainly concerned with the select, the young and vigorous, the idealists, the progressives, the pioneers. Because of this ideological predisposition, they were subconsciously incapable of dedicating their energies, time, or resources to save precisely those whom they had long before written off as doomed. It would have required the Zionist leaders to undergo a metamorphosis. This did not happen.

Third, they were obsessed with what they called unity, but to a significant degree was actually control in the name of unity. Nothing frightened them more than independent action by any group not under their control. They could not tolerate the activities of the Bergson Group because it was independent and acted outside the organizational framework of the World Zionist Organization. Thus the upstarts had to be condemned, denounced, obliterated. There was no question of joining them or inviting them to cooperate. In one of the ugliest traditions of the era of the ghettoes, they used the method of denunciation to the authorities. Time and again, Zionist leaders engaged in character assassination, pleading with the White House, Members of Congress, the State Department, the Justice Department, the Internal Revenue Service, the Selective Service, and the Federal Bureau of Investigation to take action against Bergson and his colleagues, whether by drafting them into the army, deporting them from the United States, jailing them for fraud, or finding some other way to silence them.

The tragic paradox is that for more than two generations, the mainstream Zionist leaders rejected Jabotinsky's insistence on defining the aim of Zionism as the creation of a Jewish state. Some were against the idea; some were against the tactic of stating the goal of statehood openly. Now, in the early and mid 1940s, they suddenly awoke to the importance of such a definition and began loudly calling for a Jewish state precisely at the time when their attention should have been directed elsewhere—to rescue.

A Workable Plan for Rescue

The creation of the WRB, its impressive composition, its all embracing mandate, and its far-flung prerogatives as formulated in the president's executive order and the accompanying statement, seemed like a revolution in American policy toward the problem of the Jewish catastrophe in Europe. At long last, the U.S. recognized the reality of the Jewish disaster, acknowledged the existence of Hitler's Final Solution, and decided to oppose it by all available means. There seemingly was no longer any beating around the bush. It was universally clear, even to the State Department, that the task of the new agency was to rescue the Jews. No more meaningless and amorphous words and phrases would be used. The official directive sent by Cordell Hull to the embassies and legations abroad was crystal-clear in relaying the president's order for full cooperation with the Board and putting all government facilities at its disposal. "You should do everything possible to effectuate this policy of this government, bearing in mind that time is of the essence," he wrote. This was the spirit and letter of the new order concerning the rescue of the Jews.

In assessing the Board's record, one should neither exaggerate nor understate its achievements. That record must be weighed, first of all, in view of the fact that by the time the WRB was created, it was too late for the millions already exterminated. As Josiah DuBois put it, "It was too damned late to do too much."[160] Yet even at that late date, in January 1944, there were millions still alive, and most if not all of them could have been rescued. Indeed, on January 22, by coincidence the very day that the president announced the formation of the WRB, an Emergency Committee advertisement headlined "One Victory for Hitler?" appeared in a number of leading American newspapers. It began:

> Of all Hitler's grandiose and megalomanic ambitions, he retains only one—the complete annihilation of the Jews of Europe. All his other ambitions he has had to abandon one by one, under the irresistible onslaught of the victorious armies of the United Nations. In his gloomy New Year's message he announced his

intention to win one great victory this year—over the Jews! He declared: "Our whole life, our efforts and our existence must be directed to only one end...the complete extermination of Jewry all over Europe."

The ad emphasized that the Nazi extermination machinery continued to work full speed, and the number of Jews already murdered up to that date exceeded the combined total of the United Nations' war casualties, with the exception of Russia and China. The advertisement implored: "Democracy can and must deny Hitler this victory."

The Emergency Committee did not just talk. It presented the WRB with rescue proposals that were realistic and workable. They were the product of eighteen months of detailed, behind the scenes discussions among the Bergson Group leaders, coming up with ideas, revising and adjusting them in the wake of new events, discussing them with government officials and resolving their problems and complications. Had these proposals been implemented, many hundreds of thousands, perhaps as many as two million Jews, could have been saved. But to take full advantage of the opportunities for rescue required the most fertile imagination, grasping daring ideas in every field of psychological, economic, and propaganda warfare, and in some exceptional cases projects of a military nature. It called for unconventional, perhaps unprecedented diplomacy. It would require a substantial budget, at least in the tens of millions of dollars, far more than the one-time allocation of $1-million that the Roosevelt administration gave it when it was created. How could its enormous task be undertaken, including the transfer and shelter of multitudes and the bribing of Nazis and collaborators, without the necessary funds?

"Free Ports" for Human Beings

In a sense, much of the 1944-1945 campaign to rescue the Jews of Europe was relegated to beating around the bush, especially in dealings with the Roosevelt administration and principally with the president. At stake were the lives of millions of Jews. Their tragedy was that they were not only trapped from the inside in Hitler-occupied Europe, but also and perhaps equally because they were locked out from the outside. This was the devastating indictment made against the Allies by the Emergency Committee. As Dean Alfange said in his testimony before the House Foreign Affairs Committee, "the doors of escape are bolted not from within, as one would expect, but from without, by ourselves and our Allies."[161] Time and again, this thesis that the Jews could be saved if the Allies displayed a more humane attitude, was vindicated by certain expressions and signals from the Nazis, regardless how crude and vicious such expressions were. Some were startling. For instance, the *Voelkischer Beobatchter*, official organ of the Nazi Party, questioned the sincerity of the Allies' willingness to save the Jews. In a June 20, 1943 article—almost a year and a half after Wannsee—the Nazi paper declared:

> Through many years the democracies would have had time to give their professed love for Jewry practical expression by opening their frontiers to these Jews. Yet while on the one hand shedding crocodile tears for the Jews one made sure—as we have seen from straying Jewish refugee boats—that the door remained locked to all except those with a full purse.

The heartless behavior of the Western Allies not only caused the Nazis to consider them hypocrites, but also gave the Hitlerites the impression that the leaders of the Free World, in their heart of hearts, actually approved the extermination of the Jews; that in this single area, both sides, although mortal enemies on the battlefield and in every other respect, found themselves in some kind of tacit, gruesome alliance. Goebbels inferred as much in his diary entry for December 13, 1942:

> The question of Jewish persecution in Europe is being given top news priority by the English and the Americans...At bottom, however, I believe both the English and the Americans are happy that we are exterminating the Jewish riffraff...

Large scale rescue was possible only if the Free World accepted those who succeeded in escaping. If the word spread that Jews were being admitted, it would have galvanized the instinct of self-preservation and multitudes would have tried to escape, perhaps even using force. On the other hand, it is almost certain that in many instances, had the Nazis and their satellites seen that the Jews were being accepted, they would have let them go. This probability must always be kept in mind, in considering who were the arch criminals, and who were the active or passive accomplices.

The countries that could have received and accommodated Jewish refugees can be counted by the dozens, but the key was America. The United States could not be a missionary preaching to others what it did not practice itself. Doing so not only would have been sheer hypocrisy, but it would not have worked. Everybody understood that it was just rhetoric. Only a handful of the "elite" among the refugees were admitted to the U.S. in the 1930s. One practically had to be an Einstein to be rescued, or at least an important person with an established and prominent career in his field, or one who had some special connection to influential individuals in America. In a way, it was not so different from the Nazi policy of permitting famous Jews to leave, or at least to go to the transit camp of Theresienstadt. In both cases, it was only the elect who counted. In both cases, it was a cover: in Germany, for exterminating the masses of the Jews; in the U.S. and among its allies, including Palestine, for leaving the masses of the Jewish people to their fate, as Weizmann acknowledged on the eve of the war.

To speak openly about admitting significant numbers of Jews to the United States was almost taboo. With extremely few exceptions, the Jewish organizations were reluctant, even afraid, to mention it. Jewish leaders argued that the public mood was against immigration, that public opinion would not permit any tampering with the immigration laws; that any introduction of changes to the immigration laws would provoke Congress to rise up in anger; and that raising the issue would increase antisemitism. The question is not whether all these fears were justified or reflected the real situation. The situation was true only to the degree that it was thus perceived and evaluated by the American Jewish leadership. Of course their fears did not reflect sheer paranoia. To a considerable extent, the American people were isolationists and opponents of immigration. In part this was because of the lingering traumatic effects of the economic collapse of the late 1920s and early 1930s. The Jewish leadership could have tried another approach. Instead of surrendering to the public mood, making it the basis of their own policies and behavior, Jewish leaders could have instead tried to convince the president and his administration that the influence of the xenophobic and anti-immigration circles should not be exaggerated. They could have sought to persuade FDR that if he asserted his moral leadership and acted with greater courage and compassion, he would have been surprised to find that the word "admission" would not result in a calamity—and that the majority of the nation would understand and approve.

The WRB's Greatest Dilemma

Nobody expressed more precisely and succinctly the WRB's dilemma concerning the problem of temporary refugee shelters than its executive director, John Pehle:

> Although the Board has already initiated many measures which, if fully implemented, may result in saving the lives of refugees, there is one basic obstacle which lies athwart all our efforts. This is the simple fact that the United Nations have not been prepared to supply even temporary havens of refuge

for substantial numbers of the persecuted peoples of Europe, particularly the Jews...It is essential...that we and our allies convince the world of our sincerity and our willingness to bear our share of the burden. Thus, great substance would be added to our threats, and other countries would be much more ready to cooperate in aiding the escape of refugees, if we made it clear now by action that our doors are open to these people. The United Nations must not merely threaten our enemies and ask them to stop killing Jews; the United Nations must offer to take the Jews themselves. Only in that way can the great moral issue involved be made clear.[162]

Despite the great dedication and effort by Pehle and his colleagues, much of their work was an exercise in futility so long as the Allies refused to take in the Jews. The WRB was in a predicament comparable to that of the Jews in ancient Egypt, who were ordered by Pharoah to make bricks but not given the straw to do so. Without a decision to receive and shelter refugees even on a temporary basis, no agency or individual, regardless of their compassion or zeal, could accomplish anything on a significant scale. That is why the Evian conference in 1938 failed. That is why the Bermuda conference in 1943 failed.

Had the U.S. and Britain offered asylum, the neutrals would have followed suit. Ultimately some of the neutrals did admit certain numbers of Jewish refugees, despite the dismal example of the major Western powers, but within the confines of their small countries and small populations. Other neutrals were willing to admit a steady flow of refugees if they would be removed promptly to areas under Allied control. Instead, the pernicious example of the big powers stood out as a gigantic tower against a bleak background, always of prohibition and warning not to trespass, not unlike Kafka's prophetic vision, in his novel *Amerika*, of the Statue of Liberty not with a torch in her uplifted arm in a gesture of welcome, but with a drawn sword.

It certainly was difficult to understand the decision to transport 335,000 Nazi German prisoners of war to the United States, and shelter and feed them in the U.S., while failing to do the same for their victims, the Jews. The Nazi prisoners were brought to the United States from Europe and North Africa, not on visas, not within the sacred quota system, not according to immigration laws. Establishing temporary shelters for the Jews did not involve violating existing immigration laws, or pressing for new legislation, but merely taking emergency measures in order to address a problem that lawmakers could not and did not foresee.

The objective was not to flood the U.S. with hundreds of thousands of Jews. It was primarily to achieve the vital need of America setting an example for others to follow. Still, it could not be just a token admission of a handful of refugees, but rather a considerable number, proportionate to the size and population of such a huge and rich country. To be effective and convincing, the admission had to be at least in the tens of thousands. In a such a case, the rescued, regardless of their number, could have been later relocated in smaller numbers to several Latin American countries, or wait and have their ultimate fate decided after the war. Such an act of statesmanship and compassion would have given the United States greater moral authority to ask neutral countries to do their share, and above all it would have strengthened America's hand in asking the British to admit, on the same temporary basis as expediency demanded, all Jews who succeeded in reaching Palestine by land or by sea.

From the Emergency Committee's earliest days, it campaigned for setting up emergency rescue camps in areas under Allied control as well as in neutral countries. This demand was expressed time and again in personal contacts with administration officials, in memoranda presented to the president and the State Department, and in a series of full-page advertisements in newspapers around the country. The proposal became especially timely upon the creation of the WRB, because such a plan was explicitly within the declared purview of the new agency. Certainly Turkey, Palestine, North Africa, Spain, and Portugal, as well as Switzerland, were the most logical places for such emergency shelters for escapees from occupied territories in both eastern and western Europe. But regardless of geographic accessibility (and here accessibility must be understood in the most relative sense, since every route was fraught with endless obstacles and the greatest of dangers), without the United States leading the way there was little, if any, hope that other countries would agree to open their doors at all. Without establishing a model, the U.S. could hardly use its influence on allies and neutrals to do what she herself refused to undertake.

Despite the widespread opinion of Jewish leaders that one should not raise such questions with the administration or the American public, the fact remains that when the idea of rescue shelters in the United States was presented to the public, it met with a great deal of understanding and sympathy among wide circles. Major newspapers and magazines supported it. Samuel Grafton, a very popular and influential syndicated columnist, coined a phrase for this demand: "Free Ports." He wrote: "A free port is a place where you can put things down for a while without having to make a final decision about them...We do it in commercial free ports for cases of beans so that we can make some storage and processing profit; it should not be impossible to do it for people."[163]

"Free Ports" was a catchy phrase that captured the imagination. From a propaganda point of view, its impact was tremendous. The *New York Times*, supporting the idea, assured its readers that "the plan had nothing to do with unrestricted and uncontrolled immigration. It is simply a proposal to save lives of innocent people."[164]

Significantly, the labor movement, which traditionally followed a restrictionist policy regarding the admission of foreigners, enthusiastically supported the idea. Both the AFL and the CIO publicly endorsed the plan. So did the Jewish Labor Committee and numerous prominent Jewish personalities such as Lessing Rosenwald and David Dubinsky, as well as the American Jewish Conference, umbrella for most of the major Jewish establishment groups.

In May, the Emergency Committee launched a campaign of newspaper ads, congressional lobbying, and appeals to President Roosevelt in support of the "Free Ports" temporary havens idea. A May 13 telegram from the committee reminded the president of his commitment "to take all measures within [the] power [of the U.S. government] to rescue the victims of enemy oppression who are in imminent danger of death." The remaining Jews in Hungary and in the neighboring Balkan countries were in precisely such danger. The telegram emphasized:

> [T]he German murder squads and gas chambers again show the efficiency they demonstrated in Poland. The WRB...is doing a splendid job under serious handicaps...The greatest of these...is to find places of refuge for those who can escape if a welcome awaits them on Allied ground. (...)
>
> We urge you to again take action and provide a place of refuge by establishing temporary rescue camps in the U.S. These "free ports" should also be established by our Allies in Palestine and North Africa and throughout the free world. This would give helpless victims of Nazi frightfulness some chance of survival even though in effect it is only what we advance to Nazi prisoners of war we now hold.
>
> Out of all the territory controlled by the UN and by friendly neutrals a total of 25 square miles allocated for this purpose would provide safety for countless thousands of condemned Jewish people of Europe.
>
> Post war status of people in camps can be settled then and assurance given that no immigration law will be violated...[165]

That same week, the Emergency Committee placed a full page advertisement in newspapers around the country, headlined 25 SQUARE MILES OR 3,000,000 LIVES...WHICH SHALL IT BE? It read, in part:

> The tragedy of the Jewish situation in Europe has rested not alone upon the cruel strategy of the Nazis—its diabolic success lay with the germ of racial fear that was spread among all the peoples of the earth.

This fear was that a flooding of refugees would be loosed upon many nations, complicating not only their internal political stability, but threatening as well their citizens' economic balance with an alien competition.

This fear was always a fiction—for there was always the possibility of setting aside a number of internment camps for people faced with the alternative of death—as there is always room found to contain, temporarily, the brutalized prisoners captured from our enemy.

Now, in the eleventh hour of the reign of death, a way has been found—a political "Penicillin," if you wish, that can accomplish the miracle of rescue with the guarantee that no after effects at all will be risked by the rescuers.

It is suggested the approximately 25 square miles of rescue camps in the whole world—five temporary mercy reservations, located in Palestine, Turkey, North Africa, and some of our own abandoned military training camps in the United States and some of the territories of Great Britain can hold all the Jews who can immediately escape from Nazi Europe. Assuming that, with the further shrinkage of the German frontier, more can escape—the liberated territories themselves would stabilize the problem.

Action on Capitol Hill

At the urging of the Bergson Group, Senator Guy Gillette (D-Iowa) introduced a resolution, on June 2, 1944, urging President Roosevelt to yield to "the will of the American people" to set up temporary havens in the United States. Noting that "the American tradition of justice and humanity demands every possible measure to save the surviving Jews of Europe from extermination by Nazi torture," and that two million Jews "are in immediate peril for want of a temporary sanctuary from their persecutors," the resolution asked the president to declare "that Jews and other special victims of Nazi hatred...be received on Ellis Island and other designated reception centers for temporary detention and care until the President has determined that they may be returned to their homeland without undue risk of their personal safety; and that transportation and other facilities be made available for this purpose, consistent with the effective prosecution of the war." The resolution was referred to the Senate Foreign Relations Committee, of which Gillette was a member, and plans were made to introduce a companion resolution in the House.

NEW YORK POST, MONDAY, MAY 15, 1944   18

25 SQUARE MILES

..*Which Shall It Be?*

*Since this advertisement was written, the news report about Hungary appeared.
Read it. It is not a story of the two or three million already dead. It is the dreadful challenge that plans are under way to slaughter a million more human beings—right under your
very eyes. Will you keep silent—when a way has been found to save some or maybe all of
them, or will you raise your voice so that the men who can do something stop twiddling
their thumbs—and do it now!*

THE tragedy of the Jewish situation in Europe has rested not alone upon the cruel strategy of the Nazis—its diabolic success lay with the germs of racial fear that was spread among all the peoples of the earth.

This fear was that a flood of refugees would be loosed upon many nations, complicating not only their internal political stability, but threatening as well their citizens' economic balance with an alien competition.

This fear was always a fiction—for there was always the possibility of setting aside a number of internment camps for people faced with the alternative of death—as there is always room found to contain, temporarily, the brutalized prisoners captured from our enemy.

Now, in the eleventh hour of the reign of death, a way has been found—a political "Penicillin", if you wish, that can accomplish the miracle of rescue with the guarantee that no after effects at all will be risked by the rescuers.

It is suggested that approximately 25 square miles of rescue camps in the whole world—five temporary mercy reservations, located in Palestine, Turkey, North Africa, and some of our own abandoned military training camps in the United States and some of the territories of Great Britain can hold all the Jews who can immediately escape from Nazi Europe. Assuming that, with the further shrinkage of the German frontier, more can escape—the liberated territories themselves would stabilize the problem.

A Practical Plan

These camps—or "Free Ports," as they have elsewhere been called—would be as temporary as our war prison camps will be.

They can be supervised and guarded by the military establishments of the several countries in which they are created.

They can be administered and financed by funds and the contributions of those men of goodwill who inevitably dedicate themselves to the task of human salvation.

They can be operated from within, by the willing and grateful men, women, and children in whose behalf they are established.

They would be temporary—for God willing, it is only a question of a little time before the powerful armies of freedom will rid the world of the deaths-head that roams the territories of the world.

Survival—Not Politics

Under this specific plan offered here, neither Great Britain, Turkey, Free France, nor the United States need fear that those who will have escaped to havens in their territory will involve as benefactors with political commitments.

As to Palestine itself, no one but a sadist or a Nazi would suggest that, Palestinian Jews themselves can put political considerations above the gnawing fear that their parents or children may inevitably perish in the horrible extermination camps of Germany or Hungary—or that they would sacrifice their kin to any postwar ambitions.

ISTANBUL, May   1944

According to official diplomatic dispatches, the Hungarian government of Premier Deome Sztojay has launched a program of torture and extermination of the wandering Jews now in that country. Vast gas-chambers (and gas baths) of the Nazi pattern are being erected for carrying out this mass execution.

The present large number of Jews in Hungary is in part due to the fact that many refugees, escaping from Poland and other countries, found temporary safety, in that country. Now that the Nazis have taken over, the picture has changed overnight.

It is reported that a total of five and one-half million Jews have been put to death—one way or another—since the war began. Of these, literally hundreds of thousands of men, women and children perished in the so-called gas baths of Poland. A common Nazi practice was to herd the intended victims into sanitary baths as they came off the cattle trains in Poland, on the pretext of cleansing them before their transshipment to the Ukraine for "colonization." Actually, these "sanitary" baths were lethal chambers from which no one came out alive.

A neutral diplomat, writing in official press dispatches, condemns the present Hungarian government saying: "Were I not here to witness it with my own eyes, I would never have believed that Magyars were capable of perpetrating such inhuman acts against honest, law-abiding citizens, whose only sin is that they are members of the faith which is the mother of Christianity. Never in my career was I so eager to be relieved of my post as I am today. The cruelty of the Government is beyond my comprehension, and I fail to understand how men calling themselves gentlemen and aristocrats can be so heartless and brutal to their fellow men.

(From newspaper reports).

OR 2,000,000 LIVES

Still Homeless—But Alive!

5 MILES

← 5 MILES →

The United States Must Show the Way

Palestine, Turkey, and North Africa are graphically nearest—that is a visible fact. Just as important as geography is the role which the United States must play—just because dating back to the settlement of New England, this country is the recognized leader in every fight against tyranny and oppression.

The establishment of a few rescue camps in America has nothing to do with immigration laws, because the people who would be brought into such a camp would not be immigrants, nor even visitors. They would be retained there only until some final destination will be found for them—a destination which would be found in due time, whether the lands whence they came, or some other and definite settlement which would be solved at by the victorious powers. Since such a rescue camp would in no way touch on existing immigration laws, there is no need for any legislation. Nothing stands in the way except the all important element of time.

We know that it will not be practical to save the Jewish people of Europe in tens of hundreds of thousands by transporting them to rescue camps in the United States. We know that first and foremost they will be evacuated to territories close to the Balkans—principally Palestine, but also Turkey, Cyprus, and North Africa.

In order to bring pressure effectively on all other allied and neutral countries to offer such havens, it is vital that the govern-

ment of the United States can show with clear conscience that we have done more than our share—that our country has shown the way and created the pattern. A rescue camp established in the United States will be a compelling precedent for all the members of the United Nations and the neutral countries involved.

This then is our formula—*temporary rescue camps*—so called "Free Ports" where "human cargo" can rest a brief interval until these unfortunate people can resume their journey to an ultimate destination.

The President's War Refugee Board should endorse the objective of this formula fully, for it is clear now that without such rescue camps established to receive those who can escape Europe's hell, the very objective of the President's merciful move, no matter how heroically this Board works, must inevitably fail.

The people of America have already expressed in country-wide approval this life-saving formula. It needs only the great vocal demand of the rank and file. You and your neighbors and all the decent people of this country can make a great work of salvation an immediate fact.

A Race Against Death

It is not in the tradition of our great country to talk and not act—swiftly. The

Congress and the President will move—they are in sympathy. The world is agreed and will follow their leadership. Inform them by the flood of your expressed feeling—write—telegraph, so that they count your approval. It is a race against death, and minutes count.

How You Can Help Effectively

You can help us mobilize public opinion from coast to coast. You can help spread our appeal among many more millions of Americans in order to arouse them to their responsibilities. It is imperative that we place this message in hundreds of newspapers throughout the country and through national hookups. For each day dooms thousands that might otherwise be saved.

This Committee asks the American people for substantial financial support to enable it to carry on its work for the rescue of millions of martyred human beings.

We need this financial help immediately. NOW! You can sign your name below and enclose your contribution to speed the effectiveness of our fight to save the Jewish people of Europe.

EMERGENCY COMMITTEE TO SAVE THE JEWISH PEOPLE OF EUROPE
25 West 45th Street, New York 19, N. Y.

I enclose the sum of _____ to enable you to carry out your tremendous task.

NAME _____

ADDRESS _____

(By a ruling of the Treasury Department, contributions to this Committee are tax exempt) Please make checks payable to Mrs. FRANCES GUNTHER, Treas.

The resolution did not speak of just one camp or a token admission, but referred to all Jews who succeeded in escaping Nazi dominated Europe. There was no restriction stated as to the number of persons to be granted sanctuary.

The sequence of events preceding the creation of the War Refugee Board, in which the buildup of public and congressional pressure convinced the president to act, repeated itself. Once again, the president did not wait for Congress to take action, but moved to preempt it. At a press conference on May 20, FDR spoke somewhat ambiguously about the proposal, saying that he favored the establishment of "Free Ports" but that they did not need to be in the United States. This declaration, of course, had the potential to vitiate the whole meaning of the plan. No other country could be expected to establish rescue camps in their territory if the United States refused to establish them in its own. Roosevelt's remark was, in truth, preposterous. But on June 2, the day Gillette introduced the resolution—about which the president was certainly forewarned—FDR made another statement, which in effect reversed his position: he said that an unused army camp in the U.S. might be converted into a temporary haven for war refugees from abroad. He had in mind the Oswego army camp, in Fort Ontario, upstate New York. The president explained: "In the face of this attitude of our enemies, we must not fail to take advantage of any opportunity, however limited, for the rescue of Hitler's victims. We are confronted with a most urgent situation."[166]

Regardless of how much one would like to make allowances for a president who carried on his shoulders the many responsibilities of the major belligerent in a world war of unprecedented brutality and carnage, one cannot but react with astonishment to Roosevelt's continued cynicism concerning the Jewish disaster. To abstain from taking any effective steps for rescue was bad enough, but to cloak all this in a mantle of supposed righteousness and humanitarianism, must trouble any decent person. Consider FDR's directive on June 9—just one week after this "one unused army camp" statement—to Robert Murphy, his envoy to the southern front in Italy and North Africa. The U.S. was "ready to share the burden of caring for refugees," Roosevelt announced—but only to the tune of "approximately 1,000 refugees." He emphasized to Murphy: "I should like the group to include a reasonable proportion of various categories of persecuted people who have fled to Italy."[167] Only a tiny handful would be admitted, and not all of them would be Jews.

Roosevelt's requirement proved to be a problem for Murphy, since finding non-Jewish refugees was no simple task. In the end, more than ninety percent of the selectees were Jews. In an attempt to satisfy his boss, Murphy did manage to make sure that eighteen "nationalities" were represented, that is, the refugees came from eighteen different countries, even if nearly all of them were Jews.

Why was the project restricted to less than a thousand? Why not a hundred thousand? Why not empty out all the makeshift refugee camps in southern

Italy and remove the refugees from Spain, Portugal, and Switzerland so that many more could try to reach those countries? If the subject matter were not so tragic, one could characterize Oswego as a farce. The justification for the small number that could come was the problem of transportation. Where would the Allies find ships to bring over so many Jews? The answer was given by the Allies prior to Oswego: the less than one thousand refugees would be brought in by the same procedure as that of the bringing in of the 325,000 Axis prisoners of war. They, however, were not sent to upstate New York, with its harsh winters, but to the pleasant climate of the West Coast. They were treated almost with tenderness because the Roosevelt administration hoped for good postwar relations with Germany and its partners. The author Thomas Lask, who observed the Axis POWs, wrote later that they were "in good shape, and from the relaxed and easy way they went about their labors, they looked neither harried nor driven."[168]

The Nazi prisoners of war were not the only aliens admitted to the U.S. outside the immigration laws during this period. The Germans and other Axis powers sent many thousands of their own nationals to various Latin American countries for subversive activities, espionage, propaganda, and especially to influence businessmen and manufacturers, including many from America who ignored the wartime boycott and blockade restrictions against doing business with Nazi Germany. The State Department made arrangements with some Latin American countries to round up thousands of these undesirable aliens and send them to the U.S., where they were interned for the duration in special camps.

Once again, the Allied leaders proved how good they were at taking great ideas promoted by the Bergson Group and whittling them down to pale versions of their original conception. The idea of a Jewish army with a quarter of a million soldiers fighting the Nazis was transformed by the British into a five thousand-man brigade that did not see action until the war was almost over. The idea of a rescue agency with the necessary funds and freedom to act was reduced to an agency given a tiny amount of government funds and little cooperation from the State Department. The proposal for Free Ports that would shelter hundreds of thousands was transformed into one camp for 982 refugees.

When the Bergson Group first formulated the idea of temporary shelters, as articulated in its July 1943 Emergency Conference, the proposal had two purposes: first, to let the Jews know that they had places to which they could escape; and, second, to obtain from Allied and neutral governments the consent to receive those who succeeded in fleeing. In order to obtain such consent, it was necessary to reassure them that the refugees would be admitted only on a temporary basis. Countries such as Turkey or Spain, where access was easiest for the fleeing refugees, had to be reassured that the burden would not fall only, or mainly, on them, but that the refugees admitted to their territory would be systematically relocated to territories under Allied control.

The Emergency Committee suggested first to the president, and then to the WRB, that the Allies and primarily the U.S. should undertake to help feed and clothe the refugees residing temporarily in the neutrals, and should further undertake to make arrangements for their relocation during the hostilities and within a reasonable time after cessation of hostilities. It was a vast plan for a mass rescue operation through escape, transfer, evacuation, and relocation. What Roosevelt adopted had very little to do with it, and in fact was a perversion of the plan not only because it came so late—Oswego, in August 1944, was more than a year after the original proposal, and 1943-1944 was the crucial year—but also because the refugees were brought not from neutral countries but from Allied occupied territory, southern Italy.

It did not help that during the course of the debate over temporary sanctuaries, some American Zionist officials sowed seeds of doubt as to the viability of the proposal, for fear that it would undermine their postwar goal of a Jewish commonwealth in Palestine. In their contacts with administration officials and members of Congress, some Zionist leaders undermined the proposal. One called the plan "an Audobon Society for Jews"—that is, an attempt to preserve the Jewish species by saving just enough to keep the species from becoming extinct. Even those Zionist spokesmen who favored temporary asylum made their consent contingent on unlimited immigration to Palestine. The result was that they wasted their considerable organizational force, and their influence on the major political parties, by continuing to focus on a goal that was irrelevant at that moment and was rejected in Washington. It also made it harder for the advocates of Free Ports to convince the president to establish shelters on a large scale, as per the Gillette resolution.

The ironic footnote to the Oswego episode was that the fear—shared by the administration and the Jewish leadership alike—that the American public would resent and oppose an influx of refugees proved to be completely false. In fact, the citizens of Oswego and surrounding areas treated the refugees with kindness and respect, helped them find work and accommodations, and in general did what they could to welcome them to America.

9   MISSION TO TURKEY

One of the earliest proposals that the Emergency Committee made to the War Refugee Board was to send one of the committee's leaders, Eri Jabotinsky, to Turkey. Eri was one of the very few experts in organizing migration under emergency circumstances, having helped smuggle thousands of Jews from Europe to Palestine during 1938-1940. His record in this regard was outstanding, almost legendary. John Pehle was eager to dispatch Eri to Turkey as soon as possible, and assigned his assistant, Ward Stewart, to obtain the necessary clearance from the State Department.[169] But the days dragged into weeks as Stewart encountered one State Department excuse and obstacle after another. Along with the inexplicable delays came claims that the British or the Turks were opposed to Eri's mission. Finally, after six weeks of waiting, the Emergency Committee informed the State Department that it would publicly expose the department's obstructionism unless action was taken. Lo and behold, the permission for Eri suddenly appeared and he left for Turkey in May, aboard a U.S. bomber.

Although technically not acting as a U.S. government representative, Eri was undertaking his mission with the full approval of the U.S. government's War Refugee Board, and in Ankara he quickly established cordial relations with the American ambassador, Laurence Steinhardt. Eri's correspondence with the WRB and the Emergency Committee was sent by the ambassador in diplomatic code and via his diplomatic pouch. From Eri's reports[170] back to Bergson Group headquarters it became obvious that in contrast to other U.S. diplomats, who were generally either indifferent or hostile to the Jewish refugees, Steinhardt made substantial efforts on behalf of Jewish rescue. According to Eri, "any backing that has been given our work by the local Government is due solely to the personal efforts and prestige of Mr. Steinhardt."

Eri was not only a man of courage but also of fertile and original mind. His help was invaluable for facilitating the WRB's rescue work. When he arrived in Ankara, he found representatives of four different American organizations, as well as Jewish Agency representatives from Palestine, competing to help the refugees and duplicating each other's efforts, with each considering themselves the most important person to the rescue activity. He also found some familiar faces:

> [T]he whole thing is open and above board for all the local and German authorities to see. There exist in every country people who organize the evacuation locally. They are, to an astonishing degree, the same people who worked with me on

the evacuation in 1937-1940. And even the evacuation from Greece was organized by one of my ex-collaborators, a personal friend of Abrasha [Irgun immigration activist Avraham Stavsky].

The governments of the satellite countries not only did not oppose the Jews leaving but encouraged them to do so, and were disappointed by the lack of comprehensive action by the international Jewish organizations. It reached the point where the Rumanian government decided to sell a charter to a private Greek ship owner named Pandelis to give him the exclusive right to take Jews out of the country. "This extraordinary document made him an absolute dictator of our work in Rumania," Eri reported. Pandelis was a notorious character from whom Eri had chartered a number of ships in the 1930s. He was in the refugee business for financial gain, not for any ideals, but he was considered reliable in the sense that he could "deliver the goods"—that is, ships that could be used (although not without risk) to navigate for several days in the sea from one port to another. Typical of his modus operandi was to make a contract with one or another of the Zionist groups, telling them that the "capacity" of the ship was, for example, eight hundred, six hundred of which the Zionists could fill with whomever they wished, without charge, but the remaining two hundred he would recruit professionally, that is, each would pay such a high sum that it would cover his expenses and profit. It was a racket in a double sense: first, the evacuation was strictly partisan, only Zionists, and only those affiliated with certain Zionist parties were chosen as candidates, thus excluding the majority of Jews who did not belong to any party. Second, Pandelis's profits surpassed anything reasonable. No wonder various Jewish leaders in Rumania protested and even influenced the government to cancel Pandelis's "charter" for a time (later the government renewed it). This cruel system of partisanship aroused Hirschmann's indignation and he felt he had to do something about it.

Apart from shipping difficulties, there was, of course, the problem of getting the refugees admitted somewhere. The Turkish government was willing to let people pass through Turkey only if they possessed visas to enter another country. By mid-June 1944, the Turkish government was spooning out only a limited number of visas each month, and those were not always utilized because of British restrictions on entering Palestine, even on a transit basis. Other countries, assuming they were willing to grant asylum to refugees (which seldom was the case), were out of reach because of lack of transportation. (From Turkey, refugees could reach Palestine by train.) According to Jabotinsky's reports, four factors were involved in facilitating immediate mass evacuation: exit permits from the Balkan countries; transit permits through Turkey; entrance permits to Palestine and Allied and neutral countries; and transportation.

The first two problems were relatively easy to solve. There were no serious obstacles to getting Jews out of the Balkans. Jabotinsky was confident he could obtain large-scale exit permits from Rumania. He also believed that, thanks to Ambassador Steinhardt's friendship with the Turkish foreign minister, the transit problem could be solved.

Even the transportation problem was not insurmountable: ships were available, but at a premium. In June 1944, transportation from a Balkan country to Palestine cost about $500 per person. He believed it could be reduced to about $250. One million Jews could be evacuated for $250-million. At that time, no private institution or Jewish fundraising apparatus could provide that amount of money. The WRB depended on funds from private Jewish organizations, which limited its operations greatly and reduced its effectiveness.

Nonetheless, Eri threw himself into his familiar kind of activity: smaller scale evacuation projects from the Balkan countries. He had two ideas for solving the transportation problem. The more ambitious one was to persuade the WRB to get the State Department to offer Turkey a grant or lend-lease a number of railway cars, locomotives and ships for the use of the refugees. He also suggested diplomatic activities on the part of the WRB and the State Department to impress upon the Turkish ambassador in America the benefits—political, financial and in terms of public opinion—of being generous in permitting Jews transit on a mass scale.

It was in this spirit that in July 1944, the Bergson Group's allies in the House of Representatives introduced a resolution urging the Turkish government to speed up the entry of refugees from the Balkan countries and to establish an emergency camp as a temporary haven for people escaping from Nazi controlled territory. The resolution charged that full advantage had not been taken of the "great opportunities for the evacuation from the Balkan countries through Turkey." The resolution asked the State Department to make it clear to the Turkish authorities that they should act "in the interest of humanity," since the U.S. "has made clear by its action that it is determined to take all measures within its power to rescue the Jews and other victims of enemy oppression who are in imminent danger of death at the hands of the Nazis."

His other plan was a more modest one, but could be carried out almost independently, that is, without massive diplomatic intervention in Washington, and without close cooperation with the WRB, only with its tacit blessing, taking into consideration that as a government agency it had to work within the legal restrictions of British immigration policy in Palestine. Although 75,000 Jews should have been admitted between the declaration of the White Paper policy in May 1939 and the end of the prescribed five year period, in 1944, only about 40,000 of the immigration slots had been utilized. Tragically, some 35,000 had not been used, due to the various obstacles put up by the Mandate authorities.

One of the most sordid aspects of British policy was to deduct from the unused certificates anyone who managed to enter Palestine illegally. At the same time, the British increased their vigilance and intensified the patrolling of the shores against Jewish immigrants. As a result, all but 3,000 of the quota places were used up.

Eri wanted to expedite the slow, uncertain process by a dramatic undertaking—to challenge the quota system altogether, without waiting for the British to release the last 3,000 certificates. He sought to arrange an "illegal" steamship service to shuttle 2,500 refugees each week from among the 10,000 Jews remaining in Rumania and 50,000 in Bulgaria. If operated twice each week, it would evacuate almost all the Jews from those two countries, which would establish a pattern to be used in Hungary and perhaps elsewhere. It was intended to defy, once and for all, the quota system, by forcing the hand of the British at a time when world opinion would have understood, sympathized, and perhaps even financially supported it. The political climate in Europe at that moment was propitious. At this late hour of the war, the governments in the Balkans went out of their way to accommodate Allied public opinion and believed they could do that by showing understanding for Jewish needs and aspirations. The Rumanian foreign minister expressed support for the aim of Jewish statehood, and promised freedom of emigration for all Jews who wanted to leave. The Bulgarian propaganda minister, Dymo Kadasoss, declared: "The Bulgarian Government has a positive attitude to the formation of a Hebrew state in Palestine, because every people has a right to its own country. The Bulgarian government will not hinder immigration to Palestine." Of even greater significance was the attitude of the Soviet authorities in Rumania. Their sympathy was unmistakable. Perhaps it was a prelude to their support for Jewish statehood in 1947-1948.

Pressure to Disavow Eri

There is plausible, albeit indirect, evidence that the Jewish Agency or other Zionist leaders sought to have Eri pushed out of Turkey. They apparently did this by trying to persuade Pehle and Ambassador Steinhardt that Eri was pretending to be an official representative of the WRB. Pehle and Steinhardt both received requests to disavow Eri. On June 27, 1944, Pehle cabled Steinhardt:

> Board has received several inquiries as to whether Eri Jabotinsky represents the Board in Istanbul. Impression seems to be rather current that he is our representative. While the matter is not serious enough to warrant a public statement, we, of course,

have denied that Jabotinsky represents the Board in any capacity. I would appreciate your advising me whether Jabotinsky is holding himself out as a representative of the Board.

In his June 30 reply, Steinhardt reported that he did "not know of any occasion on which Jabotinsky has directly held himself out to be a representative of the Board." He speculated that Eri had "sought and succeeded in giving this impression," since in their first meeting, Eri "expressed surprise that you had not informed me of his impending mission. Subsequently he asked to transmit to you by Diplomatic pouch which was done." Steinhardt agreed that no public action should be taken.

As noted earlier, Pehle and his aides had pressured the State Department to arrange priority air transportation for Eri on an Army bomber to Turkey, which certainly indicated the urgency of Eri reaching Turkey as soon as possible. The WRB also obtained a Turkish visa for him, even though the State Department claimed, probably with justification, that the Turks were not eager to issue it. In his letter to the Turkish ambassador in Washington at that time, Pehle wrote:

> As you know, the evacuation of refugees from the Balkans is most pressing. Ambassador Steinhardt and the Board's representative in Turkey, Ira Hirschmann, have been working closely with the Turkish Government in this matter.
>
> The Board desires to take advantage of the services of any private agency which can be of help in this task. I believe that Mr. Jabotinsky, working in close consultation with the Board's representative in Turkey, could be of assistance in the efforts of our two Governments to save some of the persecuted people of Europe from death.[171]

Moreover, at the WRB's request, the Treasury Department granted the Emergency Committee a special license to transfer funds for Eri's work in Turkey. He was also obliged to submit to the American ambassador in Ankara periodic reports about his activities, and that money could be spent "only as authorized by the American ambassador and/or Mr. Ira Hirschmann." There was no doubt that Eri went to Turkey with the full endorsement and assistance of the WRB. There was no reason to give him an official title. In fact, precisely because Eri was an official of the Bergson Group and might engage in activities that might not be within the purview of the WRB as a government agency, it was preferable that he be dispatched to Turkey as an individual rather than a WRB representative.

Eri never pretended to be an agent of the WRB. He did not have to, not only because he would have been disavowed instantly by Ambassador Steinhardt, but also because his semiofficial status was already evident from the fact that the WRB had arranged his transportation and visas, and from the assistance extended to him by the U.S. ambassador. Why would an experienced diplomat such as Steinhardt spend so much time with a stranger, and forward in diplomatic code and pouch the most confidential information, about governments, organizations, and individuals, and even plans of extralegal activities? He did it because he knew exactly who and what Eri was. As did Pehle. No wonder they agreed that the matter did not a warrant a public statement. If Eri had indeed been an impostor, falsely claiming to be something he was not, in such sensitive matters and at such a crucial time, surely Pehle and Steinhardt would have acted against him.

The British Target Eri

On December 7, 1944, Eri cabled the Emergency Committee that he was expecting Turkish authorization to use the ship *Tari* for "a Constanza-Haifa service." The operation of the first trip would require $200,000. The Emergency Committee cabled authorization.

So long as the actual number of people being rescued through Turkey and sent to Palestine was limited, the British authorities in Turkey did not interfere. When Rumania and Bulgaria were liberated by the advancing Soviet armies, thousands of Jews in those countries, completely destitute and starving, clamored for a chance to leave the scene of horror and extermination which they miraculously survived, and not be forced to live in the vast cemetery that Europe had become for them. The British thought these cries of despair could be muffled one way or another, and their hope to reach Palestine could be frustrated simply by ignoring it. Jabotinsky's plan would have unleashed a new dynamic and set a pattern to rescue survivors on a large scale in the shortest possible time. The British, for their part, decided that should not happen.

In January 1945, the Emergency Committee received a radiogram from Eri: "TURKISH GOVERNMENT WAS WILLING AUTHORIZE USE SHIP OF REFUGEES, BUT BRITISH SENT NOTE CANCELING PROMISE PALESTINE VISAS JEWS ARRIVING IN TURKEY, ALSO REQUESTED PREVENT SHIPS FROM TRANSPORTING REFUGEES."

Eri, dispirited, concluded that his mission had been unsuccessful and proposed to leave Turkey. Bergson, however, instructed him to remain and explore further rescue possibilities. But the British intervened with the authorities to get rid of him. First, they informally asked the Turkish authorities to cancel his visa. When that request failed, they accused Eri of being linked to the Stern Group's November 1944 assassination of the senior British official in the Middle East,

Lord Moyne. That would compel Ankara to deport him. Friendly Turkish officials privately told Eri of the British request and advised him to leave voluntarily before they would be forced to arrest him. Eri thanked the Turks for their courteous treatment, sent a letter of protest to the local British ambassador, and on February 24 boarded a train for Palestine. When he reached the border, the British arrested him.

The Emergency Committee immediately launched a protest campaign, starting with an open letter to the British ambassador in Washington, Lord Halifax, which was placed in various newspapers. Authored by Ben Hecht, it declared:

> In my bid for information, Excellency, I should like to know particularly whether my friend Eri ran into trouble...because of his work as a refugee-saver. I understand, of course, that the British policy to date has been to refuse haven to the survivors of Treblinka, Maidanek and Oswiecim. As I know, also, that not even the three million corpses have been able to remove the tweedledum boys presiding over the doors of Palestine. I have read considerable in the past about the antics of the notorious Colonial Office in helping turn back the desperate refugees from Europe—to die at sea—rather than be allowed to defile the shores of a British colonial port—etcetera, etcetera. I am, therefore, not naively excited about the absence of common decency and elementary humanitarianism from the annals of the British Colonial Office...

He concluded:

> I know that there is some sort of a bullheaded British determination to chalk up a bloody and depressing anti-Hebrew record for your Empire. But surely this determination is not as idiotic as it seems. Surely the British know as well as I do that whisking people off to concentration camps and stuffing gags in their mouths at the same time isn't cricket...It would confuse me...to believe that the English have taken to bedeviling fine Hebrews like Eri Jabotinsky—*pour la sport*...

Eri was not the only Bergson Group official arrested by the British. Arieh Ben-Eliezer actually preceded him by two months. In April 1944, a telegram from Bergson and Will Rogers, Jr. to Ben-Eliezer, in Tel Aviv, instructed him: "IMPERATIVE YOU PROCEED TURKEY IMMEDIATELY TAKE CHARGE

OF RESCUE ACTIVITIES THERE VERY URGENT CABLED EXPENSES THOUSAND DOLLARS VIA AMERICAN EXPRESS." Ben-Eliezer began making preparations for the mission. But two days before his departure, the British arrested him. He was kept incommunicado and interrogated for several weeks by British intelligence, first in Palestine, then at headquarters in Cairo. After that, he was sent to a prison in the Egypt-Sudan desert area, and then later transferred to a detention camp in the jungles of Eritrea.

A Unique Weapon for a Unique Situation

As information about the mass slaughter of Hungary's Jews reached the West, the Bergson Group looked for new and more effective ways to interrupt the killing. Allied warnings of retaliation after the war did not seem to have the desired effect. A Hungarian cabinet minister, boasting on the radio about how many Jews had been annihilated, dismissed the threats as "nothing but Anglo-Saxon bluff." On July 3, a telegram from the Emergency Committee to President Roosevelt argued that threats of retaliation needed to be "backed up by concrete example specifically indicating that it is made in retribution for mass murder" of the Jews. The message was passed to the State Department, and more than two weeks later, George Warren, one of its advisers on refugee matters, replied that the administration had already "exerted every effort to bring these barbarous cruelties to an end." He rejected the idea of acts of retaliation, insisting that the Allies needed to focus exclusively on "the major business of bringing about the early defeat of the Nazi enemy as the really effective way to end the sufferings" of the Jews.[172]

The claim that the Allies had "exerted every effort" to help the Jews was absurd and hypocritical. The disingenuous State Department official was resorting to the tired old formula of claiming that rescue was possible only through military victory. He did not even consider that the defeat of the German armies while liberating France, Poland, and the other subjugated countries, might not save the Jews.

The Bergson Group then appealed directly to the Joint Chiefs of Staff to use a unique weapon in this unique situation. At a July 1944 rally in New York City, Bergson first articulated this proposal. Referring to threats by Churchill and Roosevelt to use poison gas against the Nazis if Germany used it against Allied targets, Bergson said: "Since poison gas has been used against the co-belligerent Hebrew Nation," he said, the Allies should use poison gas against the Germans unless the mass murder of the Jews was halted.[173] After receiving George Warren's rejection letter, the Bergson Group prepared a more detailed proposal for military intervention against the Holocaust. Sent to the White House on July 24, over the signature of committee vice president Johan Smertenko, it proposed:

1. Railways and bridges leading from Nazi-occupied territory to extermination centers in Poland can be destroyed by bombing, specifying that the action is taken in order to prevent the transportation of the Hebrew people of these Axis countries to Hitler's slaughter house. These railways also serve military purposes and their destruction will be of great benefit to our ally, Soviet Russia.

2. The extermination camps themselves can be bombed, destroying the gas chambers where thousands of people are assassinated daily. This would enable the Hebrew people gathered in these camps to escape and offer them an opportunity to join the underground resistance forces where they can be of help in sabotage and resistance activities.

3. In accordance with the reiterated statements of the American and British Governments that the use of poison gas by Germans and Japanese would be followed by retaliation in kind, a specific statement can be issued that the extermination of Hebrew men, women, and children by the continued use of poison gas will be considered a provocation for retaliation in kind. We respectfully call your attention to the fact that authenticated reports from Czechoslovakian and Polish underground sources have disclosed that over a million and a half persons have been murdered in the poison gas chambers of Auschwitz and Birkenau camps and that the threat of widespread use of the same medium upon the German population will contribute to the disaffection of the German people and may result in a speedier collapse of Hitler's home front.

All these are measures that will not require any additional exertion of military forces nor call for any deviation from the successful military campaigns now in progress. On the contrary, they can be of substantial aid to the campaign of psychological warfare that is being waged simultaneously against our enemy.

After considerable internal debate, the Joint Chiefs ultimately replied to the Bergson Group that matters of this nature were a matter of policy that needed to be addressed by the top levels of the administration.

Did the War Refugee Board Live up to Expectations?

John Pehle was a man of vision and compassion, determined to do his job as executive director of the War Refugee Board to the best of his ability. His colleagues in the new agency were admirable men and women, inspired by the loftiest ideals and untiring in their efforts. They have to their credit considerable achievements. As Secretary Morgenthau later wrote:

> All over Europe the Board has carried on its work with the great care necessary in such complex operations. It has participated in the rescue of thousands from the Balkans across the Black Sea to Palestine—in the rescue of many weary victims of Hitler's persecution who had found sanctuary in Sweden and Switzerland. It has cooperated in establishing many refugee camps in Africa and through the President's leadership, an Emergency Refugee Shelter at Oswego in the United States. It has taken the lead in sending food packages from this country to helpless internees in European camps. In the Hungarian crisis it took many steps which undoubtedly helped stay the deportation of Jews and relieve their condition. It has used all the old techniques and invented some new ones. It has applied them all to the saving of human life.[174]

There is no doubt that the WRB and its agents were instrumental in rescuing a significant number of Jews, which was, of course, tremendously important. The life of each individual is precious. As the Talmud teaches, he who saves one life is as if he preserved a whole world. Yet it did not live up to what was envisioned by the Emergency Committee. Its record was magnificent, but the problem in its larger dimension—saving the Jews who were still alive when the WRB was created in January 1944—was not solved.

Why? The reasons were multiple.

First, of course, was the objective situation, which was extremely difficult: it was a total war and the WRB could not control the situation; it could not easily stay the hand of the executioner.

Second, the WRB was not created because Roosevelt experienced some sudden revelation and transformed his basic attitudes. The president's executive order creating the WRB was issued under the pressure of public opinion, impending Congressional action, and Morgenthau's intervention, all of which came about to a decisive extent because of the energetic efforts of the Emergency Committee. Were it not for those efforts, the president would not have lifted a finger. But if, at last, he did so, it was not because of personal conviction of its necessity from a moral point of view, but because of expediency and internal political considerations. If the creation of the WRB had been the signal for a genuinely new, aggressive U.S. policy against genocide, it would have been natural to appoint as its chairman a personality of international renown who was not part of the administration which had behind it such a dark record on the moral front. Morgenthau thought the answer was Wendell Willkie, but the president's advisors counseled against doing anything to enhance the reputation of a political adversary. Since time was of the essence, Pehle was chosen instead, and the idea of a finding a big name was discarded as not essential. Whether Willkie or another personality of that caliber would have accepted is difficult to say.

One of Pehle's first and most difficult problems was how to dispel the conviction held by the British government and the other allies, as well as the neutrals, that the new agency was just a repeat of Evian or Bermuda, an empty gesture on the part of President Roosevelt to give the impression that something of tremendous importance was created to alleviate the plight of the Jews, while in fact it was nothing of the sort. Pehle explained to one refugee advocate:

> I think that the greatest single contribution you can make to the WRB's program...is to convince interested groups [in England], both within and outside the Government, that there has been a real change in this Government's attitude on refugee matters, and that the WRB really means business. It seems to me that in an entirely unofficial manner you may be able to make clear the fact that the creation of the WRB was not a political move in an election year, but an expression of our determination to do everything in our power to rescue the Jews...who are being systematically exterminated by the Nazis.[175]

Allied strategy never took into account the Jewish dimension, and the war operations from beginning to end were planned and carried out as if there was no Holocaust. No one in high places paid any attention. At best it was considered a *fait divers* which deserved an occasional sigh. Throughout the years, the excuse was "rescue through victory." But when victory came at last, there were practically no Jews left to rescue. Another reason the War Refugee Board was less effective than it could have been was that the major Jewish organizations, instead of concentrating all their effort on strengthening and expanding the WRB, instead continued to waste time and energy fighting the Bergson Group.

10 THE CAMPAIGN TO RESCUE THE JEWS OF HUNGARY

By the beginning of 1944, Hitler was in mortal danger and his fate was sealed. The situation on all fronts pointed to defeat and disaster, yet in his madness he refused to recognize reality and called upon the German people to dedicate their remaining forces to defeat the Jews. His insane obsession with the Jews at that time may sound strange and frankly incomprehensible even within the confines of his own logic. Instead of voicing despair, he should have congratulated himself that at least on one front, he was victorious: that of massacring the Jews. One of his main war aims was achieved. The Final Solution was carried out almost completely in all countries under his occupation, in western, central, and eastern Europe. Nonetheless Hitler was greatly perturbed: his victory over the Jews was not quite complete. There remained one glaring exception in the very heart of his domain: Hungary. In that country, there still were nearly one million Jews alive, and in many respects continuing an active and productive life—a veritable island of safety in an ocean of destruction.

Hungary, although an active ally of Germany, and at war with the Allies, fighting on the eastern front against the Russians, refused almost until the end to toe the Nazi line as far as dealing with the Jews was concerned. The Jews were not ordered to wear the yellow star, and continued, with some exceptions, to play an extremely important part in the economy of the country. Of a total of 100,000 commercial stores and industrial enterprises, an estimated 40,000 were owned by Jews. Among these were some of the mighty industrial concerns not only of Hungary, but of the whole European continent. Most prominent was the Manfred Weiss steel combine, which produced a wide variety of items, from bicycles to trucks to airplanes. Eleven Jews were members of the Hungarian parliament. Most fantastic of all, Hungary even had a Jewish army of sorts— 130,000 strong, serving in auxiliary units but in Hungarian uniform, fighting on the side of the Nazis on the eastern front.

Prime Minister Miklos Kallay not only tolerated the Jews but protected them with unusual courage. He defied the Nazis as no other government in Europe did, except for the Danes. Not only were Hungarian Jews exempt from wearing the yellow star, but the Hungarian Minister in Berlin, Dome Sztojav, actually lodged an official protest, on behalf of his government, against that German policy. In May 1943, the Hungarian prime minister declared in a speech that "resettlement" as a "Final Solution" of the Jewish problem was unacceptable so long as the Germans were not providing a satisfactory answer as to precisely where the Jews would be resettled.

In a May 8, 1943 diary entry, Goebbels expressed his indignation at Hungary's position, which he blamed in part on the fact that the wife of Hungarian dictator Admiral Horthy was Jewish, and her family was prominent in the country's financial and social affairs:

> The Jewish question is being solved least satisfactorily in Hungary...The Hungarian State is permeated with Jews, and the Fuhrer didn't succeed during his talk with Horthy in convincing the latter of the necessity of more stringent measures. Horthy himself, of course, is badly tangled up with the Jews through his family, and will continue to resist every effort to tackle the Jewish problem aggressively.

Hitler himself found it necessary to summon Horthy in April 1943 to his headquarters at Klessheim Castle, and vented his anger and dismay at the policy of Budapest toward the Jews. Yet it had no effect on Horthy or Prime Minister Kallay. Not unlike the Rumanians, they knew Hitler had lost the war, and the best interests of Hungary would be to seek peace both with the Soviets and the Western Allies. And also like the Rumanians, they thought that proof of their good faith would be to demonstrate a more humane attitude toward the Jews. Hitler summoned Horthy again in March 1944, asking him to bring along both the prime minister and members of the cabinet. Kallay excused himself; he was determined not to apologize or plead with Hitler. During the confrontation again in Klessheim Castle, the Fuhrer accused the Hungarians of treachery and told them he had no choice but to occupy their country. Hitler kept Horthy incommunicado for twenty-four hours and when he returned to Budapest on March 19, the country was already occupied by German troops and the Gestapo.

Another remarkable aspect about this situation was that Hungary was traditionally and legally a virulently antisemitic state. Widespread anti-Jewish sentiments were evident from the early 1920s, in the wake of the unsuccessful Bolshevik revolution launched by a Jewish communist, Bella Kun. A good number of his cohorts were also Jewish. It was a traumatic experience for the Hungarian people.

The government that ruled the country during the Hitler period was an incongruity replete with paradoxes. Constitutionally a kingdom, but without a king; headed by a Regent supposedly representing a sovereign, but there was none in existence; and though Hungary is a landlocked country without a navy, the Regent was an admiral—Miklos Horthy, surrounded by a host of courtiers in a nonexistent court. Horthy was a great admirer of Mussolini and himself fascist-oriented.

A strong fascist movement, the Arrow Cross, came into being. Antisemitic excesses occurred, and a restrictionist policy against the Jews evolved. The number of Jewish students was limited in the universities. Early in 1938, before the war and before Hitler's occupation of Austria, the then-prime minister, Kalman Daranyi, initiated laws limiting Jewish participation in certain professions to twenty percent. Almost all factions in parliament, including the anti-German deputies, both conservatives and democrats, voted for the laws.

Anti-Jewish legislation increased in intensity in the years to follow. In 1939, new restrictions were passed based on racist criteria for determining who was considered a Jew. By 1941, the racial criteria were virtually identical with Nazi Germany's Nuremberg Laws. Although a Catholic country, the racial laws in Hungary applied also to baptized Jews who were converted after 1919, and three years later, the laws were extended also to those who were converted after that date. In some cases, the laws were even harsher than those in Germany.

Thus, legally Hungary was an all-inclusive antisemitic country. Yet it constituted a bizarre dichotomy: rabid antisemitic laws on the one hand, and tolerance and protection on the other. The fate of the Jews in Hungary reflected the contradictions and vagaries of the successive cabinets, ranging from violent fascist and savage antisemitism of the Arrow Cross regime, to the toleration and protection of Prime Minister Kallay.[176] It would be erroneous to suggest that no Jews were molested, even under Kallay. In fact, on some occasions certain categories of Jews were treated ruthlessly, chased on foot across the border, and while on their forced march robbed of their last few belongings by Hungarian guards. Many were beaten and some were killed.

To some extent these contradictory modes of behavior can be explained by two factors. One was the existence of the very vocal and aggressive fascist movement, the Arrow Cross. With the emergence of Hitler as overlord in Europe, this movement mimicked Nazism and tried to apply in Hungary both its ideology and practical policies as much as possible. Second, the country's Jewish population almost doubled since the outbreak of the war. In 1938, they numbered about half a million. (Of these, about 100,000 Christians were regarded as "racial" Jews and subjected to anti-Jewish laws, even before Hungary was occupied by the Germans.) Nonetheless, they considered themselves a privileged class and felt secure.

In 1941, Hungary joined Germany in the war and as a reward received additional territories from neighboring Slovakia, Rumania, and Yugoslavia. These territories included several hundred thousand Jewish residents, among them thousands who fled from Poland and the Czech areas in order to seek safety under Horthy. Hungary treated these newly-acquired "foreign" Jews as if they were a different species from its own. In August of that year, thousands were deported to the Kamenetsk-Podolsk region in Nazi-occupied eastern Poland. Atrocities were committed against them and many perished. The following year, thousands more were pressed into forced labor battalions and sent to the Rumanian front.

The Horthy government even asked the Nazis to lend it a helping hand to get rid of the "foreign Jews who infiltrated" Hungary. Thus there were present in Hungary two kinds of Jews: the native and the foreign. Nonetheless, the brutal measures taken against the foreign Jews ceased in 1942. Hungary once more became a place where Jews were not molested, and where refugees from Poland and Slovakia desperately tried to cross the frontier to reach safety in Hungarian territory.

When the Germans invaded Hungary in March 1944, those differences between the two categories of Jews were completely disregarded by Adolf Eichmann and his gang of killers. All Jews fell into the same category, to be dispatched to Auschwitz and gassed. Eichmann and his entourage arrived on the day of the invasion and occupation. It was an almost complete assembly of all the SS officers who were in charge of exterminating the Jews all over Europe. With incredible speed, he set up the machinery and put into motion the Final Solution on the pattern he and his colleagues practiced in other countries. His first priority was to establish a *Judenrat*, a council of local Jewish leaders, whose task was to assist in carrying out the smooth deportation of the Jews to the death centers.

Most amazing was the behavior of the Jewish notables, the leadership of the Jewish community. Although by that time, everyone knew what was in store for the Jews in a country occupied by the Germans, and everyone understood (from what had happened in other countries) what the role of the *Judenrate* would be, the leading Hungarian Jewish personalities who were invited to form themselves into a *Judenrat* behaved as if they were born yesterday. Eichmann encountered no difficulty in establishing the *Judenrate* immediately upon his arrival. This is said without any value judgment, and it would be wrong for anyone who was not there to criticize the behavior of any Jews under Nazi domination. Nobody is in a position to know how he would have behaved had he been in their shoes. Nevertheless it is difficult to understand why the leaders of the Jewish organizations who were summoned by Eichmann did not find it necessary to immediately burn the files containing the names, addresses, and personal information of their members. They did not try to circumvent the order to wear the yellow star. They did not attempt to change their addresses, to whatever extent it was possible. Nor did they flee. With fatalism and even with some trust, they went straight into Eichmann's trap. Thus was the war of extermination extended to the last Jewish community in Europe under Nazi control. And it happened in full view, without any pretense. Two days after the Germans entered Budapest,

Swedish news correspondents in Berlin were told by a spokesman for the German Foreign Office that "complete elimination" of the Jews from various phases of life would be carried out in Hungary. The reports told of mass arrests and confiscation of Jewish homes and stores by the Gestapo, together with Hungarian fascists. Jews in Budapest committed suicide by the hundreds. These were only third hand reports obtained indirectly by the reporters; the reality was much more disastrous.

Eichmann really outdid himself in this short period of time. It was the peak of his murderous career. It seems that everything went his way. He later boasted that the operation in Hungary "was like a dream," smooth beyond all expectations. The Jews unconsciously organized themselves thoroughly for the task of being liquidated. The Hungarian authorities, especially the police, cooperated with the greatest of zeal under the direction of Laszlo Endre, the newly appointed State Secretary for Political [Jewish] Affairs, in the Ministry of Interior.

At a time when the Nazi hierarchy did everything in its power to mobilize resources for the army that was in retreat on nearly all fronts and suffering appalling losses, a special conference was convoked by Eichmann in Vienna with the Reich State railroad officials to divert resources to the mass murder process. It was decided to make available all the necessary rolling stock for carrying out an unheard-of task, the transportation of nearly half a million people from the concentration centers in Hungary to the death camp of Auschwitz, where twelve thousand were gassed daily. To meet the magnitude and speed of the operation, Eichmann arranged a new "emergency" rail line to bring the incoming trains within a few yards of the crematoria. The number of gas chamber operators was increased from 224 to 860 so that the quota of killings could be met. The campaign was not only efficient but was carried out with lightning speed. In less than two months, one hundred and forty seven trains transported more than 434,000 Jews to Auschwitz.

The Emergency Committee in Action

Upon publication of the news about the German occupation of Hungary, the Bergson Group immediately turned its attention to the problem of how to save this last remnant of European Jewry. It was clear that it would be of little use to concentrate only on long-range plans of mass evacuation, even if there were countries willing to receive hundreds of thousands of Jews on a temporary basis (which, in fact, there were not). Of greatest urgency was the need to frustrate the Nazis' intention to deport the Hungarian Jews to the death camps. The Emergency Committee was well aware that the Germans were no longer the awe-inspiring military masters that they had been several years earlier, and that the satellites knew Hitler was losing the war and were therefore looking for ways to disengage themselves from the Axis. Thus the Emergency Committee decided to focus on putting pressure on Hungary itself to refuse cooperation with the Nazis in carrying out the murder plan, and where possible to actually sabotage each phase of the Nazi enterprise. At the same time, Budapest should be urged to permit Jews to leave the country without hindrance.

Against this strategic and psychological background, the Emergency Committee sought the most effective way to influence the Americans and other Allied governments and international agencies to pressure Budapest. The committee held mass protest meetings throughout the country, organized the writing of thousands of letters to the White House and Congress, and sent several thousand telegrams to newspapers, urging them to speak out against the slaughter of European Jewry. This resulted in the publication of numerous editorials urging U.S. intervention to help the Jews.

Another important angle was to mobilize Hungarian-American organizations and personalities. There were in the U.S. large Jewish and Christian communities of Hungarian origin, which included outstanding individuals in various fields. The Bergson Group held two emergency conferences, one of leading members of Jewish Hungarian groups, the other of leading Hungarian Christian clergymen and lay people. The first took place on April 2, 1944, at the Waldorf Astoria hotel in New York City, presided over by the renowned academician and historian Dr. Emil Lengyel. More than eight hundred delegates, representing 150,000 American citizens, participated. In his opening remarks, Dr. Lengyel urged the three major Allies to send the Hungarian leaders a warning to desist from carrying out the Nazis' extermination program:

> The Hungarians have not passed through the Germans' school of fanatical hatred. They will kill the trapped people only if that seems to them the safest way to save their own necks. The Allies must make it clear that every life will be accounted for, and that the guilty ones will have to pay with their own blood. The people employed by the Germans are the type who can be scared into sabotaging the murderous tasks entrusted to them if our warning is broadcast to them by every possible means, and is repeated with such emphasis as would leave no doubt in their minds that we mean what we say.

Additional speakers of note at the conference included political leader Dean Alfange; the pastor of the First Magyar Presbyterian Church, Dr. Ladislas Harsany; U.S. Congressman Samuel Dickstein (D-New York); Hungarian activist Dr. Geza Takaro; and Ferenc Gondo, editor of the Hungarian American publication *As Ember*.

THE NEW REPUBLIC   AUGUST 21, 1944

NOW IT IS UP TO DEMOCRATIC ENGLAND AND NOT TO FASCIST HUNGARY

Whether 800,000 Hebrews Will Live or Die

The 800,000 Hebrews in Hungary can be saved. This is a fact. Regent Horthy officially informed the Government of Great Britain through the International Red Cross that all the Hebrews will be permitted to leave Hungary if only they possess visas to Palestine. In the meantime, the deportation of Hebrews from Hungary to extermination centers in Poland has been suspended. Thus a new situation has arisen where the fate of 800,000 human lives is not any longer the responsibility of <u>Fascist Hungary</u> and its German masters, but has become ours and above all that of <u>Democratic England</u>. Destiny has placed before England a fateful choice—to become either rescuers or accomplices in murder.

No Politics

Of course Palestine is now one of the countries whose political status and boundaries are a matter of controversy between different parties and interests, but the Hebrew Committee of National Liberation has offered a generous compromise to the British Government. The Hebrew Liberation Committee has conceded that the British Government need not admit the Hebrews of Hungary and other Balkan countries as permanent immigrants, but that it need only establish EMERGENCY RESCUE SHELTERS IN PALESTINE under the same principle as the Emergency Rescue Shelters proclaimed by President Roosevelt at Fort Ontario, New York. This proposal, made to the British Government through the British Ambassador, Lord Halifax, on June 10th, places this tragic human problem on a plane of pure humanity, taking it out of the realm of political maneuvering. The permanent fate of the Hebrew evacuees will be decided at the end of hostilities when other and similar problems of migrations and political boundary matters are dealt with.

No Financial Burden for England

It is not suggested that the people of Great Britain be burdened with the task of transporting and feeding the evacuees. We are justified in assuming that the War Refugee Board, the International Red Cross, Jewish relief organizations like the Joint Distribution Committee, to say nothing of the Hebrew population of Palestine, will assume the onus of transportation, care and feeding of the evacuees. The only thing required from Great Britain is a declaration that such Emergency Rescue Shelters will be established in Palestine, so that the news can spread to the Balkans.

Failure in the Past

Although nearly two months have elapsed since this situation was first brought to the British Government's attention, nothing has yet been done. No decent and fair-minded person will be shocked at our statement that if Great Britain fails now to declare the establishment of Emergency Rescue Shelters in Palestine, *the Government of Great Britain will share the guilt of the death of those Hebrews who remain trapped in the Balkans*.

Although the Red Cross communication brought us great relief and satisfaction, it was by no means surprising, for it was always the policy of Germany's Balkan satellites to release Hebrews if only they had somewhere to go. As early as January 1943 the

Rumanian Government offered to release 70,000 Hebrews from Transnestria. At that time, Mr. Peter H. Bergson (now head of the Hebrew Committee of National Liberation) made official representations to our government in Washington, and Captain Jeremiah Helpern (now member of the Hebrew Liberation Committee) to the Foreign Office in London. We widely publicized a dramatic appeal by the incomparable Ben Hecht under the headline, "For Sale to Humanity 70,000 Jews." But these efforts were of no avail, and these voices were crying in the wilderness. Countless thousands of human beings who might have lived perished in the most horrible manner.

A Fight to the Finish

This time this cruelty must not be repeated. The Hebrew Committee of National Liberation has proclaimed the campaign to save the Hebrews of Hungary to be a sacred fight—*and a fight to the finish. We are behind them in this fight. We will support it with all our energies as good Americans must, in whose heart humanity has not been extinguished and who cherish the ideals of this beloved democracy.*

For this is not a matter of concern to the Hebrew people alone. In this global war that we are fighting, the interests of all peoples are closely interlocked. We believe that only a situation wherein millions of Hebrews could be ruthlessly and atrociously slaughtered with no more than futile expostulation rendered possible the savage indiscriminatory robot bombings of London. Unless the United Nations prove themselves willing to act in forthright fashion with brutality, there is no telling to what lengths the German savages will go in their last desperate hours.

Play Your Part In This Crusade!

We are confident that in this mobilization of public opinion there is a place waiting for you—regardless of your national origin or religious creed. Join us. Help us to spread this message among many millions of Americans in order to arouse them to their responsibility. It is imperative that we place this message in hundreds of newspapers throughout the country and broadcast it to the entire nation, for the very principles for which we are fighting this war are at stake. We, therefore, need not only your voice, but also your financial help, immediately, NOW! You are invited to sign your name below as a member of the American League for a Free Palestine, and, to enclose your contribution to speed our great human venture.

The conference issued resolutions urging the opening of Palestine to Jewish escapees from Hungary, the establishment of temporary havens in Allied and neutral territories, the provision of food and medicine to Jewish refugees, and renewed threats by the Allies to punish all Nazi collaborators. The conference also decided to create a special Hungarian section of the Emergency Committee to keep attention focused on the unfolding catastrophe.

It was significant that the conference was held on April 2, because coincidentally, that was the day the Russian army entered Rumania. The war now entered a new phase and presented new rescue opportunities. Psychologically, the Russian advance was of tremendous importance. It weakened the Nazis' hold over the satellites and greatly increased the chances of permitting large numbers of Jews to leave Hungary. But where could the Hungarian Jews go if permitted to leave? A quick glance at the map sufficed to show that with the opening up of Rumania, the main practical possibility of large scale evacuation was through Rumania to the port of Constanza, and from there by ship either directly to Palestine or with a stopover in Turkey—and from there by train to Palestine. The Emergency Committee thus focused part of its activities on pressing the British to cooperate in rescue efforts by admitting refugees to Palestine, at least on a temporary basis. The committee emphasized that it was seeking such arrangements not on political grounds but out of purely humanitarian considerations, leaving the decision of Palestine's political status open until after the war. In a series of newspaper advertisements, the committee argued:

> Rescue is mainly a problem of geography. Even were the U.S. wide open to all escaping Jews, it would be of little immediate help because of the barriers of national boundaries, and an ocean to be crossed. The rescue, therefore, has to proceed along shorter and safer roads. These lead to Cyprus, to Turkey, to Spain. One road, however, is shortest and surest. It leads to Palestine.
>
> Palestine is the closest and most practical haven for the escaping Jews...[I]t is only a few days removed from the Axis countries by short, quick water-routes, by train, or even by bus.
>
> Palestine is the only country where a [Jewish] population is ready and waiting to receive their escaping brethren, to share with them their bread and their homes...
>
> The Emergency Committee believes that a united public opinion must appeal to a democratic government and the oldest parliament, which holds the key to the salvation of the Jewish people, to open wide the doors of sanctuary—Palestine.

For tactical reasons, the Emergency Committee did not advocate admission of Jews into Palestine out of political considerations, but rather only as a "sanctuary." It consistently sought to avoid arguments concerning the rights of the Jewish people to Palestine, or referring to the international commitments undertaken in the past by Great Britain concerning the upbuilding of a Jewish national home. The Emergency Committee tried to separate the political aspects of Palestine and ultimately its status from the urgent humanitarian need to save lives, to offer merely a "sanctuary" to those fleeing death. Bergson once explained to Rabbi Stephen Wise, in a private conversation, that if the rabbi was trapped in a house that was on fire, his main concern would be how to get out alive, not how to get to the Waldorf Astoria.

Thus, just as the Emergency Committee urged the U.S. government to establish "free ports" in America, it did not hesitate to ask the British to respond to the Hungarian crisis by establishing similar havens in Palestine. Although a number of prominent figures in the United States and England supported this demand to separate the humanitarian imperatives from political considerations, it was of no avail. The British government persisted in playing politics in the most cynical and inhumane manner, right until the bitter end. Perhaps nothing illustrates this better than the cruel manipulation of unused immigration certificates. The British White Paper of May 1939 had limited Jewish immigration to a maximum of 15,000 per year for five years. Although those five years were the most disastrous in the history of the Jews of Europe and the need to escape was most desperate, a strange thing happened: at the conclusion of the appointed period, that is, in April 1944, 30,000 immigration certificates still remained unused. How is this mystery explained? The British conceived a fiendish procedure of preventing the Jews most in need of these certificates from obtaining them. For a Jew to receive an immigration certificate, he had to present himself in person before a British consular official and fill out the requisite application forms. But where could a Jew find a British consular official in Nazi-occupied Europe?

Although the Germans were at various times willing to let the Jews leave, they were not willing to renew consular relations with their British enemy for this particular purpose. They had only been willing, up until some point in 1941, to let Jews cross the frontier into a neutral country. Later, however, it became extremely difficult for Jews to flee, except from some of the satellites into the Balkans. But whatever the prevailing conditions, there were always some Jews who succeeded in reaching the frontiers of a neutral country, mainly Turkey, but also Spain and Portugal. These countries were not always obdurate in their refusal to permit refugees to enter their territory, on condition that their stay would be temporary. In the case of Turkey, the authorities demanded that the refugees show an entry certification to Palestine as proof that they would soon move on. But the fleeing Jews did not have such documents. This created a vicious cycle. The Emergency Committee proposed breaking the cycle by the simple expedient of transferring the 30,000 unused certificates to the

British consuls in Turkey and Spain, with explicit instructions that each refugee presenting himself to the consulate in Istanbul, Madrid, or other neutral countries be given a certificate without delay or chicanery, until the quota was exhausted. This would reassure the governments of those countries, but especially the Turks, to let in approximately the same number of Jewish refugees as the number of certificates at the disposal of the local British consulate.

The Emergency Committee repeatedly made this argument in letters and telegrams to British officials, petitions, and newspaper advertisements, but received only evasive replies. The War Refugee Board took up the idea and had some limited success. It did not succeed in freeing up all 30,000 certificates, but it did manage to pry loose a small number. Of course, even if the British had accepted the proposal in full, it still would not have offered a solution to hundreds of thousands of Jews in the shadow of death. Still, every avenue had to be tried.

On April 19, the committee brought a delegation of fifteen Hungarian-American rabbis, Christian clergy, political leaders, intellectuals, and community activists to Washington to plead for the rescue of Hungarian Jewry. They met with Senators Gillette, Downey, and Mead, as well as with John Pehle, executive director of the War Refugee Board. The senators promised to actively press the administration for rescue action. Pehle likewise pledged to do everything possible to expedite the rescue of Hungary's Jews.

The committee also sought to reach out to the Soviets. A May 15 telegram to Stalin was signed by an array of prominent educators, scientists, former diplomats, clergymen of various denominations, and Nobel Prize laureates. They urged:

> [T]he victorious Red Army poised at the very gates of Hungary can induce the Hungarian puppet government to listen to your warning and to desist from executing its diabolical intentions. We beg also to draw your attention to the fact that among the Jews trapped in Hungary there are some 50,000 refugees from Western Ukraine who may be exchanged for Hungarian prisoners of war.
>
> We further beg to suggest that the offices of your diplomatic representatives in Sofia be employed to alleviate the tragic situation of the [surviving] Jews in Balkan Countries.

To gain maximum publicity for this appeal, it was read aloud at a special conference at the Hotel Biltmore, in New York City, at which a number of the prominent signatories spoke. One was Mrs. Ruth Bryan Owen Rhode, the former U.S. Minister to Denmark, who declared that if the U.S. and its allies failed to prevent the liquidation of the Jews of Hungary, they would become "accessories before the fact" of murder. She said "Stalin himself might issue an order warning and threatening the Hungarians with severe punishment if the deportations or executions are not stopped immediately." She explained that "a warning from Stalin to Hungary would have special influence upon the Hungarians, taking into consideration that the Russian armies are at the gates of [that country]; that Russia has a considerable number of Hungarian prisoners of war against whom it can retaliate; that Russia has [already] proven its policy of punishment of criminals who were guilty of the slaughter of civilian populations; that about 50,000 or more Jews of the Western Ukraine who fled to Hungary are considered Russian nationals by the Soviet government because it considers the Western Ukraine Russian territory, and that diplomatic relations between Russia and Bulgaria are not severed and therefore it can deal with the Balkans situation directly without the need for intermediaries."[177]

Stalin did not answer. The War Refugee Board likewise tried to persuade the Soviets to issue such threats, but its efforts, too, were unsuccessful. Stalin did not believe in warnings and threats. He practiced swift revenge without much regard for legal or diplomatic niceties. His armies entered territories previously occupied by the Nazis and carried out large scale executions of those responsible for the atrocities.

Pressure on the Vatican

Since Hungary was officially a Catholic country, the Vatican was certainly in a position to exert some influence on the Hungarian government, regardless of the political orientation of its leaders. Volumes have been written about the godless behavior of the Catholic Church during the years of the Holocaust. The silence of Pope Pius XII has been well documented. Nonetheless, at that late hour, when everyone knew that Hitler's defeat was inevitable, the Emergency Committee believed that despite the shocking and abhorrent record of the Vatican, no effort should be spared to bring about a last-minute awakening of the highest religious and moral authority in the Christian world. The committee initiated several appeals to the pope, directly and through other channels, asking him to intervene. In late May, the committee requested an audience with the Apostolic Delegate to the United States, Amleto Giovanni Cicognani. Finally, on July 7, he received a joint delegation from the Emergency Committee and the Union of Orthodox Rabbis of America. The group presented the Vatican representative with a memorandum on the perilous situation of the Jews in Hungary and asked him to transmit an appeal to the pope to use his influence with the Hungarian regime. In the hour-long conversation, the Jewish delegates also called Msgr. Cicognani's attention to the plight of Jews in other largely-Catholic countries under Nazi domination, and urged papal intervention there as well.

A second emergency conference, this one of Christian Hungarian-Americans, was held on June 17. Numerous prominent personalities, both Catholic and Protestant, took part. It concluded with a powerful message to Pope Pius XII which, coming from leading Christian figures, carried particular weight. It read, in part:

> We representatives of Christian Americans of Hungarian descent, assembled in a national conference in New York to express our sympathy with the persecuted Jews of our Motherland, most respectfully entreat Your Holiness to use the weight and authority of your exalted position to convey and emphasize to the Hungarian Government our sentiments in condemning and deeply resenting the action of that Government and of all those who are now torturing and murdering the Jewish people. We most humbly implore Your Holiness to authorize and advise the active cooperation of all pious Catholics in Hungary in the work of rescuing the Jewish people from the hands of their persecutors and in aiding them to reach places of safety.[178]

The conferees sent a message to their fellow-ministers in Hungary appealing for "help to remove the shame with which traitors besmirch the Hungarian name by persecuting the Jews! Help to redeem Hungary's honor, for only an honorable Hungarian nation may rise! Its millennial past is free of filth, and so also must be its future." In a message to the Hungarian government, the conference denounced Hungary's leaders for having "betrayed every Hungarian tradition" and proven themselves to be "the most repulsive examples of robbers, murderers, and pagan barbarians." In response to a recent invitation by Hungary to Hungarian-Americans to return after the war to their native country, the conference stated: "We are not coming back to homes, farms, factories, and mines spattered with the blood of the Jewish friends we left behind when we departed from Hungary. The horrible thought that any civilized American would return to take a place made for him by robbery and murder could have been born only in the depraved mind of a Nazi maniac."

The conference also sought to rally the masses of Hungarian-Americans, by issuing a call to Hungarian churches in the U.S. to hold special prayer services for rescue of the Jews. Sunday, July 9 was designated for these Services of Intercession, in which numerous churches took part. Particularly impressive was the gathering at the First Magyar Reformed Church of New York, on East

66th Street. Some five hundred people crowded into the little church. Midway through his sermon, the pastor, Dr. Geza Takaro, instructed ushers to distribute arm bands printed with the star of David, which were supplied by the Bergson Group. Messages of support from Mayor Fiorello La Guardia, Governor Thomas Dewey, Senator Robert Wagner, and Archbishop Francis J. Spellman were read aloud. Prof. Louis Toth of Cornell, who chaired the Presbyters of the church and was active in the Emergency Committee, was one of the speakers:

> We are profoundly shocked and dismayed that in the land of our birth, men could be found to serve as accomplices of Hitler's murderous gang. We shall not rest until we of Hungarian flesh and blood shall be able to lift our bowed heads again, and that cannot be until every one of these men who are now besmirching the good name of the Hungarian people will receive the kind of punishment that the world will not soon forget: the punishment of common, ordinary murderers.[179]

The Emergency Committee's energetic campaign of public pressure, rallies, and newspaper advertisements, and the mobilization of Hungarian-Americans, took place in parallel to an effort behind the scenes by the War Refugee Board to convince the pope to speak out for Hungarian Jewry. This was consistent with the position that the Bergson Group articulated at the very inception of the Board, that there needed to be ongoing efforts by the Emergency Committee aimed at public opinion in order to support and strengthen what the Board was doing.

All of the pressure on the Vatican, from whatever source, finally had an effect. In July, the Pope issued strong statements urging the Hungarian government to stop collaborating with the deportations and instructing Catholic leaders in Hungary to oppose the atrocities. In a July 6 letter, Msgr. Cicognani informed the Emergency Committee that after meeting with the committee's delegation, he had forwarded their appeals to the Vatican's secretary of state, Cardinal Maglione, and that Maglione had replied that the Vatican's representatives in Budapest were "carrying on an intense activity in behalf of the non-Aryan Hungarians, and in every way seeking to aid and protect them." He wrote that the pope had sent a telegram to Regent Horthy, urging him to "do everything possible in favor of the many unfortunate persons who are now suffering because of their race or nationality." Msgr. Cicognani assured the committee that both Pope Pius XII and his representatives throughout Europe "will continue to take every possible measure" to oppose the mass murder. He concluded by asking the committee to refrain from publicizing the letter, "lest untimely publicity prove a detriment to the work of the Holy See for the cause of the Jewish people of

Europe." A second letter from Msgr. Cicognani to the Emergency Committee, later that month, reported that the pope's appeal had led Horthy "to assume a more determined attitude of opposition to the racial laws" and influenced Hungarian Catholic leaders to "carry on a more intense activity in favor of the victims of persecution." As a result, "the whole racial situation is somewhat improved," he concluded.

Amidst the positive change in tone and attitude, the two letters reflected many of the long-standing problems with the Vatican's response to the Holocaust. First of all, the awakening of the Vatican's conscience, if that is what it was, came too late to be of help to the vast majority of the Jews in Hungary. The claim that the pope would "continue" to help the Jews had a hollow if not hypocritical ring to it. The word "continue" implied that he and his representatives had been exerting themselves all along, which was simply not true. If there were any exertions at all, they were less than a drop in the bucket. The use of euphemisms such as "non-Aryan Hungarians" and "unfortunate persons," rather than the word "Jews," indicated that the Vatican was still reluctant to explicitly acknowledge the specifically Jewish dimension of the catastrophe. Finally, there is the request to refrain from making the pope's intervention public out of fear that it could have detrimental consequences. To the very end, the pope persisted in this false claim that "publicity" would harm the Jews. This position, adopted by the pope, the hierarchy of other Christian churches, and the governments of the Allies, was one of the main causes of the Jews' undoing. Still, as these letters indicated, the Vatican did belatedly intervene and the moment it did not, it could not fail to at least partially succeed. Under pressure from the Allies, the Vatican, and world public opinion, Horthy ordered a halt to the deportation of the Jews before the over 100,000 Jews in Budapest could be reached.

Hungary of course remained under German occupation, Horthy was losing control, and in the chaotic conditions that prevailed, Eichmann still hoped to finish the job. At the same time, there were indications that the appeals from the Vatican and other Christians abroad were beginning to have an impact on the Hungarian population. In July, there were reports of Christians being arrested for helping Hungarian Jews. A Catholic priest named Egon Tuscanyi was reportedly arrested for supplying Hungarian Jews with forged identification papers. A member of the Hungarian nobility, Count Mihaly Andrassy, was prosecuted for hiding Jews on his estate. In Nagyvarad alone, more than one hundred and sixty citizens were arrested for aiding Jews, and in Szabadka a leading municipal official was jailed for helping Jews escape. The vice-governor of Pest complained that five high ranking officials in his province had sheltered Jews in their homes and helped rescue their property. These were only a few examples of the changing atmosphere in Hungary, and no doubt there were hundreds more instances of compassion and self-sacrifice. They were certainly not all due to the pope's intervention, nor did they all occur after that intervention. There was not a country in Europe in which there were not at least a few non-Jews who maintained their humanity and risked their lives to help individual Jews—neighbors, acquaintances, sometimes even passing strangers. But they were so rare and exceptional that numerically, they could not make an impact. Had the number been greater, even the Nazis would have relented at least to some extent. After all, the Nazis' mass executions began not with the Jews but with the euthanizing of mentally ill and handicapped Germans. Enough Germans had the courage to express their revulsion to force the Hitlerian authorities to abandon the practice. No such outburst of indignation took place when the lives of millions of Jews were at stake.

The Role of the Red Cross

The record of the International Red Cross with regard to the Jewish disaster was not much better than that of the Vatican. The Emergency Committee undertook a series of initiatives, in Washington and through its representative in Geneva, Dr. Reuben "Rudi" Hecht, to remind the international charitable organization of its moral and legal duties.

One of the major arguments that ICRC representatives often trotted out, to explain why they could not intervene on behalf of European Jews, was that it was beyond the parameters of the ICRC's mission to take action on behalf of citizens persecuted by their own government. The Bergson Group countered that the Nazi extermination of the Jews had nothing to do with internal affairs. The vast majority of the victims were not citizens of Germany, but civilians from foreign countries conquered by Germany, and that foreign internees have rights protected by international law. Even with regard to German Jews, the Red Cross's argument had no legal validity, because the Nazis had robbed the Jews of their citizenship and thus made them into alien civilians, and as such they could ask for protection. For the Red Cross's position was cruel and senseless. That the Nazis made a mockery of international conventions was no excuse for the humanitarian world organization to fall for it. But at this stage it was, tragically, a theoretical discussion, because now there were no more German Jews to speak of. The vast majority had been murdered and only a very few survived from among those who were deported. The Red Cross had done little or nothing to help them, even though under international conventions they were entitled to the ICRC's protection, vigilance, and intervention.

The case of Hungary was somewhat more complicated, although after March 19, 1944, when the Germans occupied the country, Hungary was still technically ruled by its government. This fact had to be taken into consideration in the committee's approaches to the Red Cross. To avoid losing time in the argument over whether or not the ICRC had a right, according to its own criteria, to protect the 800,000 Jews in Hungary, the Emergency Committee decided to call to its attention the hundreds of thousands of Jewish refugees, citizens of other nations, who fled during the previous years into Hungary. The committee believed this would be the best entering wedge for the Red Cross to get involved. A June 5 telegram from the Emergency Committee to the international Red Cross headquarters in Geneva pleaded:

> We draw attention to the perilous situation in Hungary of the Jews, citizens of belligerent Allied countries, Russia, Poland, Yugoslavia, Greece, and Holland. They are interned in camps and are being gradually exterminated or deported to slaughterhouses. Taking into consideration that interned foreign citizens according to international agreements are entitled to the same protection of the Red Cross as war prisoners, we urgently request the International Red Cross to intervene with the Hungarian Government in order to avoid new murders of interned foreign civilians. Please inform us of your decision.

It took the ICRC five weeks to reply and even then the response was based on worn out, pious clichés. It claimed the Red Cross "has no right and means to intervene with any government; the committee can appeal to the public conscience but with that its means to exercise any influence on any government are exhausted." The ICRC insisted that it wanted "to come to the aid of those unfortunate people if it could see its way clear to do so," but concluded: "After due consideration [the ICRC] thought it wiser to abstain from taking any action in response to your cable [because] in doing so the general situation of the Jews in Axis-held countries would only be made worse." What would compel the leading executives of this important world organization to arrive at such a pessimistic conclusion? How could the Red Cross think that helping the Jews would harm the Jews? What could possibly be worse than being gassed in Auschwitz?

In truth, all this was old stuff. These arguments had been heard for years, not only from the ICRC but from all the pious, humanitarian, liberal democratic institutions, whether governmental, religious, or other. The excuses were all cut from the same cloth. Even the language was remarkably similar, whether issued in the name of the pope, the foreign minister of Great Britain, the secretary of state of the United States, or the president of the Red Cross. They all referred to the Jews as "those unfortunate people." They all explained that if they did nothing, it was at least in part out of their concern for the welfare of the Jews themselves. But no matter how many hollow excuses they proffered, in the end a tree is judged by its fruit, and the fruit of Allied policy toward the Jews during the Holocaust was plain to see.

The Red Cross's letter also revealed another important piece of information regarding the Allies' response to the Holocaust. It declared:

> The obstacles we met in the endeavor to help the Jewish Community in Axis-held countries do not, however, come solely from Axis governments. As a matter of fact, by dint of persistence the ICRC succeeded ultimately in obtaining permission to send relief to detainees in concentration camps, etc., if nominatively addressed, but the blockade authorities on their part would not allow such relief, in goods or in funds, to come from Allied countries.

For the past year, the Bergson Group had been urging the State Department and Foreign Office to permit sending food to the Jews in Europe. These pleas fell on deaf ears, with Washington and London claiming that the food would be confiscated and that would strengthen the Nazis. Perhaps. But as long as it was not tried, the argument was invalid; it was not proven one way or the other. It is impossible to judge any action which has not been tried. But the polemical ingenuity of the Allies, especially the British, was not exhausted with that argument. To forestall the need to answer the question "How do you know if you have not tried?," Allied officials had a ready answer: even if the Germans did not confiscate the food sent to concentration camps, it would still strengthen their war effort because it would free them from the responsibility of feeding the inmates. "Why should we ease the burden and obligations of the Nazis?" ran the pious rhetorical question.

It was impossible to prove to the public at large that the leaders of the Allies, the champions of the Four Freedoms, could be so heartless. It sounded especially incredible because it was known that the inmates in concentration camps were starved before they were gassed and burned, and at any rate the amount of money the Nazis expended on food amounted to practically nothing in proportion to the billions of Reichsmarks spent on the war. Yet here it was, in black and white, a letter from the Red Cross leadership confirming that the Allies prevented the ICRC from providing food to the Jews in Nazi concentration camps. This did not get the Red Cross off the hook, since there were many things it could have done to help the Jews if it was not so bogged down in legal technicalities and falsehoods. But it was a graphic reminder of the extent of the callousness of the Allies' response to the suffering of the Jews.

EPILOGUE

Generalization is both the weakness and the strength of analytical and historical narrative. Everyone knows why it is a weak method: it is sweeping, all inclusive, hence invariably imprecise and often invidious. When in this book it is said that the Jews were exterminated while the world looked on indifferently, it is a generalization with all its weaknesses. In that world in the midst of which the Jews were annihilated were individuals and groups and even governments who made heroic efforts to save them, and in some cases succeeded. There were countless individuals who actually sacrificed their lives in the process. But the strength of the generalization is that without it, one could hardly convey a trend and the temper of a generation and society. In the final account, the fact remains that millions of Jews were slaughtered in the twentieth century despite the humanist tradition and what we call Christian civilization: the democratic regimes, the philosophic and ideological creeds formulated and popularized in the wake of the American and French revolutions—despite all these, the Jews perished without the mighty as much as lifting a finger to prevent it. Not to use a generalization, sweeping though it is, would distort this truth. Technically, to dispense with it would be as impossible as for mankind to function without the Kantian categories. Thanks to them intellectual chaos is avoided. Otherwise the details would be overwhelming like some of the modern streets and byways, irremediably congested with traffic almost coming to a standstill.

However, generalizations, though imperative, can and must be used on condition that one is not carried away by them as if they were the absolute truth. They are legitimate if one is aware, and makes the reader aware, of the many-sided qualifications, exceptions, and even contradictions without necessarily specifying each of them, which would make the narrative unmanageable. A truth, if there is such a thing in history, will be more easily perceived when it is being stated in a sweeping generalization rather than by a jumble of detailed exceptions and qualifications.

The tragedy of the Jews is that in the time of greatest crisis and peril to the Western world and civilization posed by Hitler's onslaught, certain priorities slowly crystallized in the minds of its leaders. In this process of Allied thinking and planning, a certain attitude became quite clear: that the Jewish people in Europe were expendable. Their survival was of no great importance. Barely perceptible old and suppressed phobias became activated in the twilight sphere between consciousness and the subconscious—that the Jews are, after all, a nuisance that the world might be a better place without them. Without the rest of the world acting as de facto accomplices, the Nazis' demonic plan could never have been implemented. Perhaps civilization itself should have been put on trial, alongside the Nazis, at Nuremberg.

A CONVERSATION
WITH SAMUEL MERLIN

The text below brings together highlights from four postwar interviews conducted with Samuel Merlin.

KEY:

DSW = David S. Wyman interview with Samuel Merlin (and Hillel Kook), 19 April 1973, New York City. Wyman, professor emeritus of history at the University of Massachusetts-Amherst, is author of *Paper Walls* (1968), the best-selling *The Abandonment of the Jews* (1984) and, with Rafael Medoff, *A Race Against Death* (2002).

MNP = Monty N. Penkower interview with Samuel Merlin, 18 January 1978, New York City. Penkower is professor emeritus of modern Jewish history at the Machon Lander Graduate School of Jewish Studies, in Jerusalem. He is the author of numerous books, including *The Jews Were Expendable* (1983) and *Decision on Palestine Deferred* (2002).

MJN = Meyer J. Nurenberger interview with Samuel Merlin, in the 1970s. Nurenberger (1911-2001), an activist in the Bergson Group, was an editor of the *Morgen Zhurnal* in the 1940s and, later, founder and editor of the *Canadian Jewish News*. He authored *The Scared and the Doomed* (1986).

LJ = Laurence Jarvik interview with Samuel Merlin, July 1980, New York City. Jarvik is producer and director of the 1979 film documentary, *Who Shall Live, Who Shall Die*.

MJN: When did you begin working with Hillel Kook [Peter Bergson]?

M: Our work [was focused] in Eastern Europe, mainly in Poland, in the late 1930s, when we thought that the Jews were exposed to a catastrophe. And this was to evacuate Jews by illegal means, it means illegal from the point of view of the British, especially from the point of view of the British White Paper.[180]

The first meetings between Kook and me were not very cordial. I was then secretary general of the New Zionist Organization [the Revisionist Zionist movement, headed by Vladimir Ze'ev Jabotinsky] and Kook was a commander in the Irgun Zvai Leumi [the Palestine-based underground militia, allied with

Jabotinsky]. It was early in 1938, in Warsaw. It is not clear to me why his attitude was both suspicious and unfriendly, especially since I was known to advocate a policy of unqualified political and financial support for the Irgun. Probably his attitude has to be viewed on the background of the strained relations between the Irgun command, the New Zionist Organization, and even Jabotinsky. Everyone who was identified or organizationally linked with the Revisionist executive was an object of criticism and skepticism. It took me quite a bit of patient and tolerant perseverance before Hillel changed his attitude and accepted me for what I was.

MJN: Why was it impossible to handle the breach between the Irgun and the Revisionists in Warsaw?

M: Revisionism was, above all, a political movement. A political movement means that the objective—in our case the aim was the establishment of a Jewish state—can be achieved by political activities on various levels in various forms and in various directions. One of these means can be under certain circumstances military resistance against the British, or violent retaliation against Arabs in case the latter conduct terrorist activities against the Jews of Palestine. But, and this was the crux of the argument, military acts of violence should be considered at best only one of the means to fit in with the general scheme of the wide spectrum of political activities. The leaders of the Irgun and their supporters within the Revisionist organization and its youth movement, Betar, considered—or so [Jabotinsky] understood them—that violence should be the predominant if not the exclusive means of achieving the political aim, the establishment of the Jewish state. Here was the deep divergence as to opinion as well as an emotional attitude between the father of the Zionist revolutionary movement and his spiritual children.

M (to MNP): I was secretary general of the World Revisionist organization, stationed in Paris until I resigned in 1938, split with Jabotinsky—I joined the Irgun later—because I thought that political activism was not enough, that we needed direct action. Jabotinsky was skeptical about it—his view was *bereshit bara elokim hapolitika*,[181] and once in a while, you can use violence. I wanted to combine the two. He would say, "You have to walk on two legs, right and left, right and left, but political activity is the determining factor." My view then was that political activity had run its course, and now we have to fight the British. I joined the Irgun right after [Irgun member Shlomo] Ben Yosef was executed [by the British, on June 29, 1938, for carrying out a retaliatory attack against Arabs].

MJN: When did you arrive in the U.S.?

M: I arrived here in early 1940. I came here together with the late Zvi Hirsch Wachsman, a Jewish journalist, active in the New Zionist Organization in Paris. We came on a mission for a newly established Ministry of the French government called the Ministere du Blocus et Boycottage, the Ministry of Blockade and Boycott. The French had decided to employ us because they knew that, beginning in 1933, immediately following Hitler's ascent to power, the Zionist-Revisionist world executive proclaimed a worldwide boycott of Nazi Germany. Wachsman was the head of that special boycott department of the New Zionist Organization executive in Paris; I was then secretary-general of the executive.

In 1940, Wachsman negotiated with the French government; they were impressed by our experience in this field. This is how the special mission was appointed. The purpose of our mission was, first, to find out who in the U.S. and in Latin America was doing business on a large scale with Nazi Germany; and, second, to mobilize public opinion against these firms so as to pressure them to desist. The French government submitted to us a list of such firms they knew were dealing with Germany; they also explained to us the technique of the business transactions with Germany. What was most disturbing—in that list figured some of the most important and the largest Jewish owned firms in the U.S. However, very little came out of this mission because only a few weeks later France was invaded, Paris occupied, and there was no longer any contact between us and the French government.

MJN: So when France fell, in 1940, you had no more connection with Paris. Was Jabotinsky already here [in the U.S.] at the time you arrived?

M: We arrived almost simultaneously...I came here in a double capacity. One was the mission on behalf of the French government. The second, my contacts with the Irgun. More precisely, my contacts will Hillel Kook, who was at that time in London. He was eager to see the materialization of my transfer to the U.S. While I was in Paris, Hillel was in London. We corresponded. He was thinking of ways and means how we, that is, he from London and I from Paris, could come to the United States. Hillel Kook was the commander of the Irgun outside of Palestine. And he, as commander of the Irgun, wanted me to come to the U.S. as an emissary of the Irgun. We arrived almost simultaneously in the U.S. I arrived first, then, within a couple of weeks, came Hillel and Alex Rafaeli...A delegation of the Irgun had [already come] to the U.S. in 1938, composed of the Jewish mayor of Dublin, Robert Briscoe; the former commander of the Jewish Legion during World War I, Colonel [John Henry] Patterson; and Chaim Lubinsky. Arieh Ben-Eliezer and Yitshaq Ben-Ami arrived in 1939, [and established] an organization called the American Friends of a Jewish Palestine. The others came in the spring of 1940.

MJN: How did you evaluate the situation and the opportunity for activity in the U.S. at that time? What were your and Hillel Kook's first impressions of the Jewish community and the general atmosphere prevailing in the country?

M: First of all, I cannot myself take any credit for realizing how important American Jewry would prove to be in the struggle for the rescue of the Jews of Europe and the liberation of Palestine. It isn't that I was skeptical; it is just that I was not enthused. But the people who were animated by a great vision of the possibilities in this country were Arieh Ben-Eliezer, "Mike" Ben-Ami, and Hillel Kook. It is only with my own participation in the work and in the proportion that I got involved deeper into the various activities that I became aware in concrete forms of the numerous potentialities in this country.

What struck me most when I arrived in this country was the fact that somehow news about Jews and about Palestine were relegated in the *New York Times* and the *Herald Tribune* to the religion or obituary pages. When I asked for the reason, I was told that it was a longstanding practice. The Jews, and everything concerning Jews, even the political activities of the old Zionist movement, were somehow considered as connected with religion. At that time the Jewish people were considered in liberal circles, especially those dominated by assimilated Jews such as the Sulzbergers [publishers of the *New York Times*], as a religious community. As to mixing up obituaries with news of Jews, I had a suspicion that it had some kind of psychological connection; that the Jews were doomed; that the most characteristic news about Jews is that they were dying.

A second thing that struck me was the fact that Zionist activities were limited to the Jewish East Side and Manhattan Center—the smaller hall; that meetings were held in *landsmanshaften*, in synagogues and within the framework of rather insignificant groups. I was curious to know whether these mostly Yiddish-speaking groups represented a majority of the Jews of America. I was told that they represented a significant minority, but though a minority, they were the most concerned and committed to Jewish affairs. One has also to keep in mind at that time the Yiddish press was still an impressive and influential institution with a readership of hundreds of thousands. What I tried to clarify at that time was why there were not activities aimed at interesting the majority of the Jews who were English-speaking and probably socially differentiated from those of the East Side and in other Jewish districts. I don't remember what explanation I received but I do remember that I was asked earlier upon my arrival to help organize a meeting in a small hall on the East Side. I asked, "Why not in a large hall where thousands of people could congregate?" I was told that this is how work was being done there and propaganda on a mass scale was being attempted only in exceptional cases. I wasn't given to understand what these exceptional cases could be.

To me, the whole explanation was strange because I felt that the predicament of the Jews at that time was an exceptional case, and indeed the Jewish problem reached the dimensions of crisis and emergency...I raised the possibility of transferring the Jewish problem from the small, limited, esoteric groups to the wide open consciousness of American Jewry as such, and I also raised the problem of transferring the Jewish news from the religion and obituary pages in the newspapers to a level of international concern and immediacy.

MJN: When did you come to the conclusion that you couldn't do anything with the existing Jewish organizations, and that you would have to start from scratch any activity that would help the Jews of Europe? With whom did you speak among the Jewish leaders before you too the road to independent activity?

M: In answering this question, two things have to be kept in mind. We had a dual background of dissent and independent action. First, as Revisionists who acted independently of the Old Zionists, and then the Irgun which acted independently of the Zionist-Revisionists at a later stage. We took it for granted that there was an emergency and if we were not going to do what was necessary, nobody would. On the other hand, we never came to a final conclusion that it was not worthwhile trying to achieve cooperation between us and the established Zionist and Jewish organizations, even if it implied certain subordination on our part. Throughout the years of our work in this country, we repeatedly renewed one initiative after another to achieve some cooperation and invariably it came to nothing. However, at the very beginning of our activity, we not only decided but actually almost made a vow not to enter into public disputes with the Old Zionists regardless of how nasty and destructive the provocation. On the whole, I believe the record shows that we kept that vow.

MJN: You must have decided at a certain moment that you are talking to a blank wall, because the differences of opinion between you and the Jewish establishment were such that an observer like me came to the conclusion very early that you were speaking the language of the Jews in Europe threatened by extermination, while most of these leaders spoke in terms of certain vested interests.

M: It isn't correct to say that we came to the conclusion that we spoke to a blank wall. This was not the conclusion but the starting point. What we tried time and again was to see whether there was a change in the mentality and attitude of the Jewish leadership under the impact, first of the tragic events in Europe and then, our example that important activities can be carried out on a large scale. To give you an example, quite early upon our arrival, and this was probably in 1940, Nahum Goldmann [co-chairman of the World Jewish Congress] organized a meeting between us and several leaders of the Jewish organizations. I don't remember exactly the speeches, except that they presented the case for discipline. When we tried to explain that the problem of discipline arises only because the Zionist organization does not dedicate its resources and capabilities to the Jewish army campaign, a leader of the Labor Zionists, David Wertheim, answered—and this I remember very clearly: "What is there to talk with you? You don't even understand that such a campaign as yours will only bring about the State Department to decide to have you all arrested." I remember this remark so vividly because I couldn't understand how the [equivalent of a] foreign ministry in a democracy can "arrest" anybody.

MJN: What did you answer?

M: Our main spokesman was Hillel Kook. He always spoke very cautiously and diplomatically, in a tone of conciliation. At one juncture, we even achieved an agreement [on the Jewish army campaign] with the Emergency Council for Zionist Affairs, and then they reneged on this agreement even before any attempt was made to carry it out.

MJN: Were you ever able to convince them that you were not out to capture their positions, or their jobs, or that you are not competing with them to become professional Jews?

M: It is a difficult question to answer, not because we had some intentions or achieving a status of leadership in this country, or to wrest their positions, but on the contrary, because it didn't occur to us; it didn't enter our minds. Our interests were centered on rescue of Jews and the future of Palestine and our eyes were always on the target to be achieved, with no interest whatsoever in our personal status in any community outside of Palestine. Maybe it was because we were so disinterested in this kind of thing that they couldn't believe us, or actually couldn't understand us.

* * *

M: In the first days of the war, 133,000 young Jews [mostly in Palestine] registered as willing to serve in the British armed forces. So here we have already a nucleus, you have already what is necessary from all the world, from all other countries and at that time America was still not in the war and here the reservoir of volunteers would have been very great. Since the Middle East was from the beginning a very important theater of war, the problem of shipping was, would be, would have been much easier to have soldiers right on the spot. And what is important is that the motivation in the First World War for Jews to volunteer and to fight Germany was very weak because Germany was a friend of the Jews and the enemy of that time was Russia, which was the ally of Great Britain. This time the motivation was tremendous, was maximum, one cannot even find the right words in order to define the power, the emotional power, of the motivation of young Jews everywhere to volunteer.

J: What happened to these volunteers in Palestine?

M: Now the British didn't want to make use of them. They thought that this would annoy the Arabs. So they decided that at that time that they will create small units of Arabs and Jews on the basis of parity. If an Arab volunteers, then a Jew is also accepted. But the Arabs didn't want to volunteer, therefore the number had to be kept very low, according to the numbers of the Arabs who had volunteered.

LJ: What would have happened had they accepted [all the Jewish volunteers]? Would the Arabs have revolted?

M: Now one of the myths was that Great Britain couldn't have accepted the Jewish army because the Arabs would be annoyed and angry, and rebel. We argued at that time, not because we were clever and we discerned the situation more clearly than others, but the facts were that the Arabs are against the Allies anyhow. You can lose something that you have, but you cannot lose something that you don't have. You don't have the Arabs. The Arabs were not your allies. Whenever they could betray you, whether it was King Faisal, or whether it was the government in Iraq, they did it. Whenever they could sabotage physically the war effort, they did it.

LJ: How would a Jewish army change--

M: The Jewish army not only would have been a very important contribution to the war effort; not only would it have had an effect upon the Jewish condition in occupied Europe; not only would it influence the strategy of the Allies; but a Jewish army would have also, perhaps—and it stands to reason—aroused the interest of the Arabs also to join the Allies from their own point of view, in order to compete with the Jews. If there was a Jewish army of a quarter of a million people, the [Arabs] would understand that their situation would be very bad if their contribution is nil, which it was. [All] of their contribution is rebellion and sabotage. The policy of the British, which was accepted in toto—lock, stock, and barrel—by the State Department [and] the White House, that one shouldn't do it because of the Arabs, was plain stupid.

If a Jewish army would have been used, in Europe, then such large numbers have enough autonomy to do things which are not exactly prescribed by the higher authorities.

LJ: What sorts of things?

M: They could have done all kinds of things in order to prevent the machinery, or the technique, or the method of the extermination of the Jews.

LJ: Commandos?

M: They could have attacked the railroads; they could have cut the bridges; they could have flown missions in order to bomb the crematoria, the gas chambers. And actually, if one was in the army, one knows that such things happen and no great tragedies after that occur. Very few Jews, Jewish officers would have been court-martialed. They wouldn't have disbanded the Jewish army because they have done something in order to rescue their own people which were in the very process of being exterminated.

* * *

MJN: Can you tell me something about the preparations for the Emergency Conference to Save the Jewish People of Europe [in July 1943]?

M: What we tried to achieve at that conference was to impress public opinion and the government of the U.S. about three imperatives:

(1) That the disaster is of such magnitude that all the previous concepts of charity, of palliatives, of helping individuals or groups, or members of parties, are no longer valid; that the task at hand was no less than the rescue of the whole people that was condemned by the Germans to extermination;

(2) Having stated the magnitude of the problem, that is, that the rescue is intended not for individuals but for a people, and should be carried out on a mass scale, it therefore can no longer be handled by private organizations regardless of how rich and powerful. Neither the [American Jewish] Joint [Distribution Committee] nor any other organization of that kind could ever be in a position to tackle the problem, not only because of financial considerations, though this, too, was an important prerequisite. In order for rescue to be commensurate with

the need, the mass character of the catastrophe, it could only be undertaken by the government of the Allied powers, and first and above all, the government of the U.S. Hence, the aim of our campaign was to convince and to impress and, if necessary, to impose by public opinion, upon the government of the U.S., the consciousness of this imperative to take action to save the Jewish people of Europe. We summarized this whole idea in the concept of a governmental authority with the specific and exclusive task to save the Jewish people of Europe. We knew that if this task, even if it were accepted by the government in Washington, were given to one of the existing departments, nothing would come out of it because it would be lost in the shuffle. Each governmental department, each secretary in the cabinet, was overburdened by the war effort and it couldn't be seriously expected for any of them to assume an additional task.

(3) The third objective was to divorce the imperative of rescue from ideological considerations. In contradistinction to the Jewish establishment and often in clear opposition to them, we insisted that the rescue of the Jews in Europe should be divorced from any ideological considerations. To us what was more important than anything else was to save Jewish lives per se. We did not insist that they should go to Palestine; we made several alternative propositions—for example, establishing temporary camps wherever possible, in several countries, and to keep them there in safety until the end of the war. Because of the combination of these three main postulates—the rescue of the Jews as a people and on a mass scale; that it should be undertaken by the government as a direct responsibility within the framework of the war; that it should be undertaken on purely humanitarian grounds—made an impact both upon a considerable part of public opinion as well as of important members of the Roosevelt administration, including such men as the secretary of war, [Henry] Stimson, secretary of the navy, [Frank] Knox, and secretary of the interior, [Harold] Ickes. We had the ear even of some people in the State Department, like Adolph Berle, Jr., though he was always cautious not to stick his neck out. But perhaps most important of all was the impression our philosophy and attitude had upon the secretary of the treasury, Henry Morgenthau, Jr. When Roosevelt ordered the creation of the War Refugee Board, it was to a great extent due to the insistence of Morgenthau. It was also he who appointed the members of that board and its apparatus.

MJN: I remember whenever I came up to your office at West 45th Street, I was saddened. I saw that you weren't concerned only what to do next about the Jews of Europe, but you had to do something immediately, not to be deported from the U.S. as people who "obstruct the war effort"; and next, how to save the Emergency Committee because every day, a few members of the committee were resigning, under the pressure of the Jewish establishment...Whenever I use to come back to my office at the Yiddish daily *Morgen Zhurnal*, the editor kept asking me, "Nu, those thieves, those embezzlers of Jewish money, are they still free, are they still around?"

M: This reminds me of a little story that is quite amusing. There was in 1948, in Israel, a Mrs. Zacks, a liaison officer between the government and the foreign missions. She was glamorous, she was elegant, and she spoke foreign languages. It was June or July of 1948, the war was still on and Tel Aviv was being bombed every day, usually by a single Egyptian plane. Nothing could be done about it because Israel at that time had no air force at all, nor did we have any anti-aircraft guns. So daily, the plane, or a couple of planes, arrived and dropped their bombs with impunity. At that time, I was still bedridden as a result of the wounds I received on the *Altalena*. So I was lying in bed at the Hotel Gat Rimon, on the upper floor, and Irma [Jeremiah Helpern] was my roommate. He tried to convince me that I should go down to the ground floor whenever there was an air raid alarm. But I couldn't do it because any slight movement caused me excruciating pain.

It happened that the last day before a ceasefire was proclaimed, the Egyptians, instead of bombing Tel Aviv as usual, only once, they kept repeating it practically all day and even in the evening. One of the bombs fell at the back of the hotel where I was, and Irma got quite excited and actually forced me to go down the steps. When I was down, I lay on the tile floor in the lobby; it was blacked out and in one corner close to where I was lying on the floor was sitting Mr. Knox, the American Charge d'Affaires, and two of his assistants, the first and second secretaries. With them was Mrs. Zacks. During the conversation that I overheard because of the proximity, at a certain point Knox asked Mrs. Zacks what she thought of the activities of the Bergson Group in the United States, leading up to the proclamation of the State [of Israel]. She said that the group was no good; that they were self-seeking adventurers whose only interest was to enrich themselves by raising public funds under false pretenses; and the fact that proves more than anything else their worth and character is that Merlin and Bergson [Kook], who were the two central figures of that group are now, when Israel is at war, in Switzerland, where they bought a castle and support a harem. Bergson was at that time detained [by the Haganah] in a camp, in Bet Shean. This story was published at least twice in the Israeli press, and she never denied it.

Actually, the more time goes by, the more firm I am getting in my conviction that the Jews of Europe, or at any event its vast majority, could have been saved if the "recognized" Jewish organizations had been concerned with the tragedy of their brethren in Europe instead of being concerned with a combination of ideology and fanatical defense of their status. I remember as early as December 1942, a young rabbi, Dr. Max Nussbaum, in Los Angeles, told our friend Bernie Fineman of Metro Goldwyn Mayer, "You must forget that you have stolen the show from the Jewish organizations; their leaders will never forgive you regardless of what happens or what is involved." Nussbaum tried to explain to us how we should go about in order to reach a certain agreement with the Jewish leaders in this country. He argued that regardless of how dramatic the public presentation of our case was, with recognized and famous Jewish leaders supporting us and speaking to the government, and in particular to President Roosevelt—leaders like Dr. [Stephen] Wise and Dr. [Abba Hillel] Silver—we will not be in a position to achieve our aims, whether short range or post war. He therefore suggested a "psychological approach" to the Zionist and Jewish leaders. He said that we have to convince the Jewish leaders that we are aware that without their support we can go nowhere. Only with such a confession, made with a great power of conviction, could the wounds of pride we inflicted upon them be healed.

* * *

M: Hearst was the only newspaper owner who supported us without any qualifications or reserv[ation]s. *All* his papers. He gave us pages after pages free. He gave us the whole editorial page—Hearst himself. He gave *orders* to print our material. So the advertising agent called us: you are giving ads to everybody; why shouldn't you give once to the *Journal-American*. The *Journal-American* had a circulation of six million, four million, I don't know. At that time the *New York Times* had a circulation of only 600,000 during the weekdays. We felt somehow obliged to place an ad—the same ad that we placed in other newspapers. And it didn't bring any results. Well—I am speaking from memory, so I'm not sure—the same ad brought in from the *New York Times* $5,000. This ad [in the *Journal-American*] brought in less than $500.

DSW: The *New York Times* was your best source?

M: The best source was the *New York Times*, except Sundays. Sunday was the worst day...There was [also] *The Nation* and *The New Republic*. *The Nation* had a better circulation than *The New Republic* at that time. We had better results from *The New Republic* always than from *The Nation*. Next on the results which were satisfactory, in the sense that they covered the expenses plus, was the *New York Post*. When *PM* still appeared and we publicized in *PM*, [that] was less successful than the *New York Post*. There was a time when the *New York Times* refused to publish our ads. This was a great controversy.

DSW: Because of the shortage of newsprint?

M: No, no. They refused. They said that our facts may not be proven. All kinds of things…We argued with them. We negotiated…[T]hey didn't take every ad automatically, especially if it had political connotations or political contents. So there was a fellow there—and I used to argue with him—sometimes a sentence, a phrase, a word, and this and that. And we were always under pressure. We wanted to the ad to go in the same day, which means tonight for tomorrow's paper. And then at a certain point, they stopped. They said, "We aren't going to take any more of your ads."

DSW: What reason was there?

M: The reason—well, they gave all kinds of reasons. That we make political statements without substantiating them, especially against the British. So we thought that this is the end of the world. Without the *New York Times*—but, strangely enough, the *New York Post* picked up. And we started to give them very often. Sometimes every week an ad. Sometimes twice a week an ad.

* * *

M: [American Jewish leaders] identified themselves with Roosevelt and Churchill and later Bevin and everyone who said that one can do nothing serious during the war [to rescue European Jewry]. They said, "How are we going to save so many people?" You know what it means to save *one* person. They said, "Since it's impossible to do anything on an adequate scale during the war, one has to concentrate upon creating the best and most favorable conditions for the postwar period." And *we* said, "The Jews who are being exterminated on such a scale cannot wait for postwar conditions, because the situation can arrive when there will be no more Jews to enjoy those beautiful conditions for which you are fighting with so much passion." One has to look upon this controversy not only from the point of view of jealousy or whatnot, but also from the point of view of certain attitudes, a philosophy of viewing things. In many respects they were very sincere—

DSW: An honest difference of opinion—

M: There was an honest difference—even when they called us all the names under the sun. They called us impostors and embezzlers and whatever. At the same time, they actually believed that what is more important than anything else is unity. They actually believed that dissidence is a crime, because the only thing that the Jews can hope for to exploit favorably such Jewish interests—whatever the interests were—is first of all unity, discipline. They believed that without unity, without discipline, everything is lost. And, therefore, they considered our activities as a crime, as undermining Jewish power, Jewish interests, because they thought the first priority, transcending everything—they were metaphysical about it—first of all unity, unity and discipline. Where's your mandate? By whose authority are you acting? Of course it's silly, because they themselves didn't have any authority. They did without such certain authority. The only authority they had was that in the [Palestine] Mandate, it was written that there will be "a Jewish agency" to collaborate with the British. This is exactly what we said they are doing: they are an agency to collaborate with the British, and that's all there is to it. They didn't have anything—any other [authority]...In the course of the very few years that we worked here, we got contributions from almost 750,000 people. And the Zionist organizations never had such a number of contributors. We were not competing with them for leadership or whatnot, because we were always ad hoc organizations. We always had a specific purpose. We said, "This is the purpose that we are going to try to achieve." And actually we are the only group in Jewish public life that [ever] liquidated itself voluntarily.

DSW: Did you get the feeling there was a substantial amount of non-Jewish reaction or support? You say you had 750,000 people.

M: Names, we got. Figureheads. The names [on the newspaper ads and sponsoring committees] were mostly non-Jewish, because we aimed at non-Jewish. We aimed at members of the Supreme Court, we aimed at the members of the cabinet. We aimed at labor leaders. The non-Jewish labor leaders were for us. The Jewish labor leaders were against us.

DSW: But the rank and file—

M: The rank and file—of those 750,000 people who gave us money in amounts from $1 to $5,000—I mean who sent in contributions. Some contributions that we got through personal contacts...These people, I would say—of course it's only an estimate—but I would say that 95%...Of each hundred contributions, maybe one or two or three were from non-Jews. I don't know. I cannot prove it now. And I couldn't have proven it even at that time.

DSW: You can't prove it by names, anyway. But you could get a feeling.

M: The feeling is that there was a very small [percentage from non-Jews]. But on the other hand, adverse reactions from Christians, from non-Jews, were practically nil. Except a few crank letters. [W]e used to get hundreds of letters every day—hundreds of letters, hundreds. So there were a few, perhaps through the years, I don't know whether we had a hundred, one hundred, letters by cranks. By antisemites and so on.

On the other hand, we always had some expressions of sympathy. For instance, the FBI, one morning, quite early, around five minutes past nine, my secretary came in and said two gentlemen want to talk with you. They identified themselves as from the FBI. They are accountants. They came to see our books. So I said, "Of course." They said we need a room and we will use it for seven weeks. And actually they moved in. The first few days there were three guys. Then there were two guys. And they worked from 9:00 till 4:30 every day. I told our bookkeeper to cooperate and to give them everything they want. And they became a part, a feature of the office. Every day they came in, like everybody else. So after several weeks, many weeks—and they changed some teams—but the original two were still there and one of them came in and said that he appreciates greatly our cooperation with them, that of course he cannot tell us what his report will be, but in order make clear his feelings, he took out some money and he said, "This is our contribution, but it has to be anonymous. And you have to write it in your books."

* * *

M (to MNP): I was in charge of contacting various groups of rabbis [for the October 1943 march in Washington]. We never worked in the ghetto, the ghetto came to us—there were Yiddish-language journalists who were involved with us. We created a group, the National Jewish Council, whose leaders included several Jewish journalists—Samuel Rosen, Meyer Nurenberger—who was an editor of a religious Yiddish daily, the *Morgen Zhurnal*—and Isaac Zaar, who was not a religious man, he was with Poalei Zion [the Labor Zionists]. They were in touch with rabbis and community leaders. The Orthodox community showed understanding instead of hatred for our work, so we began to appreciate the potential help they could lend us. As a result, we spoke with Rabbi Eliezer Silver [and his Va'ad ha-Hatzala organization].

The march had a terrific effect in several respects. First, it was a genuine, emotional, deeply-felt demonstration of identification with what went on in Europe. This kind of identification could not be found in non-Orthodox circles. The problem, we felt, was that only Jews who would feel this very profoundly, individually, would be willing to move mountains. Second, we should not underestimate the fact that President Roosevelt had to run away from Washington, to find a funny excuse at the last moment to be away. The political pressure was such that he couldn't just say, "I have no time to meet them," but he had to say, "I'm not in Washington." Third, the march was part of the chain of events that led to the creation of the War Refugee Board, because of the pressure it put on FDR. The march had tremendous influence on congressmen, now they were faced with these exotic-looking people whom they hadn't seen before. Before, the rabbis they would meet were clean-shaven, modern-looking rabbis like [Stephen] Wise and [Abba Hillel] Silver. But these rabbis had beards, black coats, tears streaming down their serious-looking faces—some people said they looked like prophets of old. [Samuel] Margoshes wrote along these lines [in *Der Tog*].[182]

The march was originally designed as a demonstration, but then when we saw it had a good chance to be very large and impressive, we pressed, through members of Congress, for President Roosevelt to greet them. And we received a promise beforehand that the leaders of the march would be received by the president—our congressional contacts told this to me before the march. But Wise didn't want the rabbis' delegation to come. Roosevelt's Jewish advisers, such as Rosenman, urged him not to touch it. And he didn't.

* * *

M: [Mainstream Jewish leaders] were unhappy with [the Gillette-Rogers rescue] resolution for two reasons. One was, it was our resolution. This was enough. Second, and perhaps this was even more important to them, that this resolution didn't mention Palestine. When Stephen Wise testified before the [House Foreign Affairs Committee, chaired by Rep. Sol Bloom]—

DSW: Were you there when he testified?

M: No, I wasn't there. But I know—what he said was, "It is a fine resolution except it doesn't go far enough."[183]

DSW: The press reports say he said "it's inadequate."

M: It is inadequate. It is inadequate and it doesn't go far enough because it doesn't specify that the only practical solution to save the Jewish people of Europe was to open the gates of Palestine and to do away with the British White Paper...Now what was our attitude? We were interested mainly in two things. First of all, for the first time to pin down the American government to speak out clearly that what we are talking about is the Jewish tragedy, the Jewish disaster, per se. Because until then, every time one spoke in anonymous terms.

M (to LJ): They didn't call them Jews at all, they tried to avoid the word Jew. In Bermuda for instance, the word "Jew," as much as it was humanly possible, was avoided. They used words like "unfortunate people," "persecuted people," "helpless people," there was a whole vocabulary of words, I mean not even euphemisms, just words in order to disguise the fact. When the war broke out, we knew that Hitler is determined to destroy the Jews. Our first concern was to break, to destroy, the anonymity of the victim.

M (to DSW): For us it was, in order to tackle the problem, a condition sine qua non was that the problem has to be defined—as such. And therefore we formulated—or tried to help formulate it in the sense that one needs to face the problem in its realistic terms and scope. Namely, that it has to do with the Jewish people, per se, as such. And second, the bureaucracy—the United States government has so many departments, there are so many agencies, there are so many secretaries of the cabinet, that it became practically impossible to do something because it was impossible to pin down one address—where to go and what to do.

DSW: So you wanted one group that would do it.

M: We wanted one institution, one authority. We wanted a board or a commission created for one specific purpose. That is, to deal with the problem of the Jews in Europe.

* * *

MJN: What were, in your opinion, the most important achievements of the Emergency Committee?

M: I personally don't delude myself about the scope of our achievements. I am aware of our tragic failure to save masses of Jewish people. I don't underestimate the importance of the limited achievements. First, concerning "illegal immigration," and, then, our initiative in bringing about the creation of the War Refugee Board as well as our part in the rescue efforts from Switzerland and Turkey. Of course, thousands upon thousands of Jewish men, women, and children were saved, and each human life that was saved is a tremendous achievement. But at the same time, one cannot be oblivious to the fact that almost the totality of the Jewish people of Europe was exterminated.

WRITING THE BERGSON GROUP
OUT OF, AND BACK INTO, HISTORY

by Rafael Medoff

Between 1942 and 1948, the Bergson Group was one of the most talked-out about phenomena in the American Jewish community. Its eye-grabbing full-page newspaper advertisements, sensational theatrical productions, and controversial marches and rallies were the topic of frequent and often heated discussions in the Jewish press, in synagogues and other communal settings, and around dinner tables from Brooklyn to Beverly Hills. Love them or hate them, the Bergsonites were very much on people's minds.

Yet as books about that period began to appear in the postwar period, the Bergson Group practically vanished. As a result, when Samuel Merlin set out to write his history of the group, he was setting out to right a significant historiographical wrong.

Mainstream Jewish leaders who clashed with the Bergson Group simply omitted any mention of it when they published their autobiographies. Rabbi Stephen S. Wise did not mention the Bergsonites in his memoir *Challenging Years* (1949); consciously or otherwise, his friend Carl Hermann Voss left the Bergson Group out of his 1964 book about Wise. Voss's 1969 collection of Wise's letters included just one that referred in passing to Ben Hecht.[184] Nahum Goldmann, U.S. representative of the Jewish Agency and co-chairman of the World Jewish Congress, Meyer Weisgal, senior aide to Zionist leader Chaim Weizmann, and Emanuel Neumann, public relations director of the American Zionist Emergency Council, likewise left Bergson out of their autobiographies, published in 1969, 1971, and 1976, respectively.[185]

Bergson Group veterans were slow to write their own memoirs. When several finally did, they were either self-published or published by very small presses and were not widely distributed. As a result, Yitshaq Ben-Ami's *Days of Wrath, Years of Glory* (1982), M.J. Nurenberger's *The Scared and the Doomed* (1985), and Alex Rafaeli's *Dream and Action* (1993) received relatively little public attention, certainly nowhere near the attention necessary to make them an established part of the conventional historiography of the period.[186]

Mainstream Jewish organizations enjoyed a significant advantage in the effort to shape public perceptions of American Jewry's response to Nazism and the Holocaust: they had the financial resources to sponsor histories of their groups, while the Bergson Group, having voluntarily dissolved in 1949, did not. Thus the American Jewish Committee and the American Jewish Joint Distribution Committee were able to enlist two of the most prominent scholars of modern Jewish history, Naomi Cohen and Yehuda Bauer, respectively, to author the histories of their organizations. Both studies portrayed their subjects' wartime record in a strongly favorable light.[187]

In American Jewish periodicals in the 1960s, references to the Bergson Group were few and far between. One of the most interesting of those who did comment on the subject was Lucy Dawidowicz, later to gain international renown because of her book *The War Against the Jews*. The occasion of her comment on the Bergsonites was her review in *Commentary*, in 1962, of *Perfidy*, Ben Hecht's dramatic account of the Kastner trial in Israel. Dawidowicz acknowledged that the newspaper ads Hecht wrote for the Bergson Group "did shock people out of their torpor." While characterizing Hecht as a yellow journalist, she added, "As I now read the newspapers of those days, I find myself preferring the yellow journalist to the political Zionist." She then asserted that "political Zionists" such as Stephen Wise "gambled away one chance to save the Jews," by emphasizing the Palestine issue instead of rescue in 1943-1944. Dawidowicz also acknowledged that the Bergson Group's "proposal to establish a United States commission to rescue European Jews brought about the creation of the War Refugee Board."[188] Still, at that early date, Dawidowicz's references to the Bergson Group were a small ripple in a large pond which at that time was generally undisturbed by debates over the Jewish community's response to the Shoah.

That began to change in the late 1960s and early 1970s, when the first wave of books about the Roosevelt administration's response to the Holocaust typically included at least brief mentions of the Bergson.

Arthur Morse (*While Six Million Died*, 1968) called Bergson "an extraordinary firebrand [whose] attention-getting techniques were in dramatic contrast to those of the more conventional Jewish spokesman." Morse noted that the Bergson Group was supported by numerous members of congress, prominent intellectuals, and even Roosevelt's own secretary of the interior.[189]

Henry Feingold (in a 1969 essay, and in his *The Politics of Rescue*, 1970) noted the Bergson Group's "special skill in mobilizing public opinion" and credited it for the taking action in Congress that "set off a series of events that changed the direction of the flagging rescue effort."[190] Saul Friedman (*No Haven for the Oppressed*, 1973) acknowledged that Bergson's "gigantic rallies packed Madison

Square Garden and Carnegie Hall," increasing "the pressure to force the government to take more decisive action to rescue the Jews of Europe."[191]

Although these scattered references only hinted at the extent and impact of the group's efforts, they constituted the first important cracks in the wall that had shut the Bergsonites out of the historical record.

In the years to follow, several essays and a film brought further attention to the Bergson Group's efforts. The pseudonymous Daniel Charles presented the wider public with an interesting summary of the group's work, in the pages of *The American Zionist*.[192] Sarah E. Peck, in the *Journal of Contemporary History* (1980), and Monty N. Penkower, in *American Jewish History* (1981), published the first serious scholarly examinations of the group's work, after undertaking pioneering research in the Palestine Statehood Groups Papers, a large collection of Bergson documents that Merlin deposited at Yale University. Also in the early 1980s, a private group called the Stepping Stone Fund reprinted articles by Ben Hecht about the Bergson Group as a series of paid advertisements in one of New York City's largest Jewish newspapers, the *Jewish Week*.[193]

At about the same time, film student Laurence Jarvik completed *Who Shall Live, Who Shall Die*, a 90-minute survey of America's response to the Nazi genocide, with the Bergson Group in a central role and interviews with Kook and Merlin prominently featured. The film was critically important in several ways. First, it presented original interviews with the key figures of the period, including former Roosevelt administration officials and mainstream Jewish leaders, in addition to the activists. Second, it made the Bergson story accessible to the general public in more detail, and in a more interesting way, than the various articles that had appeared in print. Third, it attracted significant media attention, including reviews in the *New York Times* and the *Los Angeles Times*, not to mention throughout the American Jewish press. This galvanized a healthy debate in the Jewish community over issues that had been ignored by many for far too long.

Who Shall Live, Who Shall Die appeared just prior to the rise and fall of the Goldberg commission (discussed in the Editor's Preface to this book). These two developments triggered a series of articles and exchanges in the American Jewish press that represented the most detailed, vociferous, and revealing debates yet about the Bergson Group.

Lucy Dawidowicz, in the pages of *Commentary*, and Marie Syrkin and Bernard Wasserstein, in *Midstream*, launched the debate with wide-ranging attacks on Jarvik, Merlin, and, especially, the Bergson Group. Subsequent issues of both periodicals overflowed with letters challenging the articles and barbed retorts from the authors. A biography of Stephen Wise by Melvin Urofsky, which included passages sharply critical of Bergson, coincidentally was published in the midst of these debates, adding another layer to the discussion.

One thrust of these authors' approach was to argue that an activist response by American Jews would not have helped save Jews from the Holocaust. "[S]hould American Jews have marched in Washington in righteous fury as contemporary wiseacres suggest?," Syrkin asked. "The doors would have been slammed even tighter." In a similar vein, Wasserstein wrote that the contemporary assertion that rabbis should have marched to the White House in 1943 was "unaccompanied by any supporting evidence that might raise it to the level of a serious political proposition."

The complicating factor for Syrkin and Wasserstein was that four hundred rabbis, organized by the Bergson Group and the Va'ad ha-Hatzala, *did* march in righteous fury to the White House. That demonstration did not cause any doors to have been slammed tighter. On the contrary, the marchers' demand was received by leading congressmen as a serious political proposition and there is evidence that it galvanized greater support in Congress for U.S. rescue action.

As for the efficacy of public rallies, Wasserstein argued that "Rabbi Wise did fill Madison Square Garden with a monster demonstration—but with no discernible impact on the policy of the Roosevelt administration." He was referring to an American Jewish Congress rally on March 1, 1943. He may have been unaware that just eight days later, the Bergson Group filled Madison Square Garden twice, for back to back performances of its theatrical production, *We Will Never Die.* They subsequently staged the production in Boston, Chicago, Philadelphia, Washington, D.C., and the Hollywood Bowl, reaching not only more than 100,000 spectators, but ultimately an even larger nationwide audience when Eleanor Roosevelt, after attending the D.C. show, devoted part of one of her syndicated newspaper columns to the subject. Shattering the curtain of silence surrounding the Holocaust surely was an important achievement and a necessary prelude to changing U.S. policy.[194]

These authors also indulged in ridicule, presenting vivid caricatures of what they claimed advocates of activism had in mind. "No one can seriously suggest that [American Jews] should have...tried to force refugee ships past the Statue of Liberty," Syrkin wrote. Dawidowicz speculated that Bergson's calls for activism "perhaps meant that Jewish organizations could have outfitted ships...and sent them out against the armed forces of the Third Reich." According to Bernard Wasserstein, those who believe there should have been greater "activism" offered only two "models of activism": the 1943 suicide of Polish Jewish leader-in-exile Szamul Zygielbojm and the 1944 assassination of the senior British official in the Mideast, Lord Moyne. Needless to say, no serious commentator on American Jewry's response to the Holocaust has ever suggested that Jewish leaders should have committed suicide, assassinated foreign diplomats, or parachuted into Auschwitz. But it was certainly a colorful way of mocking those with whom Syrkin et al disagreed.[195]

A second theme of the criticism was the claim that Bergson sympathizers were being anachronistic, by proposing methods of protests that may have been realistic in recent times but not in the 1940s. Syrkin, for example, berated advocates of activism for expecting American Jews of that era to behave "in approved sixties style…young students with memories of civil rights protests have often asked me… why did we not leap into the Atlantic to free the passengers [of the *St. Louis*]?" Dawidowicz invoked the recent memory of an Israeli rescue of Jewish hostages: "These millions of Jews, in the iron fist of the S.S., could scarcely have been rescued in Entebbe-like commando operations." Wise biographer Melvin Urofsky, responding to remarks by Elie Wiesel that Jewish leaders should have "proclaim[ed] hunger strikes to the end," wrote: "Wiesel has read the tactics of the antiwar protests of the sixties back to an earlier and far different time…the protest tactics suggested by Wiesel would have accomplished little if anything in 1942."

The critics' mistake was to assess the viability of 1960s tactics in the 1940s, rather than assess the tactics that activists in the 1940s did actually use. Certainly the Bergsonites did not stage commando raids, leap into the Atlantic, or proclaim hunger strikes to the end—because in their era, much milder tactics than those were considered radical. Placing full-page newspaper ads was as scandalous as a hunger strike. Marching peacefully to the White House in 1943 and then quietly dispersing was as controversial as civil disobedience would be in subsequent decades. The tactics the Bergson Group applied were sufficient, in 1943, to achieve their goals.[196]

Some of the anti-Bergson attacks were based simply on the misreading of historical documents. Consider Syrkin's attempt to prove that the Jewish leaders, not Bergson, were the real activists, by citing a 1943 diary entry by the State Department's Breckinridge Long. There Long complained that "[o]ne Jewish faction under the leadership of Rabbi Stephen Wise" had been "assiduous in pushing their particular causes—in letters and telegrams to the President, the Secretary [of State] and [Undersecretary of State Sumner] Welles—in public meetings—in full-page advertisements." Syrkin, referring to this entry, triumphantly asserted: "Apparently Jews were uncomfortably pushy rather than the reverse."

Syrkin neglected, however, to quote the next sentence from Long's diary, which helps to clarify his intentions: "Many public men have signed their broadsides and Johnson of Colorado introduced their resolution in the Senate." What this sentence demonstrates is that Long was mistakenly blaming Wise (and Syrkin was mistakenly crediting Wise) for a series of actions that actually were taken by Bergson. "Johnson of Colorado" was Senator Edwin C. Johnson, national chairman of the Bergson Group. The "full-page advertisements" bemoaned by Long were, with very few exceptions, sponsored by Bergson. In fact, one such ad appeared in the *Washington Post* the very morning Long wrote that diary entry (April 20) and may well have precipitated the wording of the entry. The ad included the names of thirty-two U.S. generals and admirals, thirty-three U.S. senators, eight governors, and numerous other public figures, including former president Herbert Hoover, a roster that could easily have prompted Long's observation that "many public men have signed their broadsides."[197]

Ironically, Syrkin herself committed an error strikingly similar to Long's, in a 1968 letter defending American Jewish leaders' response to news of the Holocaust. She argued that the failure of U.S. newspapers to take a serious interest in the news of the mass murder made it extremely difficult for Jewish leaders to have an impact on public opinion. The press was so "impervious," she wrote, that "[t]he leaders of American Jewry were obliged to purchase advertising space in large metropolitan papers such as the *New York Times* in order to bring information about the extermination to a largely incredulous and indifferent public." In fact, it was the Bergson Group that sponsored the overwhelming majority of the ads to which Syrkin referred.[198]

Equally untenable was the attempt by anti-Bergson critics to project contemporary Israeli and Zionist politics onto the events and characters of yesteryear. Bergson was "a follower of Menachem Begin," according to Feingold.[199] In Syrkin's view Bergson considered "non-Begin Zionists" to be his enemies.[200] Wasserstein wrote that criticism of the Jewish leadership's wartime record, which originated in the 1940s with "the Revisionist Zionists and their various offshoots," had reemerged because of the Likud's victory in the 1977 Israeli elections—"since then there has grown up a new orthodoxy of Zionist history in which Jabotinsky replaces Weizmann, Begin replaces Ben-Gurion, and the IZL and LEHI replace the Haganah."[201] Dawidowicz, in her major attack on the Bergson Group in the *New York Times Sunday Magazine*, could not bring herself to use the term "Bergson Group," even though that was the name used most commonly at the time and subsequently. Instead, evidently in order to paint them into a political corner, she awkwardly called them "the Irgunists" throughout her essay.[202]

The idea of Jews marching in Washington was likewise linked to the Likud. Wasserstein wrote that the idea of a march by 1,000 rabbis in front of the White House during the Holocaust "is a picturesque scenario...which would no doubt earn the warm approval of Ariel Sharon..."[203] Syrkin chimed in that only "contemporary wiseacres" believe that "American Jews should have marched on Washington" in the 1940s.[204] Is it possible that Wasserstein and Syrkin were genuinely unaware of the Bergson Group's October 1943 march by four hundred rabbis in Washington?

Whatever Bergson may have achieved not only was more smoke than fire, but actually did more harm than good, the critics claimed. The Bergsonites "jeopardized the cause they sought to serve through a penchant for publicity and provocative gestures characteristic of Revisionism to this day," according to Syrkin.[205]

These accounts betrayed ignorance of the actual nature of the Bergson Group. To call Bergson a follower of Menachem Begin may have been a convenient way to link the Bergson group to the Israeli right of the 1980s, but it did not square with the historical record. As the preceding pages have made clear, Bergson was a follower not of Begin but of Jabotinsky. He was active in the Irgun Zvai Leumi underground but steered clear of the Revisionist party. After Jabotinsky's death in 1940, his followers in the U.S. split into separate, and sometimes, clashing organizations: Bergson and other Irgun emissaries formed what was to become known as the Bergson Group, while Benzion Netanyahu and other Revisionists opted to remain in the U.S. wing of the Revisionist party, known as the New Zionist Organization of America.

Bergson realized, early in his American experience, that the Labor-vs.-Revisionist cleavage typical of Zionist politics in Palestine and Europe would not serve his cause well. A movement hewing to a narrow ideological line was not likely to prosper among Jews who were attracted to broad Zionist goals and had never embraced ideologies of the Zionst left or right in any significant numbers. Bergson's first political action committee, created in 1941, emphasized a goal that could win support across political and religious lines: the creation of a Jewish army to fight against the Nazis. The committee successfully recruited the endorsement of more than 2,000 political figures, entertainers, union leaders, intellectuals, and newspaper publishers, most of them non-Jews and ranging across the political spectrum. Even Secretary of War Henry Stimson, Secretary of the Navy Frank Knox, as well as Knox's deputy (and later Democratic nominee for president) Adlai Stevenson expressed support, even though the Roosevelt administration did not support creation of a Jewish army. England's ambassador in Washington noted with dismay "the large collection of eminent Americans whom [the Bergson group] has managed to persuade to sign its proclamations...misguided humanitarians of every stripe and colour [are responding to its] simple and moving plea that many thousands of Jews [are] anxious to fight and die in the war against Hitler..."

In shifting its focus, in early 1943, to the need for rescue of Jews from Hitler, the Bergson Group again promoted an issue that cut across party lines. A *New Leader* columnist reported that he "nearly fell through the floor" when he discovered, "nestling cheek by jowl" on the letterhead of Bergson's Emergency Committee to Save the Jewish People of Europe, "the names of Louis Adamic (fellow-traveler)...Congressman James Domengeaux (bitter Southern reactionary)...Lowell Thomas (Big Business propagandist)...Mary Van Kleeck (leading CP fellow traveler)..."[206] In addition, prominent African-Americans such as authors Langston Hughes and Zora Neale Hurston, Atlanta University president Rufus Clement, and singer Paul Robeson also supported the rescue campaign.

The Jewish leadership's public attacks on the Bergson Group typically focused on non-political issues. When the American Jewish Conference—the coalition of all major U.S. Jewish groups—for the first time publicly criticized the Bergson Group, in December 1943, it did not brand the Bergsonites as rightwing extremists. Instead, it accused the Bergson Group of unfairly competing with existing Jewish groups, exaggerating its accomplishments, and causing "confusion" in the minds of American Jews as to which group qualified as the true spokesmen for the Jewish community. When the Bergsonites later created two pro-Irgun groups, the American League for a Free Palestine and the Hebrew Committee of National Liberation, Jewish leaders' criticism sidestepped the Irgun and focused on the Bergsonites' legitimacy, tactics, and motives. For example, a pamphlet issued by the American Zionist Emergency Council denounced the Free Palestine League as "Another Confusionist Front." It made no political characterizations, instead blaming the Bergsonites for "opportunistic impulses," "exploiting the miseries which have befallen our people," "impairing the effectiveness of the Jewish Agency for Palestine," and causing "disunity and uncertainty."[207] While Haganah-vs.-Irgun conflicts were a feature of Jewish life in Palestine, that was not the case in the United States. Once the Irgun and Stern Group joined hands with the Haganah as the United Hebrew Resistance, in late 1945, mainstream American Zionist groups began publicly justifying Irgun violence against the British.[208]

* * *

In hindsight, it is clear that the attacks by Dawidowicz, Syrkin, and Wasserstein, and the eruptions against Merlin during the Goldberg Commission episode, represented the last gasps of a vanishing mindset. By the end of 1984, such overheated verbal assaults on the Bergson Group were a thing of the past and the historiography of the Bergson Group took an enormous leap forward, with the publication of David S. Wyman's *The Abandonment of the Jews.*

Although, as we have seen, earlier studies of America's response to the Holocaust briefly mentioned aspects of the Bergson Group's activity, Wyman was the first to present the Bergson rescue campaign of 1943 in its entirety. He chronicled the fortuitous and eventful intersection of the Treasury Department staff members' efforts to expose the State Department's obstruction of rescue, and the Bergson Group's lobbying on Capitol Hill to promote rescue. Skillfully utilizing the newly accessible Morgenthau Diaries, which contain verbatim transcripts of the meetings between Treasury Secretary Henry Morgenthau, Jr. and his staff, *Abandonment* showed how Morgenthau used the spiraling rescue controversy that Bergson provoked in Congress to convince Roosevelt that he faced an election-year scandal unless he took preemptive action. As Wyman's book garnered accolades from the scholarly community and general public alike, and emerged as the definitive study of the U.S. response to the Nazi genocide, his treatment of the Bergson Group became an accepted part of the new scholarly and popular consensus regarding America and the Holocaust. The impact of

The Abandonment of the Jews was reinforced by the film *America and the Holocaust: Deceit and Indifference*, by Martin Ostrow, aired by PBS in 1994 as part of its series, *The American Experience*. Closely following the themes of *Abandonment* and featuring Prof. Wyman as its most prominent interviewee, *America and the Holocaust* included Bergson in its narrative as an important part of the history of the period.

From the start, Merlin had expected his book would fill the vacuum that other historians had left. He would tell the story of the Bergson Group that others had omitted out of bias, malice, or ignorance. He would write the activists back into history. But during the long years that Merlin labored on his manuscript, the world around him changed dramatically. The participants in the intra-Jewish battles of the 1940s passed on, and the younger generation of American Jewry did not share the partisan passions of the Bergson Group's opponents. New scholarship reshaped our understanding of America's response to the Holocaust, including the role of the Bergson Group. Wyman and Penkower filled the vacuum that Merlin had thought he would fill. These works were later supplemented by additional books such as *Shake Heaven and Earth* by the American-Israeli journalist Louis Rapoport (1999); *A Race Against Death: Peter Bergson, America and the Holocaust*, by David S. Wyman and this author (2002), an oral history in which Kook presents his story through a lengthy annotated interview with Professor Wyman; and *The "Bergson Boys" and the Origins of Contemporary Zionist Militancy*, by Judith Tydor Baumel (2005).

Merlin would no doubt have appreciated the sea change in American Jewish attitudes toward the Bergson Group, which has become even more evident in recent years. In 2008-2009, for example, two films about the Bergson Group were released, *Against the Tide* by Rick Trank and the Simon Wiesenthal Center, and *Not Idly By* by Pierre Sauvage. The *Encyclopedia Judaica*, which omitted the Bergson Group from its first edition, in 1972, invited this author to compose an entry about it in its 2007 edition. Other important reference volumes, such as the *Encyclopedia of American Jewish History* (2007), the *Columbia History of Jews and Judaism* (2008), the *Encyclopedia of the Diaspora* (2008), and the *Cambridge Dictionary of Jewish History* (2011), likewise concurred that the Bergson Group needed to be included in their descriptions of American Jewry's response to the Holocaust.

An association with the Bergson Group is now widely considered a badge of pride. The Speaker of the U.S. House of Representatives, Nancy Pelosi, wrote in her 2008 memoir of her delight at learning that her father, then-Congressman Thomas D'Alesandro, Jr., had been a supporter of the Bergson Group. The Chicago City Council voted in 2004 to name a street after Ben Hecht in acknowledgment of his Bergson Group activity. The governor of Utah in 2005 declared Elbert Thomas Day to honor the late senator's involvement with the Bergsonites.[209]

A number of mainstream Jewish leaders have publicly chastised their predecessors for opposing Bergson. In the foreword to this book and in other public statements, Seymour Reich, former chairman of the Conference of Presidents of Major American Jewish Organizations and president of B'nai B'rith International, has criticized the 1940s Jewish leadership for attacking Bergson instead of focusing on rescue. Rabbi Dr. David Ellenson, president of Hebrew Union College-Jewish Institute of Religion, said his predecessor, Rabbi Stephen S. Wise, "failed miserably" in his response to the Holocaust; Ellenson said Wise was "blinded" by his antipathy toward the Bergsonites and his "absolute and complete love" for President Roosevelt.[210]

Ellenson, Reich, Elie Wiesel, and numerous other mainstream Jewish leaders, including senior leaders of the Orthodox, Conservative, Reform, and Reconstructionist movements, signed the Wyman Institute's petitions to the United States Holocaust Memorial Museum, urging it to recognize the Bergson Group. In 2007, after five years of such petitions and other protests, the Museum did indeed redesign its panels on America's response to the Holocaust to incorporate acknowledgment of the Bergson Group's role in publicizing the Holocaust and bringing about the creation of the War Refugee Board. Other museums got it right from the start: the revamped Los Angeles Museum of the Holocaust and National Museum of American Jewish History, in Philadelphia, both of which (re)opened in 2010, included sections about the Bergson Group.

The Museum of Jewish Heritage/A Living Memorial to the Holocaust, in New York City, has held teacher training sessions about the Bergson Group; Holocaust museums in Texas, Rhode Island, and Illinois have included the Bergsonites in various ways; and the Brooklyn Holocaust Memorial Park has added a memorial plaque about the activists. The Jewish Historical Society of Greater Washington and the Jewish Historical Society of Maryland have sponsored programs and exhibits about the Bergson Group, and their parent body, the American Jewish Historical Society, has included the Bergson story in its literature. The list goes on.[211]

The passage of time, the cooling of passions, the work of a new generation of scholars, and the emergence of a new, more open-minded cadre of Jewish leaders, have combined to bring about the changes that Samuel Merlin once believed only his book could achieve. *Millions of Jews to Rescue* consequently serves not only as a corrective to a flawed historical record but also as the culmination of a decades-long process of maturation in American Jewish attitudes toward the community's response to the Holocaust.

AFTERWORD

by Jeremy Ben-Ami

Youngsters in every generation can relate to the pain of being dragged to the homes of their parents' friends and relatives, and then being forced to sit quietly through endless and often excruciatingly boring conversations about the past.

My experience was a little different. Yes, I was regularly dragged to the homes of assorted adults with whom I had little connection, but the conversation was anything but boring. Amidst the jokes told half in Hebrew and other languages that I didn't understand, and the frequent references to people and events I didn't recognize, I learned the amazing story of young men and women who changed history.

They told of breaking rules, sneaking into places they weren't supposed to enter, dodging the police, and generally causing such a tumult that one would think they were the rowdiest bunch of teenage troublemakers this side of *The Wild Ones*. Or you might have until you realized that they had been rescuing the lives of innocent people, dodging the Gestapo, and building history-making political coalitions that attracted the cream of Hollywood (including, ironically, the star of *The Wild Ones*, young Marlon Brando).

I was fortunate to have a front row seat as the veterans of the Bergson Group reminisced, and occasionally—but good naturedly—quarreled about the extraordinary battles they fought in the Jewish world and beyond in the 1930s and the 1940s. My father, Yitshaq Ben-Ami, remained close friends with Samuel Merlin throughout the post-Bergson Group decades. They were fixtures at these gatherings. Other prominent members of the group visited New York City periodically and they, too, were often a part of those conversations, including Hillel Kook (Peter Bergson), Harry Selden, and Maurice Rosenblatt. Merlin, with his professorial manner and pipe, was every bit the stereotypical European intellectual. He warmed to the role of house historian and

Samuel Merlin, circa 1965

everyone eagerly awaited the history of the Bergson Group that he was working on for as long as anyone could remember.

While waiting for "The Book," as everyone called Merlin's seemingly never-ending project, to emerge, I was piecing together their story. I was listening to their reminiscences and perusing the dusty books, periodicals, and newspaper clippings that filled my father's study and which he eventually used for writing his own memoir, *Days of Wrath, Years of Glory*.

One aspect of the story that always puzzled me was the nature of the attacks mounted against the Bergson activists. I have certainly learned that anyone who chooses to take part in public policy controversies is bound to invite critics; that's the nature of politics. What surprised me, however, was how often the Bergson Group's opponents, both at the time and in later years, tried to paint the group and the controversy it generated in narrow right-vs.-left political terms. My father and his colleagues were denounced as "rightwing extremists," "fascists," and "Irgun terrorists." I knew these men and women, and I read up on what they did in the 1930s and 1940s. Those descriptions were not even remotely close to the truth.

My father, Merlin, and their friends may have started their political activism as socialists or as members of Ze'ev Jabotinsky's Revisionist Zionist movement (or its youth wing, Betar), but they joined the Irgun Zvai Leumi, a militant underground group, to actively pursue national independence and to organize *aliyah bet* (illegal immigration of Jews from Europe) to save lives, not to advance a political agenda. Their immigration work in particular was neither rightwing nor leftwing. It was something all Jews should have agreed upon. (In fact, the Labor Zionists, after first scorning the Irgun for its *aliyah bet* activities, belatedly got into the *aliyah bet* action themselves.)

The same is true for the Bergson Group's campaign in the United States for the rescue of European Jewry, from 1943 to 1945. Rescue was a consensus issue. All Jews from right to left should have been able to support it. Critics who tried to discredit the Bergsonites by accusing them of being "covert rightwing Irgunists" were misleading the public—and jeopardizing the rescue campaign in order to score cheap political points.

The attacks scared off a few of the group's supporters, but did not resonate widely among the American public, for the simple reason that so many of the top people in the Bergson Group obviously came from the left. People such as Stella Adler, Ben Hecht, and Arthur Szyk were involved in many liberal causes. Harry Selden and Maurice Rosenblatt, whom I knew personally, were civil rights activists before they joined Bergson. Later, during the 1950s, they were leaders in the fight against Senator Joseph McCarthy. The names that appeared on the Bergson Group's letterhead or newspaper ads read like a Who's Who of liberal intellectuals and activists, among them Upton Sinclair (*The Jungle*), I. F. Stone, John

Gunther (*Death Be Not Proud*), Sinclair Lewis (*It Can't Happen Here*), Langston Hughes, and Paul Robeson. Leftwing newspapers, such as *PM*, and political magazines, such as *The Nation*, gave the Bergson Group generous coverage and strongly criticized the Roosevelt administration's refugee policies. Even the Labor Zionist youth magazine *Furrows* grudgingly praised the Bergson Group's rescue efforts. In short, rescue was never genuinely a right-vs.-left issue, despite the handful of partisans who tried to twist it for political gain.

After the war, the Bergson activists went in all political directions. Bergson, Merlin, and Jabotinsky were elected to the First Knesset as part of Menachem Begin's nationalist Herut party. But they soon fought against Begin, resigned from Herut, and left Israeli politics for good. In their views on the various major Israel-related controversies in the 1970s and beyond, the ex-Bergson activists could be found all across the political spectrum. It was obvious from the conversations I overheard in our living room and in others' homes that some of

Samuel Merlin and Peter Bergson, in the 1980s

them leaned to the right, some leaned to the left, and others came down in the middle. Any attempt to pigeonhole them all as "rightwingers" was mistaken and unfair.

As frustrated as the Bergson veterans all felt about the long delays in Merlin''s completion of the manuscript, the upside is that the story will now be read and learned by a new generation. Today's readers will be introduced to this powerful and important story without the burden of political blinders and the right-vs.-left rivalries of their parents' generation. I hope that one of the most important achievements of Merlin's book, *Millions of Jews to Rescue*, will be to put to rest the right-vs.-left myth about the Bergson Group. New readers can approach the story objectively and understand it on its own merits, without the name-calling and bitter partisanship of the past.

It's time for a clean start in reflecting on the difficult history of the last century. It is time for us to take a fresh look at what happened and why, and learn from it.

Jeremy Ben-Ami is founder and president of J Street, a pro-Israel, pro-peace lobby. He has worked and lived in Israel and has served as Deputy Domestic Policy Advisor to President Bill Clinton in his first administration.

NOTES

Abbreviations Used

BLP   Breckinridge Long Papers, Library of Congress
FDRL   Franklin D. Roosevelt Library, Hyde Park, NY
MD   Morgenthau Diaries, Franklin D. Roosevelt Library, Hyde Park, NY
MZ   Metzudat Ze'ev (Jabotinsky Archives), Tel Aviv, Israel
PRO   Public Record Office, London, England
PSGC   Palestine State Groups Collection, Yale University
RSD   Records of the State Department, National Archives, Washington, D.C.

1   Shmuel Tamir, *Ben Ha'aretz HaZot: Autobiographia* [Hebrew] (Tel Aviv: Zamora Beitan, 2002), Vol. 1, 218, cites a remark by Merlin to this effect. Miriam Chaikin, who worked alongside Merlin in the Bergson Group's New York City headquarters from 1940 to 1948, recalls an anecdote Merlin once related to her in which, as a child, he fell ill and the doctor insisted that the high fat content in pork was necessary to cure his ailment. Merlin noted that his mother followed the doctor's advice because, although she strictly observed the Jewish dietary regulations, she knew that potentially saving a life took precedence over the laws of keeping kosher. (Rafael Medoff interview with Miriam Chaikin, New York City, 18 August 2009.)

2   This description, which although pseudonymous was almost certainly authored by Merlin, appeared in *Save Human Lives: Report of Activities and Financial Statement, Emergency Committee to Save the Jewish People of Europe* (New York: Emergency Committee to Save the Jewish People of Europe, 1944), 24.

3   Joseph B. Schechtman and Yehuda Benari, *History of the Revisionist Movement - Volume 1: 1925-1930* (Tel Aviv: Hadar, 1970), 406. Friedman-Yalin (1913-1980), who later Hebraicized his name to Yalin-Mor [sometimes spelled Yellin-Mor], served from 1942 to 1948 as one of the three leaders of the militant Palestine underground group LEHI (acronym for *Lohamei Herut Yisrael*, or Fighters for the Freedom of Israel, better known as the Stern Group).

4   Natan Yalin-Mor, *Shanot B'Terem* [Hebrew] (Tel Aviv: Kineret, 1990), 21.

5   Merlin interview with Monty N. Penkower, 18 January 1978, transcript courtesy of Prof. Penkower.

6   Merlin later recalled meeting Bergson for the first time in Warsaw in 1937. (Merlin interview with Monty N. Penkower, 27 March 1972, transcript courtesy of Prof. Penkower.)

7   Ibid.

8   Merlin to Weintraub, 19 August 1981, Samuel Merlin Papers [hereafter SMP], The David S. Wyman Institute for Holocaust Studies, Washington, D.C.

9   This statement appeared on a U.S. government form Merlin filled out in 1944 to register as a foreign agent. (United States Department of Justice Foreign Agents Registration form, filled out by Samuel Merlin, F25/651, Central Zionist Archives, Jerusalem.)

10 Merlin interview with Penkower, 1972, op.cit.

11 Rafael Medoff interview with Prof. Yechiam Weitz, Jerusalem, 3 December 2010.

12 Ibid.; Rafael Medoff interview with Elisha Yalin-Mor, Tel Aviv, 9 December 2010; Rafael Medoff interview with Ruth Tamir, Ehud Duchovni and Noga Tamir Duchovni, Herzliya, 9 December 2010; Rafael Medoff interview with Uri Avnery, Tel Aviv, 13 December 2010.

13 Ibid.

14 Samuel Merlin, ed., *The Big Powers and the Present Crisis in the Middle East* (New York: Institute for Mediterranean Affairs, 1975); Samuel Merlin, *The Search for Peace in the Middle East: The Story of President Bourguiba's Campaign for a Negotiated Peace Between Israel and the Arab States* (South Brunswick, NJ: Thomas Yoseloff, 1968).

15 See, for example, Samuel Halpern, *The Political World of American Zionism* (Detroit: Wayne State University Press, 1961); Arthur D. Morse, *While Six Million Died: A Chronicle of American Apathy* (New York: Random House, 1968); and Henry L. Feingold, *The Politics of Rescue: The Roosevelt Administration and the Holocaust, 1938-1945* (New Brunswick, Rutgers University Press, 1970).

16 For example, Stephen S. Wise, *Challenging Years: The Autobiography of Stephen S. Wise* (New York: Putnam, 1949); Joseph M. Proskauer, *A Segment of My Times* (New York: Farrar, Straus and Company, 1950); Morris D. Waldman, *Nor By Power* (New York: International Universities Press, 1953); Nahum Goldmann, *The Autobiography of Nahum Goldmann: Sixty Years of Jewish Life* (New York: Holt, Rinehart and Winston, 1969); Meyer Weisgal, *...So Far: An Autobiography*(New York: Random House, 1971); and Emanuel Neumann, *In the Arena: An Autobiographical Memoir* (New York: Herzl Press, 1976).

17 For example, Naomi W. Cohen, *Not Free to Desist: The American Jewish Committee 1906-1966* (Philadelphia: Jewish Publication Society of America, 1972); Yehuda Bauer, *My Brother's Keeper: A History of the American Jewish Joint Distribution Committee, Volume 1: 1929-1939* (Philadelphia: Jewish Publication Society of America, 1974); and Yehuda Bauer, *American Jewry and the Holocaust, Volume 2: 1939-1945* (Detroit: Wayne University Press, 1981).

18 Harry L. Selden, an editor and journalist who was one of the Bergson Group's earliest and most active American supporters, was undoubtedly capable of writing such a book, but never seriously contemplated doing so since Merlin had taken on the task. (Rafael Medoff interview with Harry L. Selden, Rockville, MD, 6 June 1996.)

19 Merlin to Kook, 28 May 1972, 1, SMP.

20 Merlin to Kook, 14 May 1974, 13, SMP.

21 Merlin to Kook, 24 August 1976, 3, SMP.

22 Merlin to Kook, 16 March 1979, 2, SMP.

23 Colin Campbell, "Leading U.S. Jews to Explore Painful Holocaust Questions," *New York Times* [hereafter NYT], 27 September 1981, 1; Bernard Weinraub, "Panel on U.S. Jews and Holocaust is Dissolved," NYT, 4 January 1983, 1; Bernard Weinraub, "Study on U.S. Jews and Holocaust to Resume," NYT, 20 January 1983, 1; Walter Goodman, "American Jewish Groups Faulted In a Report on Holocaust Victims," NYT, 21 March 1984, 1.

24 Merlin to Kook, 25 February 1983, SMP.

25 *Save Human Lives: Report of Activities and Financial Statement, Emergency Committee to Save the Jewish People of Europe* (New York: Emergency Committee to Save the Jewish People of Europe, 1944).

26 Jewish socialists in interwar Eastern Europe who rejected Zionism.

27 Merlin's term means "nationalists" in German and here is intended to refer to deeply assimilated European Jews who rejected all but the most nominal connection to Jewish identity.

28 Merlin's note: "A Special Minorities Committee of the Paris Peace Conference formulated in December 1919 the basic provisions of guarantees of ethnic minorities in East European countries that gained independence as a result of the collapse of the Hapsburg and Russian Empires. After protracted resistance, the successor states agreed to sign the guarantees because the Principal Allied Powers made such agreement a firm condition to recognize the sovereignty of these states, each of which had national minorities. However, the phrase 'national rights' was not included, only the specific elements which make for quasi cultural autonomy. The suggestion that a special article be included in the Covenant of the League of Nations guaranteeing these rights was abandoned, but the supervision of the implementation of the treaties was delegated to the League of Nations."

29   Merlin referred the reader to the book *The War and the Jew,* by Vladimir (Ze'ev) Jabotinsky, and in particular the section concerning what Jabotinsky called "the antisemitism of things," that is, the confluence of objective circumstances that made severe antisemitism inevitable in Europe.

30   The first Labor Zionist organization, known as Poalei Zion and based on the principles of Socialist Zionism, appeared in Minsk, Russia, in 1900. Additional Poalei Zion groups arose elsewhere in Europe and they formed a single international organization at a convention in the Hague in 1907. Internal conflicts in the world socialist movement, especially concerning the movement's relationship with the Soviet Union, led to a division within Poalei Zion. Two rival factions arose at the world Labor Zionist conference in Vienna in 1920. The more conservative Right Poalei Zion faction merged with Hapoel Hatzair to form Ahdut Ha'avoda. The Left Poalei Zion was explicitly Marxist, viewing Ber Borochov as its ideologist. In 1930, Ahdut Ha'avoda and Hapoel Hatzair merged to become Mapai, an acronym for Mifleget Poalei Eretz Yisrael. Mapai was the largest vote-getter, and hence the dominant party in Israel's governing coalitions, from 1949 until 1977.

31   Russian Zionist leader Vladimir Ze'ev Jabotinsky launched Revisionist Zionism in 1925, as a militant faction within the world Zionist movement. Regarding the Zionist movement's strategy for achieving a Jewish national home in Palestine as too cautious and distrustful of British promises to advance the upbuilding of Palestine, he advocated revising its strategy to take a more forceful approach. Revisionism had particularly strong appeal among Eastern European Jewish youth, and its youth movement, Betar, attracted substantial numbers of adherents, especially in Poland. The Revisionists opposed the socialist economic theories of Labor Zionism, and clashes between Labor Zionist strikers and Revisionist non-union workers occurred frequently in Palestine in the 1930s. In response to Palestinian Arab rioting in the late 1920s and 1930s, Revisionists and Betar members created the Irgun Zvai Leumi, an underground militia that regarded Jabotinsky as its spiritual leader even though he was not its actual commander.

32   Established by the Fifth Zionist Congress, in 1901, as a fund for the purchasing and developing land in Palestine. One of its innovative fundraising techniques, the blue and white coin collection box, became an international Zionist symbol. By 1939, more than 60 percent of all Jewish owned-land was held by the JNF. When the State of Israel was established in 1948, it held some 232,000 acres.

33   The Keren Hayesod, or Palestine Foundation Fund, was established in 1920 to serve as the chief fundraising arm of the World Zionist Organization. It soon assumed responsibility for the entire operating budget of the Jewish Agency for Palestine, the de facto government of Palestine Jewry under the

British Mandate. Keren Hayesod played a major role financing immigration, absorption, education, housing, and development for the *yishuv* (the Palestine Jewish community).

34 The international youth movement of Revisionist Zionism, Betar was founded in Riga, Latvia, in 1923 by the Zionist leader Vladimir Ze'ev Jabotinsky. Betar is an acronym for *Brit Al Shem Yosef Trumpeldor*, or the Covenant in Memory of Yosef Trumpeldor, referring to the legendary Zionist pioneer who was killed while defending the Tel Hai outpost in northern Palestine from Arab attackers in 1920. Expecting military force to play a crucial role in the establishment and survival of a Jewish state, Betar focused on paramilitary training and preparedness. It ran Jewish naval training bases in Italy and Latvia, and Aviation training Schools in Lod, Paris, Johannesburg, and New York. Betar's themes of Jewish nationalist pride and *aliyah* as the answer to inevitable diaspora antisemitism resonated in Jewish communities suffering from poverty and anti-Jewish discrimination. At its peak, on the eve of World War II, Betar had almost 100,000 members in 26 countries. Betar played an active role in prewar efforts to smuggle European Jews into Palestine in defiance of British immigration restrictions. Betar members also figured prominently in armed resistance against the Nazis in a number of ghettoes in Europe, including the Warsaw Ghetto uprising. The majority of Betar members in Europe were killed in the Holocaust.

35 Essayist, poet, translator, and Zionist orator, Jabotinsky (1880-1940) was raised in an acculturated, middle-class family in Odessa, Russia. He conceived, and helped convince the British to create, the Jewish Legion, an all-Jewish unit of the British army that helped capture Palestine from the Turks in World War I. In response to Palestinian Arab rioting in Jerusalem in 1920, Jabotinsky helped create the Haganah, a Jewish self-defense group. In 1925, Jabotinsky created his own faction of the Zionist movement, the League of Zionist-Revisionists, which argued that the Zionists needed to revise their strategy and adopt a more aggressive approach to bringing about the creation of a Jewish state. The Revisionists later broke away from the World Zionist Organization entirely. Barred by the British from entering Palestine as of 1930, Jabotinsky spent the last decade of his life speaking to Jewish communities around the world, especially in Eastern Europe, where he warned of an incoming tidal wave of antisemitism.

36 Whether "national home" meant a sovereign state, and whether it would be in all of Palestine or just a part of it, were crucial questions left unanswered by the wording of the Balfour Declaration.

37 The Austrian-born Adolf Hitler had long dreamed of making Austria a part of modern Germany, and on March 12, 1938, the German Army, with

ample support from the Austrian populace, crossed the border to enforce the German annexation of Austria, known as the *Anschluss*. Although unification of Germany and Austria was prohibited by the post-World War I Versailles Treaty, there was no substantive international opposition to Hitler's action.

38 Weizmann (1874-1952), a Russian Zionist leader and chemist, played a key role in the lobbying that brought about the Balfour Declaration of 1917, England's promise to facilitate the creation of a Jewish national home in Palestine. He headed the post-World War I Zionist Commission sent by the British government to Palestine to advise the authorities on plans for settling and developing the country and was among the leaders of the Zionist delegation to the Versailles peace conference in 1919. Weizmann was elected president of the World Zionist Organization in 1920 and served until 1931, when his remarks doubting the need for a Jewish majority in Palestine resulted in his temporary ouster. He was reelected to the presidency in 1935 and served until 1946.

39 Merlin's note: "A hero of a parable by the great Yiddish writer Y.L. Peretz (1852-1915). He bore all the miseries and indignities of life without ever complaining or asking any questions. Working as a porter, he fell and was crushed under a heavy load. No one paid attention that he lay dead there on the sidewalk. If it were a dog, people would stop. In heaven, they wanted to compensate him, and when asked what was his desire, he answered: a warm, buttered roll."

40 Here and elsewhere in the manuscript, Merlin uses the broad term "the Zionists." A more precise term would have been "mainstream Zionists" or "Zionist leadership," since, in fact, he was referring not to all Zionists, but to all Zionists except for the Revisionist Zionists. Among Merlin and his colleagues, the sense of alienation from the Zionist world became so deep that they became accustomed to characterizing their opponents as "the Zionists," even though, of course, Jabotinsky's followers, too, were Zionists.

41 The term refers to a government policy position paper. The nickname "white paper" gained currency in 20th century England, where short position papers were bound with white covers, while longer ones were bound with blue covers and known as "blue books." The May 1939 White Paper to which Merlin refers is also sometimes called the MacDonald White Paper, after its nominal author, Colonial Secretary Malcolm MacDonald. It restricted Jewish immigration to Palestine to 15,000 annually for the next five years, with subsequent allotments to be determined in consultation with Arab leaders.

42 Gilbert's most extensive defense of Churchill is his book *Churchill and the Jews: A Lifelong Friendship* (New York: Henry Holt, 2007). Other scholarship on

Churchill's response to the Holocaust has challenged Gilbert's perspective. Michael J. Cohen, in his 1985 study, *Churchill and the Jews: 1900-1948* (London: Frank Cass), emphasized that despite Churchill's pro-Zionist rhetoric, as prime minister he approved the deportation of Jewish refugees to the remote island of Mauritius, in the Indian Ocean. He also never canceled the White Paper, which blocked all but a handful of European Jews from reaching Palestine during the Holocaust. In 2007, Cambridge University historian Dr. Richard Toye found, in the Churchill archives, an unpublished essay by Churchill containing antisemitic statements. In the article, titled "How the Jews Can Combat Persecution," Churchill denounced the "cruel and relentless" persecution of the Jews, but then criticized German Jewish refugees in England for their willingness to work for less pay than non-Jewish laborers, which, he claimed, caused antisemitism. Churchill's article also justified antisemitic responses to Jewish moneylenders: "Every Jewish moneylender recalls Shylock and the idea of the Jews as usurers. And you cannot reasonably expect a struggling clerk or shopkeeper, paying 40 or 50 per cent interest on borrowed money to a 'Hebrew Bloodsucker,' to reflect that almost every other way of life was closed to the Jewish people." (*The Independent*, March 11, 2007, 3.)

43 *Hitler's War* (London: Hodder & Stoughton, 1977).

44 At first an advocate of Jewish acculturation, Pinsker (1821-1891) embraced Zionism in response to the Russian pogroms of 1881. After the publication of *AutoEmancipation*, Pinsker became active in the early Russian Zionist group Hibbat Zion. He was elected its chairman in 1884.

45 Herzl (1860-1904), an assimilated Jewish journalist based in Vienna, turned to Zionism in response to the wave of antisemitism he witnessed while covering the Dreyfus trial in Paris. He organized the First Zionist Congress, in Basle in 1897, established the World Zionist Organization, and led the Zionist movement until his death.

46 In response to a wave of protests in Palestine and England, Lord Samuel granted Jabotinsky amnesty on July 1, 1920, and the following year the conviction was annulled.

47 Achimeir (1896-1962) led the militant Brit ha-Biryonim faction of the Revisionist movement.

48 The poet and playwright Ya'akov Cahan (1881–1960) coined this phrase in his 1903 poem, "Biryonim." He was a prominent figure in Hebrew education in interwar Poland, and helped found the Hebrew cultural organization Berit Ivrit Olamit (1931). Kahan was also an early activist in the Revisionist Zionist movement, but dropped out when the Revisionists seceded from the World Zionist Organization. He settled in Palestine in 1934.

49 In addition to Achimeir, the British arrested two young Revisionist Zionists, Avraham "Abrasha" Stavsky and Zvi Rosenblatt, and accused them of

carrying out the killing. Rosenblatt was acquitted. Stavsky was convinced and sentenced to death, but the conviction was overturned on appeal. During the course of the trial, an atmosphere of near-civil war prevailed in Palestine. The anti-Revisionist hostility incited by the Labor Zionists seriously damaged support for Jabotinsky in the 1933 elections to the World Zionist Congress and undoubtedly hastened his decision to have the Revisionists formally secede from the world Zionist movement.

50   Italian political activist Giuseppe Mazzini (1805-1872) initiated a series of uprisings that sought to bring about the unification of Italy's various regions into a single, modern democratic nation. His efforts also inspired similar movements elsewhere in Europe.

51   Tehomi's tenure with the Haganah did not go as well as he had hoped. Many of those who followed him back to the Haganah later left and joined the Irgun, and he did not rise in the ranks of the Haganah leadership. In the later 1940s, he served for a time with the Bergson Group's Hebrew Committee of National Liberation.

52   Kook adopted the pseudonym in order to shield his well-known family in Palestine, including his uncle, Chief Rabbi Abraham Isaac Hacohen Kook, from the glare of publicity resulting from his controversial activities.

53   Selden (1908-2004), the managing editor of the humor magazine *Judge*, became a dollar-a-year-man for the Bergson Group at its inception in 1940, and remained part of its leadership circle through 1948.

54   Wilf (1905-1980), a founder and leader of the Bergson Group's Philadelphia chapter, later became executive director of its American League for a Free Palestine, in New York City.

55   Rabinowitz (1916-2005) left his pulpit in Hagerstown, Maryland, to work full-time for the Bergson Group, primarily as its chief lobbyist in Washington, from 1940 to 1948.

56   The Dubiners founded and led the Bergson Group's Canadian League for a Free Palestine.

57   Horwitt (1898-1990), who was born in Russia and raised in the United States, was an award-winning inventor and industrial designer. In addition to his public activities in support of the Bergson Group, he volunteered his farm in Stockbridge, Massachusetts, in the late 1940s, for Irgun Zvai Leumi supporters to store weapons and engage in military training.

58   Untermeyer (née Antin, 1896-1983), a municipal court judge in Ohio and then an editor and author in New York City, was one of the leaders of the Bergson Group's American League for a Free Palestine.

59   A founder and leader of the Philadelphia branch of the Bergson Group, Yampolsky later became the national organization's pro bono accountant. In 1945-46, Yampolsky, assisted by his son Jack, fended off politically-

motivated attempts by the Internal Revenue Service to demonstrate that the Bergson Group was guilty of financial irregularities. The IRS was unsuccessful.

60 Ben-Eliezer (1913-1970) was part of the Bergson Group's leadership circle from 1940 until he returned to Palestine in 1943, where he served as one of the leaders of the Irgun. After Israel's establishment, he was elected to the Knesset, eventually reaching the post of Deputy Speaker of the Knesset.

61 Rafaeli (1910-1999), who earned a Ph.D. in political science at the University of Heidelberg, was active in the Irgun's *aliyah bet* efforts in the late 1930s, before being sent to the United States. He was a leader of the Bergson Group from 1940-1943, then served in the United States army before returning to the Bergson Group in 1947.

62 Eri Jabotinsky (1910-1969) was active in the Irgun's *aliyah bet* activities, for which he was jailed by the British, in Palestine, in 1940. Upon his release, he traveled to the United States, where he became a central figure in the Bergson Group.

63 Merlin is quoting from an unnamed internal Bergson Group memorandum (n.d.).

64 The proposed Jewish state would have been 2,955 square miles. By way of comparison, note that the original territory of the Palestine Mandate was 43,075 miles, and Israel within its pre-1967 borders was 8,020 square miles.

65 Quoted on page 215 of the World Zionist Organization's journal, *New Judea*, August-September 1937.

66 Patterson (1867-1947) rose to fame in England in 1898 because of his success in hunting down two huge lions that were terrorizing workers building the Tsavo railway bridge in British-occupied Kenya. That episode was chronicled in his 1907 book, *The Man-Eaters of Tsavo*, and in the 1996 Paramount movie *The Ghost and the Darkness,* starring Val Kilmer and Michael Douglas. After his experience commanding the Jewish Legion, Patterson became a staunch advocate of Jabotinsky's Revisionist Zionism and undertook numerous public speaking engagements to promote the cause.

67 Briscoe (1894-1969), an active member of the revolutionary Irish Republican Army and its political arm, the Sinn Fein, served in the Irish parliament from 1927 to 1965, during which time he also twice served as mayor of Dublin.

68 Newman (1893-1972), a disciple of Rabbi Stephen S. Wise and rabbi of Congregation Rodeph Sholom in New York City, was one of the very few Reform rabbis to support the Jabotinsky movement. He served as president of the New Zionist Organization of America, the U.S. wing of the

Revisionist Zionists, from 1938 to 1940, and was occasionally involved with the Bergson Group's activities as well.

69 The background to the creation of the Council is described by its founder, Emanuel Neumann, in his book *In the Arena: An Autobiographical Memoir* (New York: Herzl Press, 1975), 156.

70 See Rafael Medoff, "Hearst and the Holocaust," *Jerusalem Post,* 23 April 2009, 8.

71 Including three U.S. Senators, twelve members of the House of Representatives, the bishops of Los Angeles and Lexington (KY), theologian Reinhold Niebuhr, exiled German Jewish novelist Lion Feuchtwanger, actors Eddie Cantor and Melvyn Douglas, Mutual Broadcasting System president Alfred McCosker, and the presidents of Stanford University and the University of Kansas City. "Samuel A. Merlin, journalist" was also listed among the signatories.

72 Szyk (1894-1951), a Polish-born illustrator and miniaturist, so impressed British officials with his anti-Nazi caricatures that they sent him to the United States in 1940 in the hope of influencing the American public to support U.S. military intervention against Germany. Szyk became the editorial cartoonist for the *New York Post*, contributed to many other newspapers and magazines, and assumed an active role in the Bergson Group, providing illustrations for many of its advertisements and brochures.

73 Celler (1888-1981), Democrat of New York, served in the U.S. House of Representatives from 1923 to 1973. He was a panelist at the Bergson Group's July 1943 Emergency Conference to Save the Jewish People of Europe, in New York City; spoke out strongly against the Roosevelt administration's refugee policies on a number of occasions; and repeatedly sought, without success, to bring about a liberalization of America's immigration practices.

74 Dickstein (1885-1954), Democrat of New York, served in the U.S. House of Representatives from 1923 to 1945, and chaired the House Committee on Naturalization and Immigration during much of that period, but was unable to alter America's immigration policies. Dickstein was a panelist at the Bergson Group's July 1943 Emergency Conference to Save the Jewish People of Europe, a speaker at its April 1944 conference on the plight of Hungarian Jewry, and a participant in other Bergson activities.

75 Nizer (1902-1994), was a prominent criminal defense attorney in New York City. His name appeared on a number of Bergson Group newspaper advertisements. His many high-profile activities in later years included co-creating the movie ratings system of the Motion Picture Association of America; writing the foreword to the final report of the Warren Commission (investigating the assassination of President John F. Kennedy); and authoring the 1972 best-seller *The Implosion Conspiracy*, concerning the Rosenberg case.

76 Ross (1909-1967) was one of the most famous Jewish prizefighters of all time. From 1934 to 1938, he had the unique distinction of holding championship titles in three weight classes—lightweight, junior welterweight, and welterweight—at the same time. After his discharge from the Marines in 1944, Ross became a supporter of the Emergency Committee to Save the Jewish People of Europe. He also became active in another Bergson committee, the American League for a Free Palestine, heading up a proposed brigade of American Jewish volunteers to aid the fight for independence in Palestine, which was to be called the George Washington Legion. The State Department prevented it from going to the Middle East.

77 Weill (1900-1950), a world famous composer and refugee from Nazi Germany, contributed original scores to the Bergson Group's two theatrical productions, *We Will Never Die* (1943) and *A Flag is Born* (1946).

78 Rosenblatt (1915-2005), a civil rights activist, was a full time Washington lobbyist for the Bergson Group from 1945 to 1948. In later years he was a leader of the National Committee for an Effective Congress, which played a major role in bringing about the downfall of Senator Joseph McCarthy.

79 Rifkin, proprietor of a business called Global Travel Service, was a leader of the Philadelphia branch of the American League for a Free Palestine.

80 A judge for the New York City Magistrates' Court and a leader of the city's Fusion Party, Potter was active in the Emergency Committee to Save the Jewish People of Europe.

81 Betty Keane Caplan and her sister Rose grew up in Kansas City and moved to Manhattan in the 1930s, hoping to break into show business. They met Peter Bergson when he and Merlin happened to rent an apartment down the hall and imposed upon the women to use their telephone until theirs was connected. Betty and Rose gradually became involved with the Bergson Group, working in a variety of capacities from clerical work to public relations. After the war, Peter and Betty were married.

82 Philip (1902-1970) served as Interior Minister for the Free French during World War II, and later was Minister of Finance from 1946 to 1947.

83 Singh (1907-1994) served in India's cabinet continuously from 1952 to 1975, holding such posts as Foreign Minister and Defense Minister.

84 Rhee (1875-1965) served as president of the Republic of Korea from 1919 to 1925, and later as the first president of South Korea, from 1948 to 1960. He was a panelist at the Bergson Group's Second Emergency Conference to Save the Jewish People of Europe, in New York City in August 1944.

85 Sforza (1872-1952), exiled from Italy in 1926 for opposing Mussolini, returned after the Allied liberation in 1943 and later served as Foreign Minister, from 1947 to 1951. He was a panelist at the Bergson Group's July

1943 Emergency Conference to Save the Jewish People of Europe, in New York City.

86 Davila was Rumania's ambassador to the United States from 1929 to 1938. He served as a panelist at the Bergson Group's July 1943 Emergency Conference to Save the Jewish People of Europe, in New York City, and at its Second Emergency Conference to Save the Jewish People of Europe, in New York City in August 1944.

87 For more on Avuka, see Allon Gal, "Brandeis' Social-Zionism," *Studies in Zionism* 8:2 (Autumn 1987), 207-09, and Samuel Grand, "A History of Zionist Youth Organizations in the United States," Ph.D. dissertation, Columbia University, 1958, 89-131.

88 David S. Wyman, *The Abandonment of the Jews: America and the Holocaust, 1941-1945* (New York: Pantheon, 1984), 337.

89 Halifax to Foreign Office, 5 October 1942, FO 371/31379, Public Record Office, London [hereafter PRO].

90 Halifax to Foreign Office, 15 January 1943, FO 371/35031, PRO; Halifax to Foreign Office, 25 May 1943 FO 371/35035, PRO; Halifax to Foreign Office, 6 July 1943 FO 371/35036, PRO.

91 The origin and fate of the proposed statement is chronicled in Monty N. Penkower, "The 1943 Joint Anglo-American Statement on Palestine," in Melvin Urofsky, ed. *Herzl Year Book VIII - Essays in American Zionism* (New York: Herzl Press, 1978), 212-241. For an account which emphasizes the role of the Bergson Group in the affair, see Louis Rapoport, *Shake Heaven and Earth: Peter Bergson and the Struggle to Rescue the Jews of Europe* (Jerusalem: Gefen, 1999), 95-108.

92 Gruner (1912-1947), a Betar activist, came to Palestine in 1940 aboard the Irgun-sponsored *aliyah bet* ship *Sakarya* and joined the Irgun. He enlisted in the British Army in 1941 and then served in the Jewish Brigade. After his demobilization, Gruner rejoined the Irgun. On April 23, 1946, he was captured during an Irgun raid on a British police station, and was subsequently sentenced to death. The impending execution of Gruner and three Irgun comrades became a major public controversy in the Jewish world in the spring of 1947.

93 Quoted in Lucy S. Dawidowicz, *The War Against the Jews 1933-1945* (Holt, Rinehart and Winston, 1975), 142.

94 Helpern (1901-1962), a sea captain, was chief of military training for Betar and head of its Jewish Marine Legion.

95 Wyman, *Abandonment*, 98.

96 "Rumor Behind the News," *Hamigdal* 3 (April 1943), 14; Merlin to Ziff, 23 April 1943, File 1:8, Palestine Statehood Groups Collection, Yale University [hereafter PSGC].

97 Memorandum, "Views of the Government of the United States Regarding Topics Included in the Agenda for Discussion with the British Government" [March 1943], Box 203, File: Refugee Conference - Bermuda Conference, Breckinridge Long Papers [hereafter BLP], Library of Congress.

98 *Congressional Record* - Senate, 6 May 1943, 4131-4134 and 10 May 1943, 4205-4207.

99 Long to Welles et al, 4 May 1943 and 10 May 1943, Box 203, BLP.

100 Ibid.

101 *Congressional Record* - Senate, 10 May 1943, 4207.

102 R. E. Murphy to Long, 23 September 1943, Long Papers; State Department to American Consulate, Jerusalem, 15 February 1944, File 867N.20/213, Records of the State Department [hereafter RSD], National Archives, Washington, D.C.

103 Paul Alling to G. Howland Shaw, 22 April 1944, File 867 N.01/2324, RSD.

104 Loy Henderson to Joseph Grew, 12 May 1945, File 867N.01/3-1643, RSD.

105 Memorandum of Conversation with Nahum Goldmann, 19 May 1944, 867N.01.2347; Memorandum of Conversation with Morris Waldman, 10 January 1944, File 3:67, PSGC.

106 Halifax to Foreign Office, May 24, 1944, FO371/40131.5940, PRO; Balfour to High Commissioner, August 9, 1945, FO371/45399.8397, PRO.

107 Loy Henderson to Joseph Grew, May 12, 1945, File 867N.01/3-1643, RSD.

108 Fred L. Israel, ed. *The War Diary of Breckinridge Long: Selections from the Years 1939-1944* (Lincoln: University of Nebraska Press 1966), 312-313 (entry for 19 May 1943).

109 Israel, *War Diary*, 329 (entry for 13 September 1943).

110 Strong to Long, 26 August 1943, and Long to Hull , 1 September 1943, BLP.

111 Bucknell to Long, 17 May 1943, BLP.

112 *Congressional Record* - Senate, 10 May 1943, 42307.

113 *Congressional Record* - Senate, 10 May 1943, 4305.

114 *Congressional Record* - Senate, 6 May 1943, 4131.

115 Merlin's source note reads: "From a personal memo of the time by the author." The memo cannot be traced, but Bergson's account of his conversation with Truman squares with Merlin's summary: "[H]e didn't charge us with anything, he just said, 'I wish to resign from the committee as of now.' Meaning he didn't put any aspersions on the past. He didn't say 'because you used my name'—he just said—I talked to him and he said, 'I like my friends', in his crisp little voice, 'Scott Lucas is a friend of mine.' I said, 'Well Senator, you know we are right and he is wrong.' He says, 'Yes, but he's a friend of mine, and I'm loyal to my friends, and I want to help Scott Lucas.'

He took it as a politician, one politician to another." (David S. Wyman and Rafael Medoff, *A Race Against Death: Peter Bergson, America, and the Holocaust* [New York: The New Press, 2002], 85.)

116 *Congressional Record* - Senate, 6 May 1943, 4131-4134.

117 Capper to Gabriel Wechsler, 17 May 1943, reprinted in *The Answer*, 5 June 1943, 16.

118 *PM*, 7 May 1943, 6.

119 *The Answer*, 5 June 1943, 18.

120 Gillette, of Iowa, Johnson, of Colorado, and Thomas, of Utah, were all Democrats and were thus, in effect, acting in defiance of the Roosevelt administration by supporting the Bergson Group.

121 Rabbi Stephen S. Wise tried, unsuccessfully, to persuade Bishop Tucker to withdraw from the conference. (See Wyman, *Abandonment*, 144.)

122 Willkie to Lerner, 20 July 1943, File: Emergency Committee to Save the Jewish People of Europe - First Emergency Conference to Save the Jewish People of Europe - 2/1/11-chet, Bergson Group Collections, Metzudat Ze'ev (Jabotinsky Institute), Tel Aviv [hereafter MZ].

123 Morgenthau to Lerner, 20 July 1943, ibid.

124 "Hoover Urges Central African Jewish Refuge," *New York Herald Tribune*, 26 July 1943, 10.

125 "Will Rogers in London," Independent Jewish Press Service, 6 August 1943, 3a; *A Year in the Service of Humanity: A Survey of the Activities of the Emergency Committee to Save the Jewish People of Europe, July 1943-August 1944* (New York: 1944), 3-5.

126 Early to Lerner, 22 August 1943, President's Official Files, File 76-C, Franklin D. Roosevelt Library, Hyde Park, NY [hereafter FDRL].

127 In a later interview, Merlin said that he "was in charge of contacting various groups of rabbis" and that the Jewish National Council, a group created by the Bergsonites, had played an active role in organizing the protest. Three Jewish journalists who were active in the Council and in other Bergson activities, Samuel Rosen, M.J.Nurenberger, and Isaac Zaar, were particularly helpful in establishing contacts with rabbinical leaders and publicizing the march. Merlin described the event as "a genuine, emotional, deeply felt demonstration of identi[fication] with what went on in Europe, which didn't take place in non-Orthodox circles, and the problem, we felt, was that the only Jews who would feel this very profoundly, individually, were this group..." (Merlin interview with Monty N. Penkower, 18 January 1978, transcript courtesy of Prof. Penkower.)

128 The appearance of the marchers had a "tremendous influence" on members of Congress, Merlin said later. These were "exotic [-looking] people they hadn't seen before ... beards, black coats, tears that came down, seriousness

of faces; some looked like the prophets of old." Psychologically, it was a very different experience from meeting with a clean-shaven Reform rabbi in modern attire, such as Stephen Wise or Abba Hillel Silver, Merlin noted. (Merlin interview with Penkower, op.cit.)

129 Samuel Margoshes, "News and Views," *Der Tog*, 10 October 1943, 1.

130 Wyman and Medoff, *Race*,139.

131 Wyman, *Abandonment*,154.

132 Bloom (1870-1949), who served in the House from 1923 until his death, was a staunch supporter of the Roosevelt administration's refugee policy.

133 Her experiences are detailed in Rochelle G. Saidel, ed. *Fiorello's Sister: Gemma La Guardia Gluck's Story* (Syracuse, NY: Syracuse University Press, 2007). The history of the Ravensbruck is recounted in Dr. Saidel's book *The Jewish Women of Ravensbruck Concentration Camp* (Madison, WI: University of Wisconsin Press, 2004).

134 Gillette to Selden, 1 August 1944, Box 1, Folder 12, PSGC.

135 Israel, *War Diary*, 366.

136 Cannon to Atherton and Dunn, 12 November 1941, 871.4016/281, RSD.

137 Wise to Roosevelt, 2 December 1942, File: Correspondence between FDR and Wise, 1929-1945, Stephen S. Wise Pa, American Jewish Historical Society, New York City.

138 Wyman, *Abandonment*, 182.

139 From Merlin's wording, it appears that the particular statement he is quoting came from a conversation between himself and DuBois, with whom he and Bergson were well acquainted, both during the war and afterwards. However, similar statements were made by DuBois on numerous occasions, including the December 20, 1943 Treasury Department staff meeting recounted in the Morgenthau Diaries [hereafter MD], 688II/148-171, FDRL.

140 MD 688I/111-118.

141 Ibid.

142 MD 718/172-173.

143 MD 688II/148-171.

144 MD 718/172-173; also see Laurence Jarvik interview with Josiah E. DuBois, Jr., Camden, NJ, 23 October 1978, cited in Rafael Medoff, *Blowing the Whistle on Genocide: Josiah E. DuBois, Jr. and the Struggle for a U.S. Response to the Holocaust* (Bloomington, IN: Purdue University Press, 2009), 76.

145 Wyman, *Abandonment*, 182.

146 Joel Brand, the Hungarian Jewish rescue activist who was sent by Adolf Eichmann to deliver the offer to the Allies, reported that the statement was made to him by a British official, whom he initially believed was Lord Moyne, the chief British official in the Middle East. Brand later concluded

that, in fact, the remark was made by "another British statesman," whose name he did not know. (Alex Weissberg, *Desperate Mission* [New York: Criterion Books, 1958], 190) Whatever the source, the remark was typical of British responses to opportunities to rescue large numbers of Jews. For example, at a meeting with President Roosevelt, Secretary Hull, and other senior officials at the White House in March 1943, British Foreign Minister Anthony Eden, told of the possibility of evacuating the 60,000 Jews in Bulgaria, replied "that the whole problem of the Jews in Europe is very difficult and that we should move very cautiously about offering to take all Jews out of a country like Bulgaria. If we do that, then the Jews of the world will be wanting us to make similar offers in Poland and Germany." ("Memorandum - Harry L. Hopkins - Subject: Eden Visit," 27 March 1943, File: "Eden in Washington," Box 20, Harry Hopkins Papers, FDRL.)

147 Not traced, but a similar remark is mentioned in Monty N. Penkower, *The Jews Were Expendable: Free World Diplomacy and the Holocaust* (Urbana and Chicago: University of Illinois Press, 1983), 306, n21.

148 Irwin F. Gellman (*Secret Affairs: Franklin Roosevelt, Cordell Hull, and Sumner Welles* [Baltimore: Johns Hopkins University Press, 1995], 98, contends that Hull's lack of interest in the plight of European Jewry was due in part to his concern that if he promoted the rescue of refugees, critics would ascribe his position to the influence of his wife, Frances Witz, whose father was Jewish. Hull, who had presidential ambitions, feared that publicity about his wife's background would harm his electoral chances. FDR encouraged Hull's political aspirations in 1938-1939 (until Roosevelt decided to run for a third term), but considered Mrs. Hull's Jewish heritage to be a political liability. The president told Senator Burton Wheeler (D-Montana) in August 1939 that a Hull candidacy would be problematic because Mrs. Hull's ancestry "would be raised" by his opponents. FDR added: "Mrs. Hull is about one quarter Jewish. You and I, Burt, are old English and Dutch stock. We know who our ancestors are. We know there is no Jewish blood in our veins, but a lot of these people do not know whether there is Jewish blood in their veins or not." See "Confidential—Memo on conference at the White House with the President—August 4, 1939," Burton K. Wheeler Papers, Collection 2207, Box 11: File 18, Montana State University, Bozeman, MT.

149 MD 688II/92-91.

150 For more on Morgenthau's relationship with Roosevelt, see Blanche Wiesen Cook, *Eleanor Roosevelt - Volume 2: 1933-1938* (New York: Viking Press, 1999), 317-321.

151 MD 688II/148-171.

152 MD 694/194-202.

153 Ibid.

154 John Pehle, Memorandum for the Secretary's File, 16 January 1944, MD 694/190-192.

155 Ibid.

156 Ickes to Bergson, 26 January 1944, text reprinted in *Save Human Lives* (see above, note 2), 19.

157 Not traced, but the Bergson Group's strongly positive response to the creation of the WRB is evident from such advertisements as "The First Great Realistic Step Has Been Taken," *The New Republic* 110 (7 February 1944), 192, and "America Declares War Against Massacre," *The New Republic* 110 (21 February 1944), 249.

158 Ibid.

159 Pehle to Brunot, 9 August 1944, Box 8, File: Emergency Committee to Save the Jewish People, War Refugee Board Papers, FDRL.

160 Wyman, *Abandonment*, 287.

161 The transcript of the hearing was published in *Problems of World War II and Its Aftermath - Part 2* (Washington, DC: U.S. Government Printing Office, 1976). Alfange's remark appears on page 21.

162 Hull, Morgenthau, and Stimson, "Memorandum for the President" (authored by John W. Pehle), 8 May 1944, Office Files 3186, FDRL. (For the first draft of this memo, which bears Pehle's name as the author, see MD 716/171-175.)

163 Samuel Grafton, "I'd Rather Be Right," *New York Post*, 5 April 1944, 24.

164 "Port of Refuge" (editorial), NYT, 10 June 1944, 14.

165 Alfange, Rogers, Bergson, Undset, Bromfield, William, Hecht, and Ying to Roosevelt, 13 May 1944, File: Emergency Shelters, Box 7, War Refugee Board Papers, FDRL.

166 FDR press conference, 2 June 1944, *Press Conferences of President Franklin D. Roosevelt*, volume 23, 1944, #953, 212-214, FDRL.

167 *Press Conferences of Franklin D. Roosevelt*, Volume 23, #953 (2 June 1944), 212-214, FDRL; Associated Press report, "U.S. to Shelter 1000 of Europe's Refugee Horde," in File: Free Ports I-J, Box 67, War Refugee Board Papers, FDRL. For a comprehensive study of the Oswego episode, see Sharon R. Lowenstein, *Token Refuge: The Story of the Jewish Refugee Shelter at Oswego, 1944-1946* (Bloomington, IN: Indiana University Press, 1986).

168 For a study of how Axis prisoners were treated in the United States, see Lowell A. May, *Camp Concordia: German POWs in the Midwest* (Manhattan, KS: Sunflower University Press, 1995).

169 See, for example, Stewart to Medical Officer in Charge, 21 February 1944, File: Emergency Committee to Save the Jewish People of Europe, War Refugee Board Papers, FDRL.

170 E. Jabotinsky, "Report to Emergency Committee to Save the Jewish People of Europe - Ankara, June 14, 1944," in File: Emergency Committee to Save Jewish People of Europe - Jabotinsky Eri, Correspondence - 8/10-22-chet, MZ..

171 Pehle to Steinhardt, 27 June 1944 and Steinhardt to Pehle, 30 June 1944, File: Emergency Committee to Save the Jewish People of Europe, War Refugee Board Papers, FDRL.

172 Warren to Smertenko, 19 July 1944, File: Emergency Committee to Save the Jewish People of Europe, 2/1/11-chet, Bergson Group Collections, MZ..

173 Bergson to President Roosevelt, 17 October 1944, File: Emergency Committee to Save the Jewish People of Europe, 2/1/11-chet, Bergson Group Collections, MZ; John Ellis van Courtland Moon, "Pressing at the Limits: The Challenge of the Hebrew Committee of National Liberation to Chemical Warfare Policy," *Simon Wiesenthal Center Annual* 2 (1985), 139-147.

174 Henry Morgenthau, Jr. "The Morgenthau Diaries - Part 6: The Refugee Run-Around," *Collier's*, 1 November 1947, 22-23, 62, 65.

175 "America Acts: The War Refuge Board," *The Answer* 2 (12 February 1944), 6.

176 Forced out of power when the Germans occupied Hungary in March 1944, Kallay (1887-1967) spent time in Dachau and Mauthausen before the end of the war. He spent his final years in exile, in the United States.

177 Text reprinted in "Action to Save the Jews of Hungary," *The Answer* 2 (15 June 1944), 24.

178 "Non-Jewish Hungarians Confer on Rescue Measures," *The Answer* 2 (29 August 1944), 18.

179 "Non-Jewish Hungarians in New York Voice Protest," *The Answer* 2 (29 August 1944), 22.

180 These first two sentences are from the Merlin interview with Jarvik.

181 "In the beginning, God created politics." A play on the first sentence of the Hebrew Bible, Jabotinsky coined this phrase to dramatize his belief in the primacy of political action to advance the Zionist agenda.

182 Margoshes wrote that "the oldest rabbis" in the march were "remarkably reminiscent of the patriarchs in Dore's Bible." (Samuel Margoshes, "News and Views," *Der Tog*, 10 October 1943, 1.) The *New York Times* described the marchers as wearing "patriarchal vestments." ("Rabbis Present Plea to Wallace," *New York Times*, 7 October 1943, 13.

183 *Problems of World War II and Its Aftermath-Part 2* (Washington, D.C.: U.S. Government Printing Office, 1976), 220-221.

184 Stephen S. Wise, *Challenging Years: The Autobiography of Stephen Wise* (New York: Putnam, 1949); Carl Hermann Voss, *Rabbi and Minister: The Friendship*

of Stephen S. Wise and John Haynes Holmes (Cleveland and New York: World Publishing, 1964); Carl Hermann Voss, ed. *Stephen S. Wise: Servant of the People - Selected Letters* (Philadelphia: Jewish Publication Society of America, 1969). The reference to Hecht is on page 257.

185 Nahum Goldmann, *The Autobiography of Nahum Goldmann: Sixty Years of Jewish Life* (New York: Holt Rinehart & Winston: New York, 1969); Meyer Weisgal, *...So Far: An Autobiography* (Random House: New York, 1971); Emanuel Neumann, *In the Arena: An Autobiographical Memoir* (New York: Herzl Press, 1976)

186 Yitshaq Ben-Ami, *Days of Wrath, Years of Glory: Memoirs from the Irgun* (New York: Robert Speller and Sons, 1982); M.J. Nurenberger, *The Scared and the Doomed: The Jewish Establishment vs. the Six Million* (Oakville, Ontario: Mosaic Press, 1985); Alex Rafaeli, *Dream and Action* (Jerusalem: Achva Cooperative Press, 1993).

187 Naomi W. Cohen, *Not Free to Desist: The American Jewish Committee 1906-1966* (Philadelphia: Jewish Publication Society of America, 1972); Yehuda Bauer, *American Jewry and the Holocaust: The American Jewish Joint Distribution Committee, 1939-1945* (Detroit: Wayne State University Press, 1981).

188 Lucy S. Dawidowicz, "Ben Hecht's *Perfidy*," *Commentary* 33 (March 1962), 263.

189 Arthur D. Morse, *While Six Million Died: A Chronicle of American Apathy* (New York: Random House, 1968), 79-80, 99.

190 Henry L. Feingold, *The Politics of Rescue: The Roosevelt Administration and the Holocaust 1938-1945* (New Brunswick, NJ: Rutgers University Press, 1970), 175; and idem., "Roosevelt and the Holocaust: New Deal Humanitarianism," *Judaism* 18 (Summer 1969), 259-276.

191 Saul S. Friedman, *No Haven for the Oppressed: United States Policy Toward Jewish Refugees, 1938-1945* (Detroit: Wayne State University Press, 1973), 186.

192 Daniel Charles, "Peter Bergson's 'Irgun' in America," *The American Zionist*, March /April 1975, 25-28.

193 Sarah E. Peck, "The Campaign for an American Response to the Nazi Holocaust, 1943-1945," *Journal of Contemporary History* 15 (1980), 367-400; Monty N. Penkower, "In Dramatic Dissent: The Bergson Boys," *American Jewish History* 70 (March 1981), 281-309. Penkower's essay was later incorporated in his book *The Jews Were Expendable* (1983).

194 Marie Syrkin, "What Americans Jews Did during the Holocaust," *Midstream* 28 (October 1982), 9; and Letters, *Midstream* 28 (March 1982), 60-64; Bernard Wasserstein, Letters, *Midstream* 27 (March 1981), 59-63.

195 Marie Syrkin, *Midstream* 28 (October 1982), 10-11; Bernard Wasserstein, *Midstream* 26 (August-September 1980), 15; Lucy Dawidowicz, "American Jews and the Holocaust," *New York Times Sunday Magazine*, 18 April 1982, 114.

196 Marie Syrkin, "What American Jews Did During the Holocaust," *Midstream* 28 (October 1982), 9; Melvin Urofsky, *A Voice That Spoke for Justice: The Life and Times of Stephen S. Wise* (Albany: State University of New York Press, 1982), 319-320, 322; Dawidowicz, "American Jews," 114.

197 "To the Gentlemen at Bermuda..." (advertisement), *Washington Post*, 20 April 1943, 10.

198 Marie Syrkin letter, "Correspondence: Reactions to News of the Holocaust," *Midstream* 14 (May 1968), 62-64.

199 *Congress Monthly*, May -June 1985, 341.

200 *Midstream* 28 (October 1982), 11.

201 *Midstream* 26 (August-September 1980),15-16.

202 Dawidowicz, "American Jews," 48.

203 *Midstream* 26 (August-September 1980), 13.

204 *Midstream* 28 (October 1982), 9.

205 Ibid., 11.

206 *New Leader,* 8 April 1944, 10.

207 Harold Manson Papers, File II-6, Abba Hillel Silver Papers, The Temple, Cleveland.

208 See Rafael Medoff, *Militant Zionism in America: The Rise and Impact of the Jabotinsky Movement in the United States, 1926-1948* (Tuscaloosa, AL: University of Alabama Press, 2002), chapter 10.

209 Nancy Pelosi, *Know Your Power: A Message to America's Daughters* (New York: Doubleday, 2008), 97; Hadas Kroitoru, "Chicago Names Street After Ben Hecht for Saving Jews," *Jerusalem Post*, 1 July 2004, 3; Jessica Ravitz, "Late, Great Utah Senator Recognized," *Salt Lake Tribune*, 8 April 2005, 3.

210 Charley Levine, "Skeletons Rattling for US Jews," *Jerusalem Post*, June 21, 2007, 10; Etgar Lefkovits, "Rabbi Stephen Wise 'Failed Miserably' During Shoah, HUC President Claims," *Jerusalem Post,* September 25, 2008, 5.

211 Jacqueline Trescott, "A Voice Crying in the Wilderness," *Washington Post*, 1 August 2007, C1.

===================

BIBLIOGRAPHY

THE BERGSON GROUP

Baumel-Schwartz, Judith. *The "Bergson Boys" and the Origins of Zionist Militancy.* Syracuse: Syracuse University Press, 2005.

Ben-Ami, Yitshaq. *Years of Wrath, Days of Glory: Memoirs from the Irgun.* New York: Shengold, 1983.

Hecht, Ben. *A Child of the Century.* New York: Simon & Schuster, 1954.

Korff, Baruch. *Flight from Fear.* New York: Elmar, 1953.

Nurenberger, M.J. *The Scared and the Doomed: The Jewish Establishment vs. the Six Million.* Ontario: Mosaic Press, 1985.

Rafaeli, Alex. *Dream and Action: The Story of My Life.* Jerusalem: Achva, 1993.

Rapoport, Louis. *Shake Heaven and Earth: Peter Bergson and the Struggle to Rescue the Jews of Europe.* Jerusalem: Gefen, 1999.

Wyman, David S. and Rafael Medoff. *A Race against Death: Peter Bergson, America, and the Holocaust.* New York: The New Press, 2002.

THE ALLIES' RESPONSE TO THE HOLOCAUST

Abella, Irving and Harold Troper. *None is Too Many: Canada and the Jews of Europe, 1933–1948.* New York: Random House, 1982.

Abzug, Robert H. *America Views the Holocaust, 1933–1945: A Brief Documentary History.* Boston and New York: Bedford/St. Martin's, 1999.

Aronson, Shlomo. *Hitler, the Allies, and the Jews.* New York: Cambridge University Press, 2004.

Bartrop, Paul. *Australia and the Holocaust, 1933–1945.* Melbourne: Australian Scholarly Publications, 1993.

Baumel, Judith Tydor. *Unfulfilled Promise: Rescue and Resettlement of Jewish Refugee Children in the United States, 1934–1945.* Juneau, AK: The Deli Press, 1990.

Bauer, Yehuda. *Jews for Sale? Nazi-Jewish Negotiations, 1933–1945.* New Haven and London: Yale University Press, 1994.

Bingham, Robert Kim. *Courageous Dissent: How Harry Bingham Defied His Government To Save Lives.* Greenwich, CT: Triune Books, 2007.

Breitman, Richard, Stewart, Barbara McDonald, and Hochberg, Severin, eds. *Advocate for the Doomed, Volume 1: The Diaries and Papers of James G. McDonald 1932-1935.* Bloomington and Indianapolis: Indiana University Press, 2007.

Breitman, Richard, Stewart, Barbara McDonald, and Hochberg, Severin, eds. *Refugees and Rescue, Volume 2: The Diaries and Papers of James G. McDonald 1935-1945.* Bloomington and Indianapolis: Indiana University Press, 2009.

Breitman, Richard. *Official Secrets: What the Nazis Planned, What the British and America Knew.* New York: Hill and Wang, 1998.

Breitman, Richard and Alan M. Kraut. *American Refugee Policy and European Jewry, 1933–1945.* Bloomington and Indianapolis: Indiana University Press, 1987.

Dwork, Deborah and Van Pelt, Robert Jan. *Flight from the Reich: Refugee Jews, 1933-1946.* New York: W. W.Norton, 2009.

Ephraim, Frank. *Escape to Manila: From Nazi Tyranny to Japanese Terror.* Urbana and Chicago: University of Illinois Press, 2003.

Feingold, Henry L. *Bearing Witness: How America and Its Jews Responded to the Holocaust.* Syracuse, NY: Syracuse University Press, 1995.

Feingold, Henry L. *The Politics of Rescue: The Roosevelt Administration and the Holocaust, 1938–1945.* New Brunswick, NJ: Rutgers University Press, 1970.

Friedman, Saul S. *No Haven for the Oppressed: United States Policy toward Refugees, 1938–1945.* Detroit: Wayne State University Press, 1973.

Fry, Varian. *Surrender on Demand.* Boulder, CO: Johnson Books, 1997.

Genizi, Haim. *American Apathy: The Plight of Christian Refugees from Nazism.* Ramat Gan, Israel: Bar-Ilan University Press, 1983.

Gilbert, Martin. *Auschwitz and the Allies.* New York: Holt Rinehart and Winston, 1981.

Hirschmann, Ira A. *Life Line to a Promised Land.* New York: Vanguard Press, 1946.

Jackman, Jarrell C. and Carla M. Borden. *The Muses Flee Hitler: Cultural Transfer and Adaptation, 1930–1945.* Washington, D.C.: Smithsonian Institution Press, 1983.

Kaplan, Marion. *Dominican Haven: The Jewish Refugee Settlement in Sousa 1940-1945.* New York: Museum of Jewish Heritage, 2008.

Laqueur, Walter. *The Terrible Secret.* Boston and Toronto: Little Brown, 1980.

Laqueur, Walter and Richard Breitman. *Breaking the Silence.* New York: Simon and Schuster, 1986.

Lowenstein, Sharon R. *Token Refuge: The Story of the Jewish Refugee Shelter in Oswego, 1944–1946.* Bloomington: Indiana University Press, 1986.

Marino, Andy. *A Quiet American: The Secret War of Varian Fry.* New York: St. Martin's Press, 1999.

Medoff, Rafael. *Blowing the Whistle on Genocide: Josiah E. DuBois, Jr. and the Struggle for a U.S. Response to the Holocaust.* West Lafayette, IN: Purdue University Press, 2009.

Morse, Arthur D. *While Six Million Died: A Chronicle of American Apathy.* New York: Random House, 1967.

Norwood, Stephen H. *The Third Reich in the Ivory Tower: Complicity and Conflict on American Campuses.* New York: Cambridge University Press, 2009.

Ogilvie, Sarah A. and Miller, Scott. *Refuge Denied: The St. Louis Passengers and the Holocaust.* Madison, WI: University of Wisconsin Press, 2006.

Penkower, Monty Noam. *The Holocaust and Israel Reborn: From Catastrophe to Sovereignty.* Urbana and Chicago: University of Illinois Press, 1994.

Penkower, Monty Noam. *The Jews Were Expendable: Free World Diplomacy and the Holocaust.* Urbana and Chicago: University of Illinois Press, 1983.

Perl, William R. *The Four-Front War: From the Holocaust to the Promised Land.* New York: Crown, 1978.

Smith, Sharon Kay. "Elbert D. Thomas and America's Response to the Holocaust." Ph.D. dissertation, Brigham Young University, 1992.

Thomas, Gordon and Max Morgan Witts. *Voyage of the Damned.* New York: Stein and Day, 1974.

Vrba, Rudolf and Alan Bestic. *I Cannot Forgive.* New York: Grove Press, 1964.

Wasserstein, Bernard. *Britain and the Jews of Europe, 1939–1945.* New York and Oxford: Oxford University Press, 1979.

Weisberg, Alex. *Desperate Mission.* New York: Criterion Books, 1958.

Wells, Allen. *Tropical Zion: General Trujillo, FDR, and the Jews of Sosua.* Durham, NC: Duke University Press, 2008.

Wood, E. Thomas and Jankowski, Stanislaw M. *Karski: How One Man Tried to Stop the Holocaust.* New York: John Wiley and Sons, 1994.

Wyman, David S. *The Abandonment of the Jews: America and the Holocaust, 1941–1945.* New York: Pantheon, 1984.

Wyman, David S. *America and the Holocaust.* 13 vols. New York: Garland, 1993.

Wyman, David S. *Paper Walls: America and the Refugee Crisis, 1938–1941.* Amherst: University of Massachusetts Press, 1968.

Wyman David S., ed. *The World Reacts to the Holocaust.* Baltimore: Johns Hopkins University Press, 1996.

Zucker, Bat-Ami. *In Search of Refuge: Jews and U.S. Consuls in Nazi Germany, 1933–1941.* London and Portland, ME: Vallentine Mitchell, 2001.

AMERICAN MEDIA COVERAGE OF THE HOLOCAUST

Leff, Laurel. *Buried by the* Times: *The Holocaust and America's Most Important Newspaper.* New York: Cambridge University Press, 2005.

Lipstadt, Deborah E. *Beyond Belief: The American Press and the Coming of the Holocaust, 1933–1945.* New York: The New Press, 1986.

Shapiro, Robert Moses, ed. *Why Didn't the Press Shout? American and International Journalism During the Holocaust.* New York: Yeshiva University Press, 2003.

AMERICAN CHRISTIAN RESPONSES

Ross, Robert W. *So It Was True: The American Protestant Press and the Nazi Persecution of the Jews.* Minneapolis: University of Minnesota Press, 1980.

Subak, Susan Elisabeth. *Rescue & Flight: American Relief Workers Who Defied the Nazis.* Lincoln, NE: University of Nebraska Press, 2010.

AMERICAN JEWISH RESPONSES

Arad, Gulie Ne'eman. *America, Its Jews, and the Rise of Nazism.* Bloomington and Indianapolis: Indiana University Press, 2000.

Bauer, Yehuda. *American Jewry and the Holocaust: The American Jewish Joint Distribution Committee, 1939–1945.* Detroit: Wayne State University Press, 1981.

Bauer, Yehuda. *My Brother's Keeper: A History of the American Jewish Joint Distribution Committee, 1929–1939.* Philadelphia: Jewish Publication Society of America, 1974.

Berman, Aaron. *Nazism, the Jews, and American Zionism.* Detroit: Wayne State University Press, 1990.

Gal, Allon. *David Ben-Gurion and the American Alignment for a Jewish State.* Bloomington, IN: Indiana University Press, 1991.

Gottlieb, Moshe. "The Anti-Nazi Boycott Movement in the American Jewish Community, 1933–1941." Ph.D. dissertation, Brandeis University, 1967.

Grobman, Alex. *Battling for Souls: The Vaad Hatzala Rescue Committee in Post-War Europe.* Jersey City, NJ: Ktav, 2003.

Lookstein, Haskel. *Were We Our Brothers' Keepers? The Public Response of American Jews to the Holocaust, 1938–1944.* New York: Hartmore House, 1985.

Medoff, Rafael. *The Deafening Silence: American Jewish Leaders and the Holocaust.* New York: Steimatzky-Shapolsky, 1987.

Medoff, Rafael. *Militant Zionism in America: The Rise and Impact of the Jabotinsky Movement in the United States, 1926–1948.* Tuscaloosa: University of Alabama Press, 2002.

Neuringer, Sheldon Morris. "American Jewry and United States Immigration Policy, 1881–1953." Ph.D. dissertation, University of Wisconsin, 1969.

Neustadt-Noy, Isaac. "The Unending Task: Efforts to Unite American Jewry from the American Jewish Congress to the American Jewish Conference." Ph.D. dissertation, Brandeis University, 1976.

Shogan, Robert. *Prelude to Catastrophe: FDR's Jews and the Menace of Nazism.* Chicago: Ivan R. Dee, 2010.

Wolk, Kenneth. "New Haven and Waterbury, Connecticut Jewish Communities' Public Response to the Holocaust, 1938–1944." Ph.D. dissertation, New York University, 1995.

Zucker, Bat-Ami. *Cecilia Razovsky and the American-Jewish Wome's Rescue Operations in the Second World War.* Portland and London: Vallentine Mitchell, 2008.

Zuroff, Efraim. *The Response of Orthodox Jewry in the United States to the Holocaust: The Activities of the Vaad-ha-Hatzala Rescue Committee, 1939–1945.* New York: Yeshiva University Press, 2000.

ABOUT THE AUTHOR

Samuel Merlin (1910-1996) grew up in the Russian city of Kishinev and studied at the Sorbonne, in Paris. There he became active in Ze'ev Jabotinsky's Revisionist Zionist movement, rising to the post of secretary-general. In 1938, Merlin joined the Irgun Zvai Leumi underground militia and became editor of its newspaper, *Die Tat*. In 1940, he relocated to the United States, where he became one of the leaders of the Bergson Group and editor of its magazine, *The Answer*. Merlin arrived in Israel shortly after its establishment in 1948. Together with Menachem Begin, Merlin co-founded the Herut Party, served as its secretary-general, and was elected to the First Knesset as a Herut representative. Subsequently Merlin returned to New York City, where he established and directed the Institute for Mediterranean Affairs. He authored *The Ascent of Man* (1964, with Alex Wilf) and *The Search for Peace in the Middle East* **(1968).**

ABOUT THE EDITOR

Dr. Rafael Medoff is the author of twelve books about the Holocaust, Zionism, and the history of American Jewry. His textbook, *Jewish Americans and Political Participation*, was named an "Outstanding Academic Title of 2003" by the American Library Association's *Choice Magazine*. He has also authored numerous essays for scholarly journals, served as associate editor of the journal *American Jewish History*, and contributed to the *Encyclopedia Judaica* and other reference volumes. Dr. Medoff has taught Jewish history at Ohio State University, Purchase College of the State University of New York, and elsewhere. He is founding director of The David S. Wyman Institute for Holocaust Studies, which focuses on issues related to America's response to Nazism and the Holocaust (www.WymanInstitute.org).

INDEX

CPSIA information can be obtained at www.ICGtesting.com
Printed in the USA
BVOW021013190912

300866BV00013B/73/P

9 780615 439105